Ron Bowman

CLINICAL APPLICATIONS SERIES

Sheldon R. Roen, Ph.D., Editor

Family Therapy:

A Triadic-Based Approach

GERALD H. ZUK, PH.D.
Family Psychiatry Division,
Eastern Pennsylvania Psychiatric Institute,
Philadelphia

Behavioral Publications, Inc.   New York

Library of Congress Catalog Card Number 72-174269
Standard Book Number 87705-069-4
Copyright © 1971 by Behavioral Publications, Inc.

BEHAVIORAL PUBLICATIONS, INC., 2852 Broadway–Morningside Heights,
New York, New York 10025

Printed in the United States of America

CONTENTS

. . . .

PREFACE

. . . .

The central theme of this book is triadic-based processes in families and in family therapy. I selected for it what I consider my key papers on go-between process, which is a triadic-based concept of doing family therapy; and the key papers on pathogenic relating, which is a formulation about pathology in families and at which go-between process is directed.

Included are nine of my papers on family therapy, eight of which have appeared previously in journals. In addition there are included two interviews with discussions. One of the papers, "Engaging Families in Therapy; with Some Observations on American Families," appears here for the first time, as do the two interviews. Thus about a third of the material in the book is new.

Part I contains two papers, the first of which describes the main conceptual issue in family therapy today: the dyadic- versus the triadic-based approaches. This paper also contains brief descriptions of papers in the book as well as descriptions of a few that were not included. The second paper reviews exciting developments in family therapy during the later half of the 1960's, when the field entered a quite different phase from its earlier years, and when new challenges and problems were posed.

Part II is composed mainly of the papers on go-between process, but it also contains the new paper on "Engaging Families in Therapy . . . ," which departs somewhat from the theme of triadic-based processes but still reflects it. It deals with what I consider the main technical challenge currently facing family therapists seeing a wide range of families in outpatient settings and in the community: how to engage lower-income and minority families whose motivation for therapy is often mixed. In this paper I take up the question of contraindication for family therapy. It also explores an observation of mine that has piqued my interest especially during the past two or three years: the centrality of the wife-mother in the American family, which has probably been increasing concurrent with a diminution in the husband-father's role.

Part III contains three papers on pathogenic relating in families. The first is on silencing strategies, which I perceive as always potentially inflammatory. The second and third papers are on implications of laughter that occurs in family therapy or rather of inappropriate laughter.

Part IV is composed of the two interviews with discussions that consider the pathogenic relating in the families, therapy technique, and goals. An uncommon feature is that follow-up information about the families is reported. One of my aims in this section is to convey something about the therapist's working methods, his style of relating to patients.

Most of the families described in the book were seen in my capacity as a therapist associated with the Family Psychiatry Division at Eastern Pennsylvania Psychiatric Institute in Philadelphia (EPPI), where I am also a researcher in the Department of Clinical Research.

Appreciation is expressed to EPPI and to journal editors who have kindly granted permission to reproduce material for this volume. References to original sources of publication are in footnotes. Here and there I have taken the liberty to alter phraseology slightly for the sake of greater clarity and have included a few footnotes, also for clarity.

Gerald H. Zuk, Ph.D.
October, 1971

. . . .

PART I:: OVERVIEW OF THE FIELD

. . . .

Chapter 1 / TRIADIC-BASED
FAMILY THERAPY

. . . .

Early in 1967 while reviewing my three groups of studies in family therapy, it occurred to me for the first time and as something of a revelation that they were all triadic-based. For some reason I was not fully aware of this fact before and was pleased to discover a common root to the groups that had previously appeared to me related only in the fact that they were based on observations derived from family therapy.

My triadic-based work represents a contribution to a field of family therapy which has been predominantly dyadic-based during its short history. This is not to say that there has not been reference to three-person relationships by students of the field, for there has been: a common descriptive unit, for example, has been the so-called identified patient and his parents. But typically the three persons comprising this unit are examined, as it were, two at a time—mother and son, father and son, mother and father. Indeed it is possible to consider the triad as made up of three two-person relationships, but in doing this one misses key features of triadic relationships.

Aside from this introductory section in which mainly I will compare the triadic with the dyadic model as applied in family therapy and family therapy-related research, the chapter has two main sections: The first contains brief reviews of my papers on go-between process, which is a technique of family therapy grounded in triadic-based concepts; the second reviews my other two groups of papers on triadic-based pathogenic relating in families, although the first set on go-between process also develops the concept of pathogenic relating.

The nature of his work compels the family therapist to examine

This material was published in the *International Journal of Psychiatry,* 1969, **8** 539-548.

such triadic-based processes as coalitions, alliances, and cliques, and also such processes as mediation and side-taking. Coalitions and mediation cannot occur in groups comprised of less than three members, although they may occur in groups comprised of more than three. In coalitions at least two persons join together "against" at least one other. In mediation at least one person acts as mediator between at least two others.

Upon reading the family therapy-related reviews of the literature in recent years done by Jackson and Satir (1961), Zuk and Rubinstein (1965), Meissner (1964), and Mishler and Waxler (1966), one cannot help but notice how heavily family therapy has been influenced by psychoanalytic concepts and techniques. I think this is perhaps the main reason family therapy has been predominantly dyadic-based, for analysts and analytically oriented workers, when they have been interested in interaction rather than intrapsychic process alone, have characteristically focused on two-person interaction, perhaps mainly because this is the number of persons present in the analytic treatment session.

Transference, essentially a dyadic concept, has been a basic analytic model for human interaction. Even in the case of an analytic concept in which three persons are said to be involved—the Oedipus Complex for example—the analytic literature has dealt with this strictly from the perspective of one member. The child relates to his *fantasies* about his parents, not to his parents themselves; in this sense, I view the Oedipus Complex as essentially monadic-based.

The transference-countertransference concepts have been applied by a number of family therapists (see Whitaker et al., 1965), although in a broadened form. It is interesting to recall that one of the early objections to family therapy, as well as to group therapy, was the concern of analysts that the transference would be diluted by the presence of other persons. Nowadays one hears this objection less, perhaps because so many analytically oriented therapists are themselves doing family therapy.

David Levy's study (1943) of maternal overprotection set a pattern for dyadic-based investigation of the family. There was a spate of studies on dyadic family relationships, many by analytically oriented workers, in the 1940's and 1950's, some of which are reported in my review (Zuk and Rubinstein, 1965). In the realm of psychotherapy, Fromm-Reichmann (1948) coined the term schizophrenogenic mother; and Mahler (1952) described the state of symbiosis between mother and child. These dyadic-based concepts were snapped up and amplified by the early workers in family therapy. In the published reports on family therapy appearing in the late 1950's, the mother-child dyad was perhaps the central focus of interest. Even those workers in family therapy who were to make a fundamental departure from the analytic model, the so-called communication theorists, made the mother-child dyad a main focus. As Weakland (1960) says, ". . . my colleagues and I developed the concept of the 'double bind' as a pattern of communication provoking behavior characteristic of schizophrenia. Our attention there centered on two-person interaction, especially communication between mother and child" (p. 373).

A dyad that gained centrality in family therapy-related research in the 1960's was that of the spouses, husband and wife. Bowen (1960) described in some detail the pattern of "emotional divorce" between spouses with a schizophrenic child. Lidz et al. (1957a, 1957b) observed the patterns of "marital schism" and "marital skew," and made a special contribution by singling out the father-child dyad for attention, a needed balance to the surplus of studies on the mother-child dyad.

Some essentially dyadic-based studies in family therapy-related research may at first glance not appear to be so. I refer to those studies which focus on the self-other dyad or the ego-alter dyad (see, for example, Laing, 1960). The scapegoating concept, which has been especially stressed by Ackerman (1967), seems to me essentially dyadic-based, although it has some application in triadic interaction also. In my view the scapegoat, as utilized typically in some family therapy-related studies, constitutes one member of a dyadic pair, the other of which is constituted by the scapegoating group. Such concepts as Bowen's "undifferentiated family ego mass" (1966) or Wynne et al.'s (1958) "pseudomutuality" seem to me dyadic-based concepts in the same way, although these workers may themselves perceive them from quite a different perspective. I am of course expanding the usual notion of the dyad here to include cases in which one member of the dyadic pair is a *collective unit.*

Both analytically oriented workers and communication theorists have made reference to triadic interaction. In the studies already mentioned by Lidz and his associates, reference is made to the coalition formed by wives and children against husbands. The coalition was believed to constitute a deformation in family relationships that was presumed either to be a significant causal factor in relation to a schizophrenic offspring, or to reflect family disturbance accompanying the presence of a schizophrenic child. Weakland (1960) described possible applications of the double-bind concept in triads. One of his interesting references is to the work of Stanton and Schwartz (1954) who discovered a relationship between covert mental hospital staff disagreement and pathological excitement in the patient who was the object of the disagreement. These authors state, ". . . that pathologically excited patients were quite regularly the subjects of secret, affectively important staff disagreement; and, equally regularly, their excitement terminated, usually abruptly, when the staff members were brought to discuss seriously their points of disagreement with each other" (p. 345). This Stanton and Schwartz finding is a powerful example of triadic-based pathogenic relating occurring in a social system other than the family, but of course it has relevance for the family system.

Of the communication theorists, Haley has shown the greatest interest in conceptualizing three-person interaction. In his paper on marriage therapy (Haley, 1963), he posited that one function of the therapist is to serve as a mediator. More recently (Haley, 1967), he has described possible pathological outcomes of "perverse triangles" in families. Minuchin (1965) has attempted to break up pathogenic coalitions in families by removing family members from sessions and having them observe other members through one-way mirrors in the presence of a cotherapist. Satir (1964) regularly uses illustrations of pathogenic coalitions in teaching family therapy to students.

Although mainly analytically oriented, Bowen (1966) has indicated that he shares Haley's interest in three-party interaction in a statement that reads, "The basic building block of any emotional system is the triangle. When emotional tension in a two-person system exceeds a certain level, it triangles a third person, permitting tension to shift about within the triangle" (p. 368). Ackerman, another analytically oriented worker, has stated (1966, Ch. 5) that side-taking is an unavoidable function of the family therapist, and that skillfully handled it has therapeutic value.

Despite reference to triadic-based interaction and concepts, I think it is a fair statement to make that family therapists and family therapy-related researchers, especially those that are analytically oriented, have been occupied mainly with the study of dyadic interaction. It is somewhat characteristic of these workers also that when they have dealt with the triad, it is treated as if it were made up of three dyads—mother and child, father and child, mother and father—and such essential triadic concepts as coalition and mediation have been given relatively scant attention. Ravich (1967) refers to this bias in his review of the book by Friedman et al. (1965): "One major problem that inevitably confronts family therapists, because it is inherent in the nature of their work, involves a basic difficulty in dealing discriminatingly between dyads and triads. The authors repeatedly write about dyads and triads as though they were quite similar, whereas there is probably a vast difference between two-person and three-person relationships" (p. 134).[1]

A triadic-based conception of pathogenic relating will describe types of coalitions, alliances, or cliques that tend to produce "runaway patterns" that at some level of tension result in psychiatric symptoms in members of families or other groups. In papers on silencing strategies and on patterns of laughter unrelated to humor occurring in family therapy sessions, I attempt to develop a triadic-based conception of pathogenic relating.

A triadic-based technique of family therapy will describe how the therapist employs mediation and side-taking judiciously to break up and replace pathogenic relating. In such a technique, family therapy is

---

[1] According to Simmel (1902), the significance of the difference between dyads and triads is much sharper than between triads and tetrads or higher-numbered groups. The birth of a first child usually represents a dramatic change in the life of a couple, whereas the birth of a second child is comparatively less dramatic. Simmel also pointed out that it was easier for a superior to keep two subordinates at a distance compared with one, and to obtain their compliance by serving as a catalytic agent (a "third party") on the relationship of the subordinates.

defined as composed of a series of negotiations between therapist and family in which both parties vie for control.

GO-BETWEEN PROCESS

I labeled my triadic-based technique of family therapy go-between process because it sought to characterize the family therapist as taking and trading the roles essentially of the mediator and side-taker.[2] In the set of six papers on go-between process, I defined family therapy as a technique for applying leverage against pathogenic relating in families in order to break it up and replace it. When pathogenic relating in families is thus influenced, psychiatric symptoms in members may be reduced.

My first paper, "Preliminary Study of the Go-Between Process in Family Therapy" (Zuk, 1965a), was an attempt to sketch in the outline of a family therapy that would be triadic-based. It introduced and defined terms such as "conflict," "principal," and "go-between." It stated that the skill of the therapist engaging in this type of therapy consisted in his ability to catalyze conflict, then in his movement into the role of go-between or side-taker. Later papers were to correct a possible impression left in this one that go-between process was aimed at conflict-resolution. Conflict does facilitate go-between process in that it provides a climate in which the therapist can intervene forcefully. Conflict provides the crisis situation which is favorable for change. But go-between process is aimed at reducing and replacing pathogenic relating and is not essentially aimed at conflict-resolution.

"The Go-Between Process in Family Therapy" (Zuk, 1966a) described four variations of go-between process observed in family therapy, two initiated and controlled by the therapist, two initiated and controlled by the family. This paper introduced the notion that families conduct a kind of counter go-between process of their own against the therapist; that is, against his efforts to introduce constructive change.

[2] Although these are homely terms which hardly do justice to the richness of the therapist's involvement with families, and perhaps have the unfortunate connotation of labor-management negotiations, I have not been able to hit on others that more accurately convey the two basic *positions* of therapist vis à vis families.

The paper described family therapy as an active confrontation in which both therapist and family vie for power and control. Each family brings to the treatment sessions its own strategies, built up over years, to maintain the status quo and prevent change which is characteristically viewed as threatening.

The paper entitled simply "Family Therapy" (Zuk, 1967a) described three steps comprising go-between process. Step 1 is the therapist's effort to catalyze conflict. Step 2 is the therapist's movement more specifically into the role of the go-between. Step 3 is the therapist's switch from the role of go-between to the role of side-taker. In Steps 1 and 2, the therapist focuses on the current issues in the family because a focus on the past almost invariably moves the treatment away from being triadic-based toward a dyadic or even monadic framework. For the same reason the therapist usually rebuffs attempts to include in sessions talk about family members who may not be present.

"Family Therapy" used case material to illustrate pathogenic relating in one family and the therapist's employment of go-between process in an attempt to reduce it. The paper introduced the notion—although, to be sure, others have taken a similar position—that therapeutic change can be conceptualized as one of the factors present in a "bargaining transaction" between the therapist and the family, and that therapist and family negotiate with each other regarding the kind and rate of change that may be brought about. The skillful family therapist employs go-between process when he defines the type of change he wishes for the family, and then employs it to implement his definition and speed the rate of change.

The concept of change described in "Family Therapy" clearly contrasts with the psychoanalytic concept in which the therapist attempts to provide the patient with insight into his unconscious processes and explores means to overcome emotional resistances to the insight. In the psychoanalytic scheme, change is viewed as an end-result in a systematic exploration of the patient's unconscious by the analyst who employs his skill to free the trapped potential for more mature living hidden within the patient. In a triadic-based scheme, change is conceptualized as either an input into or an outcome of a process of negotiation in which the therapist takes an active role in actually defining the change he wishes for the patient(s). In other words, the therapist does not perceive himself only as a *releaser* of change which already has a certain shape and substance in the patient, but also as a *fashioner* of change.

"The Side-Taking Function in Family Therapy" (Zuk, 1968a) focused on side-taking by the therapist in conducting go-between process. Side-taking by the therapist is unavoidable in family therapy and must be considered a normal part of a group process. Even if the therapist believes he is remaining neutral, the family will perceive him to be favoring one member or the other, or one position or another on issues that may arise. Families will not let the therapist *not* take sides. The skilled family therapist learns the advantages and disadvantages of side-taking, means of avoiding undesirable entrapment in side-taking, and means of using side-taking to exert leverage against pathogenic relating in the family. This paper also amplified the concept of pathogenic relating I had been in the process of developing in earlier papers, describing a number of forms not previously noted.

"The Side-Taking Function . . . " paper and "When the Family Therapist Takes Sides: A Case Report" (Zuk, 1968b) both spelled out in general terms the way it is believed the therapist conducting go-between process promotes beneficial change: He does so by enabling or pressuring family members to define or redefine, label or relabel, structure or restructure, key aspects of the developing relationship between themselves, and between himself and family members. The therapist may be able to change pathogenic relating by influencing the family in such a manner that certain labels previously employed by family members to describe one another are discarded and productive substitutes are found. The therapist and family confront each other also on the issue of "Who is more powerful?" and "Who is in control?" and the outcome of the treatment is markedly influenced by the therapist's capacity to define and increase his power and control.

"When the Family Therapist Takes Sides: A Case Report" used case material to illustrate how side-taking may be employed by the therapist to change a label applied to a family member which the therapist perceived as a key prop for a system of pathogenic relating. In the case presentation, the therapist was shown to shift from taking the side of the parents to taking the side of their child. The object of the shift was to force the parents to discard a label they had come to use characteristically to describe the behavior of their child and which seemed an inappropriate label.

In "Prompting Change in Family Therapy" (Zuk, 1968c), I suggested that a major goal of treatment is achieved when the therapist obtains the commitment of the family to be treated on the therapist's terms. In my experience, the settling of the terms of the commitment to be treated is a major determinant of outcome in family therapy, not simply a precondition of treatment as it has characteristically been considered in psychotherapy with an individual. The paper described ways the therapist and family negotiate with each other over the terms of treatment, over the question of which family members shall be present in sessions, over which day of the week sessions shall be scheduled, over what the fee will be, and over whether other types of psychotherapy may be conducted concurrently with family therapy.

"Prompting Change in Family Therapy" also described how the therapist communicates his formulation about the pathogenic relating in a family to the family, not only using it diagnostically but actually as a means to bring pressure on the family to change. Families seek the therapist's approval and are interested in following his direction, yet they will balk when they perceive his direction to seriously threaten the status quo. The therapist must communicate his notion of pathogenic relating to the family in such a manner as to promote beneficial change while at the same time containing the family's natural tendency to reject change which appears to threaten the status quo.

PATHOGENIC RELATING

Silencing Strategies

In the set of three papers on silencing strategies, I strove to formulate a statement about what I considered at the time one of the most pervasive and pernicious types of coalition observed in families. In

"On the Pathology of Silencing Strategies" (Zuk, 1965c), I proposed that there was a causal relation between symptomatic silence occurring in psychiatric patients and silencing strategies conducted against these patients by members of their families. I outlined motives that I believed had to be present in order for silencing strategies to produce psychiatric symptoms. I suggested that the victim became silent in response to silencing only to discover the immense power to control relationships that resides in the position of one who remains silent. I hypothesized that this discovery, coming too early in development, before a capacity to integrate it into the personality exists, may precipitate a psychiatric illness in which silence is a major causal component as well as a major symptom of the illness.

In "On Silence and Babbling in Family Psychotherapy with Schizophrenics" (Zuk, 1965b), I made some suggestions to therapists working with patients exhibiting either symptomatic silence or babbling. (Symptomatic babbling is akin to silence in that essentially the patient says nothing or what amounts to nothing.) The main point was that therapists try not to limit their contact with patients to the issue of whether or not the patient will start talking or stop babbling and talk sensibly. I noted the interest of the patient in making the therapist into a silencer in order to match the power of the therapist and control him.

"The Victim and His Silencers: Some Pathogenic Strategies against Being Silenced" (Zuk, 1967b) was a paper in which I described the steps taken by silencers against their victim, and the retaliatory steps of the victim in his attempt to overcome his silencers. The silencers employ silencing as a means to obtain the compliance or conformity of their victim and as a means to punish him for lack of compliance or conformity. Each move of the silencers initiates a countermove by the victim, and a deepening and hardening of positions occurs. The paper also presented case material to illustrate that silencing strategies are also causally implicated in the development of delusional and hallucinatory states, not only in psychiatric illness involving silence as a major symptom. An account is given of a young schizophrenic woman who responded with delusional material to a silencing strategy being directed against her by her parents acting in collusion. Finally in this paper I drew attention to the fact that silencing strategies are related to brainwashing techniques.

Silencing strategies do occur in two-person situations and are of psychological significance in the dyad, but my studies characteristically considered them in three-person situations. Illustrations were typically of two parents acting in collusion against a child. The same held with respect to the next set of three papers on laughter occurring in family treatment.

Laughter Studies

In "Some Dynamics of Laughter during Family Therapy" (Zuk et al., 1963) I utilized a simple frequency count of the laughter occurring among three family members of a family containing a schizophrenic member. A pattern of laughter was found among the quarter-hour intervals comprising thirteen consecutive treatment sessions selected for examination. Both parents laughed significantly more in the first quarter-hour interval than in subsequent intervals, while their schizophrenic daughter laughed least frequently in the first interval compared with later intervals. The schizophrenic daughter laughed most frequently in the third quarter-hour interval of the thirteen sessions, precisely the interval in which her parents laughed least frequently. The negative relationship between the laughter behavior of the parents and their daughter seemed consistent with a hypothesis of a complementarity between parents and daughter in regard to laughter; that is, that laughter was serving as a signaling system between them, a means to monitor each other. It was clear from the pattern of laughter established that it was affected by different phases in the therapy hour. In the case of the schizophrenic daughter, it was demonstrated that her apparently "inappropriate" laughter was after all related to what was happening at different times in sessions.

In "A Further Study of Laughter in Family Therapy" (Zuk, 1964), I set the hypothesis that laughter often serves as a means to differentially disguise primarily spoken messages it accompanies; in other words, that laughter is a meta-message or a message about a message. For example, Person A might laugh as an attempt to invest special meaning in his spoken message delivered to Person B in the presence of Person C from whom A wishes to hide something. A's laugh may serve to alert both B and C that A wishes to disguise his spoken message; but B, standing in a closer relation to A and thus more tuned to his meaning, correctly unravels the disguise whereas C remains uneasily aware only of A's intention to disguise.

The hypothesis I suggested in "A Further Study . . . " contrasted with that of Freud who considered laughter to represent the freeing of energy once used in the service of repression. On the other hand, there is a similarity between my hypothesis and Henri Bergson's. The great French philosopher, a student of laughter and humor, held that laughter occurs when one recognizes the existence of an attempt to disguise.

"On the Theory and Pathology of Laughter in Psychotherapy" (Zuk, 1966b) reviewed my earlier work and noted that the original stimulus for my interest in the topic was an observation of how frequently "inappropriate" laughter occurred in nonsymptomatic members in family therapy. A large amount of laughter that occurs in family therapy in so-called normal members seems unrelated to the presence of humor or wit, and in this sense is "inappropriate." I finally surmised that laughter often served as a subtle screening device or monitor in the communication of family members with each other. Like silence, it is a frequent symptom of psychiatric illness. My position is that laughter, like silence, is a causal component in the process leading to a psychiatric illness and is not only a symptom that accompanies the illness.

RECAPITULATION

Triadic-based family therapy is a clinical application of the concepts of coalition or alliance, mediation, and side-taking. In its relatively brief history, approximately a dozen years, family therapists and family therapy-related researchers have focused mainly on dyadic interaction, basically in my opinion because the majority of these workers have been analytically oriented and the analytic model has its most direct extension to two-person interaction. Even though analytically oriented workers have sometimes referred to triadic-based concepts, it is evident from a review of the literature that their interest in triadic-based interaction is marginal to a main focus on dyadic interaction. While communication theorists have addressed themselves more seriously than analytically oriented workers to an examination of triadic-based interaction in family therapy, I think it is fair to state that their main focus also has been on dyadic interaction.

Go-between process is the triadic-based technique of family therapy which explores and attempts to shift the balance of pathogenic relating among family members so that new, more productive relating becomes possible. Pathogenic relating refers to such triadic-based interactions as silencing strategies, but is not limited to these: It also includes scapegoating, threats of physical violence, selective inattention, unfair or inappropriate labeling, myths or rituals of uncertain origin and accuracy, and shared family efforts at creating distraction—which may or may not be triadic based. In order to dislodge pathogenic relating, the therapist seeks to employ himself judiciously in the role of go-between or side-taker, moving from one function to the other as a means to create leverage. As go-between the therapist exerts pressure on family members to redefine and restructure their relationships with one another. As side-taker the therapist throws the weight of his authority in behalf of family members or family issues in order to shift relationships in directions he deems beneficial.

Triadic-based family therapy, *because it is grounded in the concepts of mediation and side-taking,* focuses its attention on evaluation of current, here-and-now interaction. To the extent that therapy is defined as a search for and analysis of past traumatic events, mediation and side-taking are ruled out as important tasks for the therapist. In triadic-based family therapy, family members may discuss the history of their relationships with each other, but the therapist is mainly interested in the *immediate collective reactions* of the members to the recounting rather than, let us say, its "objective" accuracy or the particular importance attached to it by the member who does the recounting. Triadic-based family therapy shares with communication-oriented family therapy an intensive focus on here-and-now interaction.

In triadic-based family therapy, change is viewed as one of the outcomes of negotiations between family and therapist. One of the negotiations described in my papers involves the therapist's efforts to get the family committed to treatment on terms he deems favorable to its outcome. Another negotiation involves the therapist's communication to the family of its manner of pathogenic relating in order to bring pressure on the family to reduce its pathogenic relating. In still another kind of negotiation, once family therapy has "taken hold," family and therapist vie with each other on the issue of termination of treatment, with favorable change a possible outcome of this negotiation also.

In the negotiations mentioned above, as well as others, the therapist conducting a triadic-based family therapy employs himself as a mediator or a side-taker in his effort to dislodge pathogenic relating. He may communicate insights to the family, or attempt to untangle disturbed patterns of communication, or employ other devices to influence pathogenic relating, all of which may be consistent with his basic functions of mediator and side-taker.

My papers are a contribution toward a triadic-based family therapy and theory of pathogenic relating, which means that they elaborate clinical phenomena associated with the group processes of coalition and mediation. In the 1940's workers studying family relationships confined their observations fairly strictly to the dyad. In the latter half of the 1950's and in the present decade, observations of triadic relationships were reported and references to coalitions, alliances, and cliques were increasing in the literature. There was a definite tendency, however, to examine triadic relationships as if they were composed of three two-person interactions (mother versus father, mother versus child, father versus child). This mode of analysis was not unfruitful, but it did neglect the systematic study of clinical phenomena associated with the formation of coalitions and with mediation, which are the triadic concepts par excellence. While some analytically oriented and communication-oriented therapists and researchers have joined me in recent years in conceptualizing the clinical phenomena associated with coalition formation and mediation, I think it is a fair judgment that my work of the past eight years is the most persistent and focused effort in this direction.

In the 1890's Georg Simmel, the great sociologist, described the profound difference between the dyad and triad; in family therapy-related research we have yet to fulfill the promise of Simmel's insight, although preliminary steps in that direction have been taken.

REFERENCES

Ackerman, N. W. *Treating the troubled family.* New York: Basic Books, 1966.

Ackerman, N. W. Prejudice and scapegoating in the family. In G. H. Zuk and I. Boszormenyi-Nagy (Eds.) *Family therapy and disturbed families.* Palo Alto, Calif.: Science and Behavior Books, Inc., 1967, pp. 48-57.

Bowen, M. A family concept of schizophrenia. In D. D. Jackson (Ed.), *The etiology of schizophrenia.* New York; Basic Books, 1960, pp. 346-372.

Bowen, M. The use of family theory in clinical practice. *Comprehensive Psychiatry,* 1966, **7**, 345-374.

Friedman, A. S., Boszormenyi-Nagy, I., Jungreis, J. E., Lincoln, G., Mitchell, H. E., Sonne, J. C., Speck, R. V., & Spivack, G. *Psychotherapy for the whole family.* New York: Springer, 1965.

Fromm-Reichmann, F. Notes on the development of treatment of schiozophrenics by psychoanalytic psychotherapy. *Psychiatry,* 1948, **11,**, 263-274.

Haley, J. Marriage therapy. *Archives of General Psychiatry,* 1963, **8**, 213-234.

Haley, J. Toward a theory of pathological systems. In G. H. Zuk and I. Boszormenyi-Nagy (Eds.), *Family therapy and disturbed families.* Palo Alto, Calif.: Science and Behavior Books, Inc., 1967, pp. 11-27.

Jackson, D. D., & Satir, V. A review of psychiatric developments in family diagnosis and therapy. In N. W. Ackerman, F. L. Beatman and S. N. Sherman (Eds.), *Exploring the base for family therapy.* New York: Family Service Association of America, 1961, pp. 29-51.

Laing, R. D. *The divided self: A study of sanity and madness.* Chicago: Quadrangle Books, 1960.

Levy, D. *Maternal overprotection.* New York: Columbia University Press, 1943.

Lidz, T., Cornelison, A., Fleck, S., & Terry, D. Intrafamilial environment of the schizophrenic patient, I: The father. *Psychiatry,* 1957a, **20**, 329-342.

Lidz, T., Cornelison, A., Fleck, S., and Terry, D. Intrafamilial environment of schizophrenic patients, II: Marital schism and marital skew. *American Journal of Psychiatry,* 1957b, **114**, 241-248.

Mahler, M. S. On childhood psychosis and schizophrenia: Autistic and symbiotic infantile psychosis. In R. S. Eissler, Anna Freud, H. Hartmann, and E. Kris (Eds.), *The psychoanalytic study of the child. Volume VII.* New York: International Universities Press, 1952, pp. 286-305.

Meissner, W. W. Thinking about the family—psychiatric aspects. *Family Process*, 1964, **3**, 1-40.

Minuchin, S. Conflict-resolution family therapy. *Psychiatry*, 1965, **28**, 278-286.

Mishler, E. G., & Waxler, N. W. Family interaction processes and schizophrenia: A review of current theories. *International Journal of Psychiatry*, 1966, **2**, 375-413.

Ravich, R. A. Review of A. S. Friedman, I. Boszormenyi-Nagy, J. E. Jungreis, G. Lincoln, H. E. Mitchell, J. C. Sonne, R. V. Speck and G. Spivack, *Psychotherapy for the whole family*. *American Journal of Psychotherapy*, 1967, **21**, 132-134.

Satir, V. *Conjoint family therapy*. Palo Alto, Calif.: Science and Behavior Books, Inc., 1964.

Simmel, G. The number of members as determining the sociological form of the group. *American Journal of Sociology*, 1902, **8**, 45-46.

Stanton, A. H., & Schwartz, M. S. *The mental hospital*. New York: Basic Books, 1954.

Weakland, J. H. The "double-bind" hypothesis of schizophrenia and three-party interaction. In D. D. Jackson (Ed.), *The etiology of schizophrenia*. New York: Basic Books, 1960, pp. 373-388.

Whitaker, C. A., Felder, R. A., & Warkentin, J. Countertransference in the family treatment of schizophrenia. In I. Boszormenyi-Nagy and J. L. Framo (Eds.), *Intensive family therapy: Theoretical and practical aspects*. New York: Hoeber, Harper and Row, 1965, pp. 323-342.

Wynne, L. C., Ryckoff, I. M., Day, J., & Hirsch, S. I. Pseudomutuality in the family relations of schizophrenics. *Psychiatry*, 1958, **21**, 205-220.

Zuk, G. H. A further study of laughter in family therapy. *Family Process*, 1964, **3**, 77-89.

Zuk, G. H. Preliminary study of the go-between process in family therapy. In *Proceedings of the 73rd annual meeting*. Washington, D.C.: American Psychological Association, 1965a, pp. 291-292.

Zuk, G. H. On silence and babbling in family psychotherapy with schizophrenics. *Confinia Psychiatrica*, 1965b, **8**, 49-56.

Zuk, G. H. On the pathology of silencing strategies. *Family Process*, 1965c, **4**, 32-48.

Zuk, G. H. The go-between process in family therapy. *Family Process*, 1966a, **5**, 162-178.

Zuk, G. H. On the theory and pathology of laughter in psychotherapy. *Psychotherapy: Theory, research and practice*, 1966b, **3**, 97-101.

Zuk, G. H. Family therapy. *Archives of General Psychiatry*, 1967a, **16**, 71-79.

Zuk, G. H. The victim and his silencers: Some pathogenic strategies against being silenced. In G. H. Zuk and I. Boszormenyi-Nagy (Eds.),

Family therapy and disturbed families. Palo Alto, Calif.: Science and Behavior Books, 1967c, pp. 106-116.

Zuk, G. H. The side-taking function in family therapy. *American Journal of Orthopsychiatry,* 1968a, **38**, 553-559.

Zuk, G. H. When the family therapist takes sides: A case report. *Psychotherapy: Theory, Research and Practice,* 1968b. **5**, 24-28.

Zuk, G. H. Prompting change in family therapy. *Archives of General Psychiatry,* 1968c, **19**, 727-736.

Zuk, G. H., Boszormenyi-Nagy, I. & Heiman, E. Some dynamics of laughter during family therapy. *Family process,* 1963, **2**, 302-314.

Zuk, G. H., & Rubinstein, D. A review of concepts in the study and treatment of families of schizophrenics. In I. Boszormenyi-Nagy and J. L. Framo (Eds.), *Intensive family therapy: Theoretical and practical aspects.* New York: Hoeber, Harper and Row, 1965, pp. 1-31.

Chapter 2 / FAMILY THERAPY: 1964-1970

. . . .

There have been some dramatic trends in family therapy during the past six years which I will undertake to describe in this chapter. The period covered will be 1964-1970. The paper brings up to date my earlier review (Zuk and Rubinstein, 1965) of concepts in family therapy, which had a special reference to therapy with families that contained a schizophrenic member, since in the earlier years of the field the published work frequently was about families with a schizophrenic member. The review coauthored with Rubinstein covered the period from the middle 1950's, when published work on family therapy first began to appear, through 1963, although it also contained reference to studies published in the 1940's and early 1950's which were not on family therapy but related to the field.

Recently (Zuk, 1969), I published a review-type paper which covered the period this chapter will cover, but from a different, more restricted perspective. I focused on a central conceptual issue in the field today; namely, the necessity to move from a dyadic-based to a triadic-based family therapy, using as an example of triadic-based family therapy my own group of studies. I pointed out that dyadic-based family therapy was largely based on the psychoanalytic model, frequently employing the terminology of psychoanalysis. Triadic-based family therapy is one of the systems-oriented therapies, as is communication-based family therapy, which is, however, mainly dyadic-based.

This paper has a broader perspective than the one referred to above. It will consider more than one main theoretical or conceptual division in family therapy, such as the dyadic-based versus triadic-based

A version of this material was published in *Psychotherapy: Theory, Research and Practice, 1971,* 8, 90-97.

dichotomy. It will consider some consolidations in positions that have been made; that is, further developments of positions by various writers that they established earlier, during the late 1950's and early 1960's. It will consider new trends that appeared in the period 1964-1970. The paper will close with some observations on the status, organization, and direction of family therapy as viewed from the perspective of the last six year period.

At the level of concepts or, one might even say, the ideological level, the major trend during 1964 to 1970 appears to be a deepening and broadening of the dialogue—one might even say, struggle—between the advocates of an individual-oriented family therapy based on the psychoanalytic model, and advocates of what, for want of a better term, might be called the systems orientation in family therapy. The first group focuses on the exploration of unconscious processes, attempts to reconstruct the historical sequence of pathology, refers often to such constructs as transference and countertransference, the Oedipus Complex, introjects and internalization, and therapeutic insight. The second group focuses on comprehending the sources of leverage and power in the immediate field of action, has a preference for explanation of change or pathology lodged in terms of positive and negative feedback rather than in terms of linear cause-effect sequences, does not invoke the concept of insight to account for change, but rather takes the position that change may be evaluated as an outcome of bargaining or negotiation between therapist and family, and attempts to catalogue the various negotiations that take place in the course of family therapy.

The ideological struggle between the camps might also be put in terms of asking, "What is the basic unit of observation in family therapy?" Is it the dyad (more accurately, dyadic process), to which the psychoanalytic model can be adapted without great difficulty? Or is it the triad (more accurately, triadic process), which requires that attention be focused on units of three persons or more, specifically on the way they form coalitions and engage in mediation? In the latter framework, the therapist may try to join a family coalition or try to break it up; or he may join the family in a coalition against a community agency such as school or police, thus bringing pressure to bear on the agency to change or at least depart from its routine handling of a problem.

At the level of development of clinical programs for patient populations, a major trend of the years 1964-1970 has been a substantial increase in the number of poor white and nonwhite minority families being seen for treatment in outpatient settings such as at the community mental health centers. This contrasts with the situation in the late 1950's and even early 1960's when, at least if the reports of those who published are indicative, there was a focus on families that contained a hospitalized schizophrenic member. Usually these families were white and middle class. In the last six years, larger numbers of families are being treated that have a wide range of symptomatology, not just schizophrenia. Presenting complaints now may range from school underachievement or delinquency in an adolescent boy, to alcoholism or drug addiction in a parent, to physical abuse by a husband toward his wife and children. There is also probably a consensus now among family therapists that it tends to be shorter-term than most of the individual-centered psychotherapies, approximating perhaps what has been the experience in group therapy, and more programs in family therapy are being geared to the short-term concept. It might be speculated that there is a tendency for psychoanalytically oriented family therapists to hold onto their families longer than systems-oriented therapists—although personally I doubt this—but in either case I suspect the majority of families presently being seen terminate, at the initiative of the therapist or the family, within 4 to 8 months of onset. There is a fairly high dropout rate during the process of engagement, particularly in lower class minority families.

At the level of therapeutic technique, a trend of the past six years has been in the direction of a proliferation of therapy approaches. Now departures are common from rules that some workers became deeply attached to in the late 1950's and early 1960's: that the nuclear family always had to be seen in toto; that appointments had to be adhered to religiously; that the optimal length of family therapy approximated the experience in individual therapy. Now there are more settings in which multiple family therapy is being done; in which crisis family therapy is

ishment. An older son often assumed responsibility for

al. distinguished two types of families: The disengaged,
al authority was abdicated; the enmeshed, in which
y was fixed, and children were allowed no indepen-
orted that 7 of the 12 families described in the study
as a result of family therapy. Improvement was
ms of such factors as ability to cope with stress,
ons between the spouses, and improved parental
trol of children.

per, Minuchin (1965) spelled out in some detail his
ng lower class families. He will order family members
niliar tasks but under conditions calculated to elicit
s. He attempts to make the rules governing the
een family members more explicit. He selects an area
s out their usual way of handling it, then arranges a
so that original responses may be elicited.

orkers in Denver, Colorado, operating under a federal
orting in the mid-1960's on family crisis therapy.
968), reporting baseline and six-month follow-up data
75 experimental and 75 control cases, pictured the
gram as encouraging. Family crisis therapy appeared
ing hospitalization in patients who would ordinarily
lized. Some cases eventually required hospitalization,
higher than the rehospitalization rate of the control
zation was subsequently required of members of the
ent family crisis therapy, the duration of their stay in
latively brief. Langsley et al. figured that the cost of
y was one-sixth the cost of hospital treatment.

has written a preliminary report on the psycho-
e refers to as the social network, after the term
zabeth Bott. By social network Speck means such
n to the nuclear family as relatives and friends, and
als with whom the members of the nuclear family
ct. He conducted six months of weekly sessions with
onsisting of from 12 to 35 members, and achieved
to be a favorable result.

being done; in which members of the extended family are being involved; in which community agencies such as the schools or courts or welfare agencies—agencies which have such a powerful influence on families—are more actively consulted and worked with.

At the level of family diagnosis and research, in the years 1964-1970 a decline is apparent in the number of efforts to demonstrate experimentally the existence of the "schizophrenogenic family." In the 1950's and early 1960's this was a focus of work, often taking place in hospital settings which offered family therapy for families with a schizophrenic member. I believe the decline is due in part to a de-emphasis on seeing in therapy families that contain a schizophrenic member in favor of a broader spectrum of families with problems; also in part due to the fact that, although statistically significant findings were reported, experimental studies on the "schizo-phrenogenic family" were based on samples that were acknowledged to be too small in numbers; and due to other methodological inadequacies. The concept of the "schizophrenogenic family" may be in need of a radical revision if it is to survive into the 1970's; it is possible, too, that it has simply served its purpose and that a new notion of family causality is needed to take its place, as it itself took the place of the "schizophrenogenic mother" concept established in the late 1940's and 1950's by Frieda Fromm-Reichmann and others.

The following selected review of studies is intended as documentation for the statements about the present condition of family therapy contained in this introductory section.

A REVIEW OF SELECTED STUDIES REFLECTING NEW TRENDS IN FAMILY THERAPY: 1964-1970

A paper by Auerswald (1968) showed how community agents and agencies influence the course and perhaps even outcome of mental disturbance in family members. He described the case of a young Puerto Rican runaway girl reported to the police by her mother. Auerswald reported how a psychiatrist colleague (Robert Ravich, M.D.)

happened to be at the police station when the mother reported the girl. He introduced himself and offered help which was accepted. The psychiatrist learned that the girl had been seeing a therapist (a social worker) and he arranged a visit to this therapist. From her he learned that at a clinic at which the girl had been evaluated, a diagnosis of schizophrenia had been made. The clinic made a recommendation of the need for a more controlled environment, which in New York, for a girl of this background, usually meant placement in a children's ward in one of the state hospitals.

The psychiatrist arranged a visit to the girl's school, where she was described by her teacher as a slow learner. He also learned that she had been involved in an after school group program at a settlement house. Upon interviewing the girl's sister, he learned of a close relationship between the girl and her grandfather. She had turned to her grandfather for warmth and affection. It was learned that with boys her own age she had used sexual play as a means to secure acceptance.

Thus, without having yet seen the girl, the psychiatrist constructed a picture of a child who had grown up relatively isolated in her own home. Communication was sparse between herself and her mother, and also with her sister. Eventually the police did pick the girl up and she was placed in an adolescent ward in a city hospital. Visiting her in the ward, the psychiatrist found her alternately childish and seductive in a degree that was bizarre for a 12 year old. The girl appeared ambivalent when faced with the alternatives of going home or to a state hospital.

The psychiatrist contructed a treatment plan and made a series of suggestions to family members and agencies involved, but a follow-up visit to the mother a month later revealed that the girl had been placed in a state hospital on the basis of the recommendation of a resident in the city hospital where she was taken by the police. The resident agreed with the diagnosis of schizophrenia that had been previously recorded. In the absence of effective countermoves, the standard operating procedures of various agencies were followed.

In concluding his paper, Auerswald pleaded for a treatment approach in which the totality of forces impinging on the patient and family are assessed, rather than the fractionated picture which is the one ordinarily developed by clinics and other agencies.

Sager et al. (1968)
adaptations of the clin
patients and their famil
The paper described
psychiatric walk-in clin
area served by the hosp
adjusting its intake proc
patients and their far
engaged in a short-term

During the first tw
three out of four of
with their families. U
high dropout rate, it v
with ambivalence and
for the symptoms ma
onus of responsibilit
them.

Then too the tear
realistic problems ass
sessions. Jobs held b
fairly rigid adherence
reluctant to reveal t
therapy. In these fai
did so during differe
sessions at school. Tl
these circumstances i

The team had t
members' backgrou
themselves also with
patients or with pati

Minuchin et al.
containing delinque
these families: Fa
missing from the
little with each ot
each other. Mother

of threats of pu
discipline.

Minuchin et
in which paren
parental authori
dence. It was re
were improved
measured in te
improved relatic
guidance and con

In a prior pa
method of treati
to engage in fai
original response
relationships betv
of conflict, poin
different context

A group of w
grant, began rep
Langsley et al. (1
on a sample of
results of the pro
effective in avoid
have been hospita
but at a rate no
group. If hospitali
group that underw
the hospital was
family crisis thera

Speck (1967)
therapy of what
introduced by El
persons in additio
other key individu
may come in cont
a social network
what he considered

being done; in which members of the extended family are being involved; in which community agencies such as the schools or courts or welfare agencies—agencies which have such a powerful influence on families—are more actively consulted and worked with.

At the level of family diagnosis and research, in the years 1964-1970 a decline is apparent in the number of efforts to demonstrate experimentally the existence of the "schizophrenogenic family." In the 1950's and early 1960's this was a focus of work, often taking place in hospital settings which offered family therapy for families with a schizophrenic member. I believe the decline is due in part to a de-emphasis on seeing in therapy families that contain a schizophrenic member in favor of a broader spectrum of families with problems; also in part due to the fact that, although statistically significant findings were reported, experimental studies on the "schizophrenogenic family" were based on samples that were acknowledged to be too small in numbers; and due to other methodological inadequacies. The concept of the "schizophrenogenic family" may be in need of a radical revision if it is to survive into the 1970's; it is possible, too, that it has simply served its purpose and that a new notion of family causality is needed to take its place, as it itself took the place of the "schizophrenogenic mother" concept established in the late 1940's and 1950's by Frieda Fromm-Reichmann and others.

The following selected review of studies is intended as documentation for the statements about the present condition of family therapy contained in this introductory section.

A REVIEW OF SELECTED STUDIES REFLECTING NEW TRENDS IN FAMILY THERAPY: 1964-1970

A paper by Auerswald (1968) showed how community agents and agencies influence the course and perhaps even outcome of mental disturbance in family members. He described the case of a young Puerto Rican runaway girl reported to the police by her mother. Auerswald reported how a psychiatrist colleague (Robert Ravich, M.D.)

happened to be at the police station when the mother reported the girl. He introduced himself and offered help which was accepted. The psychiatrist learned that the girl had been seeing a therapist (a social worker) and he arranged a visit to this therapist. From her he learned that at a clinic at which the girl had been evaluated, a diagnosis of schizophrenia had been made. The clinic made a recommendation of the need for a more controlled environment, which in New York, for a girl of this background, usually meant placement in a children's ward in one of the state hospitals.

The psychiatrist arranged a visit to the girl's school, where she was described by her teacher as a slow learner. He also learned that she had been involved in an after school group program at a settlement house. Upon interviewing the girl's sister, he learned of a close relationship between the girl and her grandfather. She had turned to her grandfather for warmth and affection. It was learned that with boys her own age she had used sexual play as a means to secure acceptance.

Thus, without having yet seen the girl, the psychiatrist constructed a picture of a child who had grown up relatively isolated in her own home. Communication was sparse between herself and her mother, and also with her sister. Eventually the police did pick the girl up and she was placed in an adolescent ward in a city hospital. Visiting her in the ward, the psychiatrist found her alternately childish and seductive in a degree that was bizarre for a 12 year old. The girl appeared ambivalent when faced with the alternatives of going home or to a state hospital.

The psychiatrist contructed a treatment plan and made a series of suggestions to family members and agencies involved, but a follow-up visit to the mother a month later revealed that the girl had been placed in a state hospital on the basis of the recommendation of a resident in the city hospital where she was taken by the police. The resident agreed with the diagnosis of schizophrenia that had been previously recorded. In the absence of effective countermoves, the standard operating procedures of various agencies were followed.

In concluding his paper, Auerswald pleaded for a treatment approach in which the totality of forces impinging on the patient and family are assessed, rather than the fractionated picture which is the one ordinarily developed by clinics and other agencies.

Sager et al. (1968) published a report which suggests that special adaptations of the clinic team must be made if poor minority group patients and their families are to be successfully engaged in treatment. The paper described a brief family therapy program based in a psychiatric walk-in clinic in a large metropolitan general hospital. The area served by the hospital was heavily Negro and Puerto Rican. After adjusting its intake procedure to suit this type of population, 75% of 79 patients and their families referred for treatment were successfully engaged in a short-term family therapy consisting of six sessions.

During the first two months of the program at the walk-in clinic, three out of four of the patients referred for therapy did not appear with their families. Upon considering the reasons responsible for the high dropout rate, it was recognized that family therapy was looked on with ambivalence and not a little anxiety. Families wanted quick relief for the symptoms manifested by the patient and were eager that an onus of responsibility for the patient's condition not be shifted to them.

Then too the team came to realize that there were many practical, realistic problems associated with the appearance of families at therapy sessions. Jobs held by members of these families usually required a fairly rigid adherence to a work schedule. Often family members were reluctant to reveal to their employers their need to take time off for therapy. In these families often both parents worked, and frequently did so during different periods of the day. Children attended different sessions at school. The team found that it had to make adjustments to these circumstances if the dropout rate was to be kept minimal.

The team had to deal with liabilities arising from the fact that its members' backgrounds were in individual therapy. Members found themselves also with some reluctance to work with poorly motivated patients or with patients of a different racial or ethnic origin.

Minuchin et al. (1967) reported on 12 poor minority group families containing delinquent members. Often the mother was the head of these families: Fathers were either peripheral members or entirely missing from the home. Communication was sparse: Spouses talked little with each other; children talked mainly to their mothers, not to each other. Mothers regulated the children's behavior, often by means of threats of punishment. An older son often assumed responsibility for discipline.

Minuchin et al. distinguished two types of families: The disengaged, in which parental authority was abdicated; the enmeshed, in which parental authority was fixed, and children were allowed no independence. It was reported that 7 of the 12 families described in the study were improved as a result of family therapy. Improvement was measured in terms of such factors as ability to cope with stress, improved relations between the spouses, and improved parental guidance and control of children.

In a prior paper, Minuchin (1965) spelled out in some detail his method of treating lower class families. He will order family members to engage in familiar tasks but under conditions calculated to elicit original responses. He attempts to make the rules governing the relationships between family members more explicit. He selects an area of conflict, points out their usual way of handling it, then arranges a different context so that original responses may be elicited.

A group of workers in Denver, Colorado, operating under a federal grant, began reporting in the mid-1960's on family crisis therapy. Langsley et al. (1968), reporting baseline and six-month follow-up data on a sample of 75 experimental and 75 control cases, pictured the results of the program as encouraging. Family crisis therapy appeared effective in avoiding hospitalization in patients who would ordinarily have been hospitalized. Some cases eventually required hospitalization, but at a rate no higher than the rehospitalization rate of the control group. If hospitalization was subsequently required of members of the group that underwent family crisis therapy, the duration of their stay in the hospital was relatively brief. Langsley et al. figured that the cost of family crisis therapy was one-sixth the cost of hospital treatment.

Speck (1967) has written a preliminary report on the psychotherapy of what he refers to as the social network, after the term introduced by Elizabeth Bott. By social network Speck means such persons in addition to the nuclear family as relatives and friends, and other key individuals with whom the members of the nuclear family may come in contact. He conducted six months of weekly sessions with a social network consisting of from 12 to 35 members, and achieved what he considered to be a favorable result.

In the last few years several settings have introduced multiple family therapy, in which members of more than one family are treated together at the same time. Laqueur et al. (1964) have reported on their experience with this technique, as has Barcai (1967).

Alger and Hogan (1969) reported on the technique of videotape replay of sessions to families. They believe that the technique promotes self-confrontation and that it increases emotional involvement in the therapy. Paul (1966) has also written on his experience with videotape playback with 11 families containing a schizophrenic member.

Some learning theory-oriented workers have made contributions that are of relevance to family therapists. Members of families are systematically trained to alter a pattern of reinforcement in their interaction with a child exhibiting undesirable behavior, with the aim of weakening and replacing the undesirable behavior. Positive results have been achieved in a study of this type reported by Patterson (1965), who has been a leader in such research.

A REVIEW OF SELECTED STUDIES REFLECTING A CONSOLIDATION OF POSITIONS IN FAMILY THERAPY: 1964-1970

Clinical Studies

Positions that began to be established in family therapy in the late 1950's and early 1960's were consolidated in the period 1964-1970. In *Intensive Family Therapy* (edited by Boszormenyi-Nagy and Framo, 1965), several of the papers elaborated positions of the contributors that basically they had been in the process of establishing earlier. Boszormenyi-Nagy continued to develop his application to family therapy of the psychology of introjects. Framo organized a review of research on family interaction. Bowen compared his treatment of schizophrenics and their families in the hospital and in private practice. Ackerman presented an interview with a psychotic girl and her family which illuminated his style of working as a therapist. Whitaker et al. discussed countertransference problems in the family therapy of schizophrenics and also suggested a scheme of assessing phases of therapy.

A contribution by Wynne (1965) in *Intensive Family Therapy* is unique because it is one of the few papers to spell out indications and contraindications for family therapy, and it is the only one to deal in such depth with the topic. In this paper Wynne distinguished "exploratory family therapy" from other types, although it bears a strong resemblance to other psychoanalytically oriented family therapies. In "exploratory family therapy" the therapist attempts to clarify and resolve structural intrafamilial difficulties. "Exploratory family therapy," according to Wynne, may be useful in adolescent separation problems, in problems in which family members trade dissociations with each other, in cognitive and communicational difficulties, in erratic or fixed distancing of relationships among family members, and in problems in which the communication among members is amorphous, vague, or undirected.

In his paper Wynne maintained that families in which the boundaries between the nuclear family and the wider family and social network are delineated and tightly organized are families for whom therapy is indicated. Conversely, those with weak or absent boundaries are those for whom therapy was contraindicated; as for example, in the case of families in which members no longer have meaningful emotional contact with one another.

A sad event in family therapy in the recent period was the death of Don D. Jackson, in January, 1968, at the age of 48. Jackson was an innovative person and possessed one of the most agile minds in American psychiatry. In two papers, Jackson (1967a, 1967b) consolidated a position for which he was well recognized. In one (Jackson 1967a) he posed a question about the basic unit of observation in psychiatry: Was it the individual patient—his symptoms, defenses, character structure, etc.; or was it the *system,* that is, the interpersonal context in which the patient's behavior occurs? Jackson presented a case for the system approach. He suggested that movement from the individual to the interpersonal framework was a discontinuous step; that it was not possible to explain one system strictly in terms of the other. He contrasted the linear, genetic, cause-and-effect psychology of the individual with the model of circular causation or causation put in terms of negative and positive feedbacks that seemed more appropriate to a psychology of interpersonal relations.

Jackson's position drew predictable fire from his more psychoanalytically committed colleagues. Wynne, in a discussion of Jackson's paper attached to it in the journal in which it appeared, took him to task for posing his question as an either/or proposition; that is, as the individual and interpersonal being discontinuous sytems. Wynne called for "open linked systems" that would bridge the gap. In a reply, Jackson wondered if Wynne's suggestion wasn't simply a device to " . . . save psychoanalytic tenets which have grown rusty and reified over the years" (p. 154).

In *Family Therapy and Disturbed Families* (edited by Zuk and Boszormenyi-Nagy, 1967), which carried several papers by workers associated with the systems wing in family therapy as well as the psychoanalytic wing, Haley, whose position is related to Jackson's, took up the theme of the discontinuity of systems (Haley, 1967a) and elaborated it in his own manner. He noted that a special contribution of family therapy and family therapy-related research has been to focus on triads as well as dyads. In his paper he considered "perverse triangles"—those arrangements that may occur among three persons that are pathological or result in pathology. In perverse triangles, at least one of the members is of a different generation than the others; a member of one generation coalesces with a member of another generation against a peer; finally, the coalition is denied. The perverse triangle, in effect, is one in which there has been a breach of generations. Psychoanalysis, according to Haley, institutionalized the perverse triangle in such a concept as the Oedipus Complex.

In *Techniques of Family Therapy,* Haley and Hoffman (1967) interviewed family therapists and elicited their comments mainly on initial interviews that the therapists conducted with families. By means of close questioning, the therapists explained their handling of the interviews. Three of the interviews were with Don Jackson, Virginia Satir, and Carl Whitaker. There are interesting interviews also with Charles Fulweiler, perhaps not as well known as the three mentioned, and with a team of therapists led by Frank Pittman of the Family Treatment Unit at the University of Colorado Medical Center in Denver. Fulweiler uses the device of leaving families alone to develop their interaction while he observes through a one-way mirror. He then returns at moments he believes especially opportune. Pittman and the Denver group provide a dramatic example of family crisis therapy.

In *Treating the Troubled Family,* Ackerman (1966) delineated his approach to families. The book, which contains lengthy transcript material interspersed with interpretive comments, is an aid to students who wish to know more about his style.

Mishler and Waxler (1966) reviewed and compared the work of Wynne and his associates, Lidz and his associates, and Bateson and his associates. The comparison focuses on the causal relationship between schizophrenia and family processes.

In a lengthy paper, Bowen (1966) developed concepts that have been associated with his name over the past decade: the undifferentiated family ego mass and the multigenerational transmission of pathology. He also outlined a scale of self-family differentiation which is intended as a measure of pathology.

MacGregor et al. (1964), developers of multiple impact therapy, reported that 75% of 62 treated families containing a disturbed adolescent maintained improvement after a period of 18 months. Multiple impact therapy exposed families to two days of extensive contact with a therapy team. First the family and team meet together, and then there is a split into different combinations of team-family according to a plan worked out at the initial meeting. The team tries to open up communication in the family and encourages role differentiation.

In *Conjoint Family Therapy,* Satir (1964) spelled out her method of treating families. Mrs. Satir capitalizes on the healthy potential in families, as contrasted with therapists who focus mainly on pathology.

In *Pragmatics of Human Communication,* Watzlawick et al. (1967) dealt with the behavioral effects of human communication, with special attention given to behavior disorders. The book emphasized the interactional model of communication as compared with the one-way model. Concepts originated by Bateson, Haley, Jackson, and Weakland were illustrated.

Paul (1967) reaffirmed his view of the importance of "operational mourning" in instances of object loss in families. He attempts to help family members work through the pain of losing loved ones through death or separation.

In *Changing the Family,* Brodey (1968) attempted to capture the flow of human interaction. The book is an extension of ideas which

Brodey (1967) presented in a prior paper on the application of cybernetic concepts to understanding family processes and family therapy.

Ferreira (1967) examined the nature of myths in families. He suggested that family myths served to solidify needs and to maintain equilibrium; and showed that myths may operate as defenses, stabilizing personalities and relationships of family members, even though they may be quite irrational.

In a series of papers (Zuk, 1966, 1967a, 1968), I outlined a triadic-based family therapy to which I gave the name go-between process. Go-between process is a systems-oriented approach in which the therapist casts himself alternately in the role of mediator and side-taker in the family in order to intervene in the pathogenic relating he observes. Pathogenic relating describes destructive processes that the therapist observes erupt in his presence in therapy sessions. One of its most pervasive forms is manifested in silencing strategies, a term I introduced. Pathogenic relating is often triadic-based in that it involves the coalition of two or more family members against a so-called victim. In triadic-based family therapy, change is considered an outcome of negotiations between therapist and family members, rather than as the working through of emotional resistance to the therapist's insights. The therapist is an active participant in the change process, rather than a releaser of the potential for change hidden within the patient.

Research Studies

Seeking to establish on sound experimental grounds a connection between pathology existing in the individual and in the nuclear family unit, a group of workers completed studies in the late 1960's that frequently contained positive results. Evidence developed to demonstrate the existence of the "schizophrenogenic family," a concept that was popularized during the 1960's. It took the place itself of another concept, the "schizophrenogenic mother," introduced by Fromm-Reichmann, which achieved currency during the 1950's.

My impression is that in the late 1960's the steam went out of efforts to demonstrate by experimental means the existence of the "schizophrenogenic family." In part this appears to be due to methodological problems, such as results based on samples that were too small. Some of the studies were based on complex designs which made replication unlikely. Also, contradictory evidence is difficult to rationalize: for example, the fact that in many if not most families that contain a schizophrenic child, there are nonsymptomatic siblings. If the pathogenic process affected one, why did it not affect the others?

If in the late 1960's there has been a decline in the number of studies on the "schizophrenogenic family," probably reflecting reduced interest in the problem, it is not that the need is any less to demonstrate the means by which pathology may be transmitted between the individual and the family. Hopefully there will be an insightful revision of the "schizophrenogenic family" concept in the 1970's that will stimulate further research; or perhaps there will be another concept to take its place, as it did the concept of the "schizophrenogenic mother."

Studies by Singer and Wynne (1965a, 1965b) were among the attempts in the middle 1960's to establish by experimental means a link between thinking disorders in parents and their schizophrenic children. Projective tests administered to the parents and children were matched "blind" by Singer at a better than chance level. Results exceeded chance also when the projective test data obtained from other family members were matched "blind" with the categories of diagnosis, forms of thinking, and severity of disorganization of the schizophrenic offspring.

Using data derived from family discussions on three topics for 15 minutes each, Lennard et al. (1965) found that schizophrenic pre-adolescent or early-adolescent sons addressed less communication to their fathers, and in turn received less from their fathers, than sons in a control group of "normals." Parents in the "schizophrenic" families communicated less than the parents in the "normals."

Reiss (1967) found significant differences in test performance among "schizophrenic" families, families in which a member had a character disorder, and "normals." Among the tests administered were puzzles and card sorts. Stabenau et al. (1965) reported test differences between families of schizophrenics, "delinquents," and "normals."

Mishler and Waxler (1968) wrote on the application of experimental methods to the study of interaction in "schizophrenic" families and "normals." The authors attempted rigorously to apply standard test procedures and to utilize reliable and valid measures of interaction. In a review of the Mishler-Waxler book, Wynne (1969) indicated that its significance should not be measured in terms of hard results, but rather it should be regarded as an example of a high standard of research design. The data were derived from Strodtbeck's revealed difference technique. Wynne's review also noted that a shortcoming of the study was the difficulty in finding adequate numbers of families for the subgroup samples. It should be noted of course that the authors did find differences between the "normals" and "schizophrenics," and reported differences of interest also within the "schizophrenics," for example, between the good and poor premorbids.

Loveland (1967) described the development of the Relation Rorschach, a technique for studying family interaction. Based on Rorschach responses arrived at jointly by a family, the evidence she presented showed that the Relation Rorschach was a useful device to assess family interaction.

Haley (1964) found differences in performance on a conversational task between 40 "abnormal" families (i.e., families containing a child who was in psychotherapy or who had been arrested) and 40 "normals." The differences occurred when a measure was taken of the order of speaking in the families. In the 1964 study, the samples consisted of parents with *one* child only. Later Haley (1967b) attempted to duplicate the procedure with samples of parents who had two children, and the result was that few differences were found. Haley speculated that the "abnormal" families may have become more normal through the addition of a nonsymptomatic sibling, and thus differences tended to be cancelled out.

Ferreira and Winter (1968) examined the decision-making process in "abnormal" and "normal" families and found that the amount of information exchanged was greater in "normal" as compared with the "abnormal" families. It was also found that the "abnormal" families spent a comparatively greater amount of time in silence during the decision-making process. In a prior study, Ferreira and Winter (1965) found that in "abnormal" families spontaneous agreement occurred less frequently than in "normal" families.

Recently Winter and Ferreira (1969) edited a book of readings with commentary on research in family interaction. The purpose of the collection was to present a coverage of the problems involved in studying family interaction, methodologies devised to handle these problems, and some representative findings in interaction research.

SOME OBSERVATIONS ON THE STATUS, ORGANIZATION, AND DIRECTION OF FAMILY THERAPY: 1964-1970

Despite, or perhaps because of, its lack of a formal organization, the family therapy movement in the United States has had an amazing vitality. If acceptance of papers on professional programs and in a wide variety of journals is any criterion, the interest level of mental health workers in family therapy is high. On the basis of my information obtained through correspondence with workers across the country and in conversations at various professional meetings, I estimate that there are perhaps 1,000-1,200 therapists who see families in conjoint treatment. Not all of these would qualify as fully experienced family therapists; perhaps two-thirds might see one or two families during a week or month. "Hard core" family therapists probably still number no more than 300-400; by hard core, I mean therapists who spend at least half of their work week seeing families and/or dealing with problems related to family therapy.

I was privileged to edit and publish (Zuk, 1967b) a listing of therapists doing family therapy in the United States and abroad. Together with the mimeographed "Supplement" of 1968, the listing contains the names of approximately 500 therapists who were willing to supply the editor with selected information about their background and experience. While not an endorsement of a therapist's proficiency, the listing does contain the names of most of the acknowledged leaders in the field and most of the workers seriously addressing themselves to family therapy.

In replying to a recent paper by Beels and Ferber (1969), I commented on the vigorous dialogue that exists between advocates of a psychoanalytically oriented family therapy and a systems-oriented family therapy. At times the dialogue has generated considerable heat, as when, in an introductory statement to the book they edited, *Intensive Family Therapy,* Boszormenyi-Nagy and Framo distinguished two types of family therapy—intensive and supportive. In their view, intensive family therapy was directed toward working through unconscious transference distortions in family relationships. It contrasted with and was a "deeper" method than supportive family therapy, by which the editors referred to the method used by therapists who attempted to change interaction patterns, clarify communication, and help families cope with concrete stress situations.

Replying sharply to the distinction made by Boszormenyi-Nagy and Framo, Haley (1966), while sympathizing with the need of psychoanalytically oriented family therapists to gain the acceptance of their more orthodox colleagues, lamented the fact that distinctions in the quality of various types of family therapy were being made on the basis of the scanty evidence that was then available.

A more recent articulation of a main conceptual difference between the two wings of family therapists is made in an article of mine (Zuk, 1969) in which the mainly dyadic-based work of the individual- or analytically oriented group is contrasted with triadic-based family therapy. A still more recent development in the ongoing debate is Haley's (1970-1971) description of certain methodological differences in the working approaches of the individual-oriented versus systems-oriented family therapists.

In October, 1964, in Philadelphia, the first nationwide conference of family therapists which assembled therapists of different persuasions was held. *Family Therapy and Disturbed Families,* edited by myself and Boszormenyi-Nagy, was based on the proceedings of this three-day conference. Also in the fall of 1964 there was a meeting in Galveston, Texas, sponsored by a regional group of the American Psychiatric Association which was attended by some leading family therapists. The proceedings of this conference were later published in a monograph edited by Cohen (1966). More recently, in February, 1969, a second nationwide meeting of family therapists took place in Monterey, California: It was named the Don D. Jackson Memorial Conference.

A survey of family therapists was undertaken in 1966 by the Committee on the Family of the Group for Advancement of Psychiatry

(GAP). The report is entitled *The Field of Family Therapy*[1] and, although it has not at the time of this writing been formally published, it was distributed by the then chairman of the GAP Committee, Dr. Israel Zwerling, to the participants of the Jackson Memorial Conference so its contents are now widely known to family therapists.

The survey was based on the replies to a lengthy questionnaire by 312 individuals who stated that they had treated families. It is acknowledged in the report that the representativeness of the survey sample could not be ascertained; still, it was believed that the results met the intended purpose to gather information about practices in the field and to identify issues that might require investigation by more refined procedures.

The survey chapter on "Techniques and Practices" offered some especially practical information about how family therapists conduct sessions. Typically, *one* therapist saw the family; only 6% regularly worked with a cotherapist. The majority saw the family once weekly in sessions lasting approximately one hour. The majority preferred to see the nuclear family in sessions, although most respondents agreed to hold sessions in the event members were absent. There was a tendency for respondents to want to include in sessions anyone the nuclear family considered an important personage. A small number did multiple family therapy (15%). Only 6% of the respondents saw families in their, the families', homes. The majority charged for family therapy at the same rate as for individual therapy. The majority did not insist on labeling the *family* as the patient. The majority excluded children when the sex life of the parents was discussed but not when sex in general was the topic.

What are the prospects for a national association of family therapists? It seems inevitable that some kind of organization will come to pass in the future. I am aware of groups of therapists, often legally incorporated, presently operating in Philadelphia, New York, Boston,

---

[1] The monograph was published during the time the article was in press originally; hence a complete reference is available and is included here. Formulated by the Committee on the Family of the Group for Advancement of Psychiatry, it is distributed by the Mental Health Materials Center, New York. It is listed as Report No. 78, Vol. VII, March, 1970.

Chicago, the San Francisco Bay Area, Washington, D.C., and Seattle; and there are probably groups in other cities of which I am unaware. There are knotty problems to be dealt with in developing a formal organization, some of which are touched upon in an editorial in the March, 1968, issue of *Family Process.* Signed by 65 individuals, the editorial took the position that there should be a few years' delay in the formation of an organization in order to prevent premature closure. A vigorous debate on the issue continues at the time of this writing.

Writing on treatment programs in the mid-1970's, Kolb (1969), who was serving during 1968-1969 as President of the American Psychiatric Association, made the interesting prediction that family therapy would become prevalent in American hospitals, particularly if the trend toward a high rate of child and adolescent admissions continues. He noted that during the 1960's family therapy was practiced mostly in extrahospital settings, but he speculated that pressure for more effective, less time-consuming methods would bring family therapy into wide use in hospitals.

There is little doubt in my mind that the trend Kolb recognized in family therapy in the 1960's will continue in the 1970's; namely, that it will continue to be practiced mainly in extrahospital settings, and become more prevalent in them, although I suspect that it will also increase, as Kolb predicted, in hospitals.

Recently Halleck (1968), a leading psychiatrist who is not recognized as a family therapist, made some interesting statements about a possible role for family therapists in relation to the status quo issue in American society. He pointed out that a successful treatment of the family of a delinquent Negro boy could result in the smothering of a family protest against injustices toward Negroes which was represented symbolically in the boy's acting out. This could constitute a use of family therapy in the maintenance of the status quo. On the other hand if, as a result of family therapy, the rebellious boy were able to confront his family with the need to express their grievances by uniting to bring legitimate economic and political pressures to bear on society, then family therapy would not have been used in the service of the status quo. Halleck speculated that candidates for a trial of family therapy might include delinquents, drug addicts, alcoholics, and alienated students. My impression is that most family therapists would not disagree with his suggestions about groups for whom family therapy is indicated.

At the present time there appears to be little activity in family therapy outside of the United States. A few foreign workers are recorded in "A Listing of Therapists Doing Family Therapy" (Zuk, 1967b). The greatest activity currently appears to be in Canada and the Netherlands. Dutch government agencies have sponsored visits by American family therapists to train mental health workers in Holland. (I was privileged to be one of these visitors during October-November, 1967). There is surprisingly little family therapy done in England.

Family therapy faces two handicaps outside of the United States: (a) As compared with the U.S., foreign societies generally are more homogeneous, less permissive, more patriarchal, less mobile; and (b) as compared with the U.S., typically there is a greater emphasis on orthodoxy among foreign mental health professionals. Both factors create a climate not especially favorable to family therapy; or rather, family therapy as it is known and practiced in the U.S.

REFERENCES

Ackerman, N. W. *Treating the troubled family.* New York: Basic Books, 1966.

Alger, I., & Hogan, P. Enduring effects of videotape playback experience on family and marital relationships. *American Journal of Orthopsychiatry,* 1969, **39**, 86-94.

Auerswald, E. A. Interdisciplinary versus ecological approach. *Family Process,* 1968, **7**, 202-215.

Barcai, A. An adventure in multiple family therapy. *Family Process,* 1967, **6**, 16-26.

Beels, C. C., & Ferber, A. Family therapy: A view. *Family Process,* 1969, **8**, 280-318.

Boszormenyi-Nagy, I., & Framo, J. L. (Eds.) *Intensive family therapy: Theoretical and practical aspects.* New York: Hoeber Medical Division, Harper and Row, 1965.

Bowen, M. The use of family therapy in clinical practice. *Comprehensive Psychiatry,* 1966, **7**, 345-374.

Brodey, W. M. A cybernetic approach to family therapy. In G. H. Zuk and I. Boszormenyi-Nagy (Eds.), *Family therapy and disturbed families.* Palo Alto, Calif.: Science and Behavior Books, 1967, pp. 74-84.

Brodey, W. M. *Changing the family.* New York: Potter, 1968.

Cohen, I. (Ed.) *Family structure, dynamics and therapy.* Psychiatric Research Report #20. Washington, D.C.: American Psychiatric Association, 1966.

Ferreira, A. J. Psychosis and family myth. *American Journal of Psychotherapy,* 1967, **21**, 186-197.

Ferreira, A. J. & Winter, W. D. Family interaction and decision making. *Archives of General Psychiatry,* 1965, **13**, 214-223.

Ferreira, A. J. & Winter, W. D. Information exchange and silence in normal and abnormal families. *Family Process,* 1968, **7**, 251-276.

Haley, J. Research on family patterns: An instrument measurement. *Family Process,* 1964, **3**, 41-65.

Haley, J. Review of I. Boszormenyi-Nagy and J.L. Framo (Eds.), *Intensive family therapy: Theoretical and practical aspects. Family Process,* 1966, **5**, 284-289.

Haley, J. Toward a theory of pathological systems. In G. H. Zuk and I. Boszormenyi-Nagy (Eds.), *Family therapy and disturbed families.* Palo Alto, Calif.: Science and Behavior Books, 1967a, pp. 11-27.

Haley, J. Speech sequences of normal and abnormal families with two children. *Family Process,* 1967b, **6**, 81-97.

Haley, J. & Hoffman, Lynn. *Techniques of family therapy.* New York: Basic Books, 1967.

Haley, J. Family therapy. *International Journal of Psychiatry,* 1970-1971, **9** 233-242.

Halleck, S. L. Psychiatry and the status quo. *Archives of General Psychiatry,* 1968, **19**, 257-265.

Jackson, D. D. The individual and the larger contexts. *Family Process,* 1967a, **6**, 139-147.

Jackson, D. D. Aspects of conjoint family therapy. In G. H. Zuk and I. Boszormenyi-Nagy (Eds.), *Family therapy and disturbed families.* Palo Alto, Calif.: Science and Behavior Books, 1967b, pp. 28-40.

Kolb, L. C. Therapeutic programs in the mid-1970's. *Journal: The National Association of Private Psychiatric Hospitals,* 1969, **1**, 46-50.

Langsley, D. G., Pittman, F. S., III, Machotka, P., & Flomenhaft, K. Family crisis therapy—results and implications. *Family Process,* 1968, **7**, 145-158.

Laqueur, H. P., LaBurt, H. A., & Morong, E. Multiple family therapy. In J. H. Masserman (Ed.), *Current psychiatric therapies: Volume IV.* New York: Grune and Stratton, 1964, pp. 150-154.

Lennard, H. L., Beaulieu, M. R., and Embrey, N. G. Interaction in families with a schizophrenic child. *Archives of General Psychiatry*, 1965, **12**, 166-183.

Loveland, Nathene T. The Relation Rorschach: A technique for studying interaction. *Journal of Nervous and Mental Diseases*, 1967, **145**, 93-105.

MacGregor, R., Ritchie, A., Serrano, A. C., and Schuster, F. P., Jr. *Multiple impact therapy with families.* New York: Blakiston Division, McGraw-Hill, 1964.

Minuchin, S. Conflict-resolution family therapy. *Psychiatry*, 1965, **28**, 278-286.

Minuchin, S., Montalvo, B., Guerney, B. C., Jr., Rosman, Bernice L., and Shumer, Florence. *Families of the slums.* New York: Basic Books, 1967.

Mishler, E. G. & Waxler, Nancy E. Family interaction processes and schizophrenia. *International Journal of Psychiatry*, 1966, **2**,, 375-413.

Mishler, E. G. & Waxler, Nancy E. *Interaction in families: An experimental study of family processes and schizophrenia.* New York: Wiley, 1968.

Patterson, G. R., A learning theory approach to the treatment of the school-phobic child. In L. Ullman and L. Krasner (Eds.), *Case studies in behavior modification.* New York: Holt, Rinehart, and Winston, 1965, pp. 279-284.

Paul, N. L. Effects of playback on family members of their own previously recorded conjoint therapy material. In I. M. Cohen (Ed.), *Family structure, dynamics and therapy.* Psychiatric Research Report #20. Washington, D.C.: American Psychiatric Association, 1966, pp. 175-187.

Paul, N. L. The role of mourning and empathy in conjoint marital therapy. In G. H. Zuk and I. Boszormenyi-Nagy (Eds.), *Family therapy and disturbed families.* Palo Alto, Calif.: Science and Behavior Books, 1967, pp. 186-206.

Reiss, D. Individual thinking and family interaction. *Archives of General Psychiatry*, 1967, **16**, 80-93.

Sager, C. J., Masters, Yvonne J., Bonall, Ruth E., & Normand, W. C. Selection and engagement of patients in family therapy. *American Journal of Orthopsychiatry*, 1968, **38**, 715-723.

Satir, Virginia M. *Conjoint family therapy: A guide to theory and technique.* Palo Alto, Calif.: Science and Behavior Books, 1964.

Singer, Margaret T., & Wynne, L. C. Thought disorders and family relations of schizophrenics. III: Methodology using projective techniques. *Archives of General Psychiatry*, 1965a, **12**, 187-200.

Singer, Margaret T., & Wynne, L. C. Thought disorders and family relations of schizophrenics. IV: Results and implications. *Archives of General Psychiatry,* 1965b, **12**, 201-212.

Speck, R. V. Psychotherapy of the social network of a schizophrenic family. *Family Process,* 1967, **6**, 208-214.

Stabenau, J. R., Tupin, J., Werner, M., and Pollin, W. A comparative study of families of schizophrenics, delinquents, and normals. *Psychiatry,* 1965, **28**, 45-49.

Watzlawick, P., Beavin, Janet H., & Jackson, D. D. *Pragmatics of human communication: A study of interactional patterns, pathologies and paradoxes.* New York: Norton, 1967.

Winter, W. D., & Ferreira, A. J. (Eds.) *Research in family interaction: Readings and commentary.* Palo Alto, Calif.: Science and Behavior Books, 1969.

Wynne, L. C. Review of E. G. Mishler and Nancy E. Waxler, *Interaction in families. Archives of General Psychiatry,* 1969, **20**, 605-608.
Intensive family therapy: Theoretical and practical aspects. New York: Hoeber Medical Division, Harper and Row, 1965, pp. 289-322.

Wynne, L. C. Review of E. G. Mishler and Nancy E. Waxler, *Interaction in families, Archives of General Psychiatry,* 1969, **20**, 605-608.

Zuk, G. H. The go-between process in family therapy. *Family Process,* 1966, **5**, 162-178.

Zuk, G. H. Family therapy. *Archives of General Psychiatry,* 1967a, **16**, 71-79.

Zuk, G. H. A listing of therapists doing family therapy. *Pastoral Psychology,* 1967b, Annual Directory Issue (January).

Zuk, G. H. Prompting change in family therapy. *Archives of General Psychiatry,* 1968, **19**, 727-736.

Zuk, G. H. Triadic-based family therapy. *International Journal of Psychiatry,* 1969, **8**, 539-548.

Zuk, G. H., & Rubinstein, D. A review of concepts in the study and treatment of families of schizophrenics. In I. Boszormenyi-Nagy and J. L. Framo (Eds.), *Intensive family therapy: Theoretical and practical aspects.* New York: Hoeber Medical Division, Harper and Row, 1965, pp. 1-31.

Zuk, G. H. and Boszormenyi-Nagy, I. (Eds.), *Family therapy and disturbed families.* Palo Alto, Calif.: Science and Behavior Books, 1967.

. . . .

PART II:: TECHNIQUE OF FAMILY THERAPY

. . . .

Chapter 3 / THE GO-BETWEEN PROCESS IN FAMILY THERAPY

. . . .

A discussion dealing with the concept and exercise of power in human relationships demands a definition of power at the onset. The suggested working definition is the capacity of a person to define, characterize, or otherwise *control* relationships with others; also, and at the same time, it is the capacity to initiate *actions* leading to a predicted increase in control. The concept of therapeutic power will mean the capacity of the therapist to define the therapist-patient relationship and to initiate actions to increase control of the relationship in ways he believes to be in the best interest of the patient.

What are the sources of therapeutic power in family therapy? Most studies touching on this question have followed the psychoanalytic view that insight and the process of making conscious what was unconscious are the key sources. The predominating influence of psychoanalytic concepts in family therapy is reported in two reviews (Zuk and Rubinstein, 1965; and Meissner, 1964). The theme of this chapter as already stated in a preliminary paper (Zuk, 1965) is that a major source having little or nothing to do with insight or awareness *per se* is the control of what may be called go-between process, a phenomenon of social systems arising particularly in the aftermath of conflict.

Go-between process presumes that conflict is a characteristic and inevitable phase of group life and that it is in the interest of the principals to take steps, secretively or publicly, to check its magnitude. One of the steps is the search for and selection of a party empowered to mediate. The power of this party, this go-between, to change the nature

This chapter was published in *Family Process,* 1966, 5, 162-178. A version was read at the Annual Meeting of the American Group Psychotherapy Association in Philadelphia in January, 1966.

of the conflict, the principals' positions vis à vis each other, and also promote personality change in each principal has not been sufficiently explored in the area of psychotherapy, or for that matter in other areas where go-between process is conducted; for example, in the relations among governments, and in business and professional organizations.

Go-between process in family therapy has special characteristics. In family therapy conflict erupts not among strangers but among individuals who have had a long history of relating to each other and who have worked out already a complex process for the mediation or pseudomediation of conflicts. The therapist is introduced into this ready-made situation; he brings his expertise to it. Some implications of the therapist's use of go-between process to bring about change, and the family's use of it to resist change, will be considered here.

Go-between process has implications for other therapies, most obviously for group and milieu therapy, and in social casework. The caseworker in particular is frequently cast in the role of go-between or mediator between individual or family and the community. The experienced caseworker probably has developed as much awareness of the powers and, to be sure, limitations of the go-between process and role of the go-between as any mental health worker to date.

DESCRIPTION OF GO-BETWEEN PROCESS

Wynne (1961) has pointed out the need for the conceptualization of important shifts and sequences occurring in family therapy. Go-between process is both a shift and a sequence: It is a shift in that it denotes a phase of eruption of conflict and a phase of diminution; it is a sequence in that the diminution follows the eruption in a regular fashion and as a separately describable phase.

Key steps in the go-between process in family therapy are proposed as follows: (a) Introduction by either therapist or family member of an issue on which there are at least two identifiable opponents or principals; (b) intensification of the conflict and the beginning of movement of a person, either therapist or family member, into the role of go-between; (c) attempts by the principals and go-between to define and delimit each other's roles or positions; (d) recession or cessation of the conflict associated with a change in the positions of principals or with a redefinition of the conflict, or both.

Distinguishing Go-Between Process from the Role of the Go-Between

Go-between process and the role of the go-between are *not* synonymous terms. It should be clear that taking the role of go-between is but *one step* or phase in go-between process. The therapist controls go-between process to the extent that he is aware of the steps. The therapist can lose control of the process in some instances by taking the role of go-between when it would have been more judicious for him to cast himself as a principal. The therapist also loses control of the process if he allows himself to be cast either as a principal or go-between by the family. To the extent that the family can determine which role he takes, it is in control of the process.

The therapist is in a position to introduce issues as potential sources of conflict. In taking the initiative to do so, he directs go-between process. He must observe the family carefully to see if the issue produces conflict, then if the conflict produces principals, then decide his own orientation vis à vis the contending parties; that is, whether he should enter the conflict in the role of go-between or principal. The therapist may decide *at the onset* to inject himself into the conflict as principal or go-between; but sometimes his gain in therapeutic leverage is greater if he waits.

As go-between process unfolds in the aftermath of conflict and the therapist and family members array themselves as principals and go-between, a struggle ensues over the definition and delimitation of their respective positions. Even though they may have empowered him to act as such, the principals often take steps to deny or severely delimit the go-between's power to mediate the conflict. He may be defined simply as one who is able to "stop the fighting." To the extent he is so defined and he accepts the definition, his power is delimited. It is up to the go-between to extend the limits of his power, if necessary even by pointing out and emphasizing fears and anxieties or expectations of the principals vis à vis each other. The go-between can also delimit his own role in the interest of therapeutic leverage; he can conclude that the principals are allowing him too much latitude in the hope that he become confused as to specific changes to demand of them.

If as has been stated, go-between process is "more than" the role of the go-between, so is the role of the go-between frequently "more than" that typically associated with the role of mediator. The mediator, say, in labor-management negotiations, typically seeks to clarify issues; but the go-between in family therapy may intentionally confuse issues. Typically the mediator is *one* person who claims and is assigned the role; the go-between role may not only shift among participants in family therapy, but the go-between may also specifically deny that he is ever acting as such.

In family therapy the go-between may be very active, intrusive, and confronting, or inactive and passive. He may move into the role of go-between by the device of attacking two parties he hopes to make into principals; or he may move into the role by calmly pointing out a difference between two parties. On the other hand, he may become a go-between by refusing to take sides in a dispute that has erupted; or he may become one by presenting a new point of view in a dispute.

The go-between must decide if he will ask the principals to change their positions; it is equally important for him to decide that his position may not be strong enough for him to do so, or that the change he might secure would be insignificant. It is important to remember that the go-between, although always a key person, can be weak or strong. He can be very weak, for example, if he has been seduced into taking the role of go-between by a principal who wishes to split an already established alliance. As has been said, power accrues mostly to the individual in family therapy who controls and manages go-between process, not necessarily to the individual who takes the role of go-between. For this reason, the therapist may decide to cast himself clearly as a principal in a conflict, in hopes of thus moving one of the family members who might otherwise be a strong opposing principal into becoming a relatively weak go-between. The therapist thus rearranges and hopefully diminishes the resistive force of the family arrayed against him.

The role of the go-between is one of considerable potential therapeutic power in family therapy, for the principals, as in other areas in which go-betweens function, empower him to secure certain changes in their positions vis à vis each other; in itself, their acceptance of a person as go-between signals a readiness to retrench from fixed positions. To be sure, each principal hopes the other will give up more. Each hopes the go-between will act mainly in his interests against an opposing principal. This knowledge is advantageous to the go-between, who can then exert leverage against the opposing principals with the aim of securing significant changes which he may deem therapeutic. The go-between may introduce initiatives not suggested by opposing principals as possible solutions of conflict. He may also exert therapeutic power by delaying or speeding up his arbitration.

DISTINGUISHING THE GO-BETWEEN PROCESS AS CONDUCTED BY THERAPIST AND BY FAMILY

In family therapy go-between process may be, and usually is, conducted both by the therapist and the family: In his conduct of go-between process, the therapist aims to change the family in ways he deems beneficial to them; in their conduct of go-between process, the family attempts to maintain the status quo, resist and undermine the therapist's attempts to change them.

Some of the devices the *therapist* may use to conduct go-between process to change the family have already been mentioned. One that has not is his use of interpretation. Apart from its function to increase understanding and awareness, interpretation may, to use a term suggested by Haley (1963), be used to maintain the therapist in a one-up position vis à vis the family. For example, a judicious interpretation may slice through a subtle maneuver of the family to oust the therapist from his role as go-between which, at the time, he may wish to play in the conduct of go-between process. Thus interpretation may be part of the armamentarium of the therapist in his exercise of go-between process.

Transference[1] or family transference, to use the term coined by
Boszormenyi-Nagy and Framo (1962), may be a significant determinant
in the *family's* conduct of go-between process to resist the therapist's
attempts at change. For example, as a result of a distorted perception
of the therapist as a parent or parent-like figure, a member or the
family as a whole may initiate action to cast the therapist in the role of
the family judge, one kind of go-between. To be sure, the family may
then systematically undermine his decisions, as if to castrate the parent
imago.

On the basis of present experience and information, it cannot be
decided whether transference or family transference are *determinants* in
the family's conduct of go-between process—as suggested in the
previous paragraph—or *consequences* of the interaction of the therapist's and family's conduct of go-between process. It may be the case,
for example, that when the therapist takes the role of family judge in
his conduct of go-between process, his doing so stimulates transference
in the family and the members then tend to distortedly perceive him as
a parent imago. Whichever the case, however, it seems clear that
transference may play a significant role in the family's conduct of
go-between process.

The descriptions to follow will illustrate how go-between process
may be used by the therapist as a technique to secure change in family
therapy, and also how it may be used by the family to resist change. It
must be remembered that in none of the examples was I as the therapist
employing go-between process systematically. Only on replaying
tape-recorded sessions did it become apparent that aspects of my work
could be described in such terms. On the basis of present experience, it
is not possible to determine the range of therapeutic changes that can
be secured through judicious and systematic application of go-between
process. The descriptions to follow simply suggest that therapeutic
change *can* follow from the therapist's skillful application of go-
between process; and also that go-between process, when controlled by
the *family,* can be a major resistance to therapeutic change.

[1] From the perspective of my thinking in 1970, this reference to transference
seems unwarranted, but at the time of writing the paper I still felt some
responsibility to relate psychoanalytic with group process concepts.

TYPES OF GO–BETWEEN PROCESS
OBSERVED IN FAMILY THERAPY

Selections from cases seen by the writer in family therapy will be used to illustrate four key variations in go-between process. The variations are as follows: (a) a family member as go-between with other family members as principals; (b) a family member as go-between with other family members and the therapist opposing each other as principals; (c) the therapist as go-between with family members as principals; (d) the therapist as go-between with family members and an agent of the community as opposing principals.

Variation 1: Family Member as Go-Between
with Other Family Members as Principals

This is a common interaction in family therapy, observed frequently in mothers who wish to pit their husbands and children against each other so as to reserve for themselves a role of benevolent go-between. The mothers "explain" their children and husbands to the therapist; they, children and husbands, the mothers report, have simply never been able to get along. Someone has always had to keep them apart, and by default that role has fallen to the mothers. They complain, perhaps with bitterness, how dissatisfied they are to be intercessors.

In these rather commonly occurring clinical encounters, the mothers are employing go-between process to control relationships with both their children and husbands. In family therapy they assume the role of go-between not only between husbands and children, but also between husbands and children and therapist. They subtly arrange to gain the therapist's acceptance as go-between. Therapists may turn to them early in treatment for further understanding of the family situation, channel direction and advice through them to the family, and may make the mistake of identifying them as allies. In reality, they may seriously undermine the therapist's efforts, for as go-between they are able to alter and rearrange his messages to the family. These mothers may actually be the strongest resisters of change in the family.

In a specific case in family therapy, a mother was observed early in sessions to jockey for the role of go-between with other family members as principals. The primary patient was an emotionally immature girl of 19 years with a history of impulsive acting out. The family was composed of the girl, a younger brother, and two parents: The mother, an outspoken, dominant person; the father, an apprehensive man, cautious, passive relative to his wife. Relatively early in the sessions the mother established herself as the family spokeswoman; in particular, she explained to the therapist the impasse that existed between her daughter and her husband. She said her husband had a history of denying and rejecting the daughter, who in turn denied and rejected him. The mother would burst into tears in recounting this story. In the seventh session, for example, the mother accused her husband of hateful behavior toward their daughter, who happened not to be present during the session. An excerpt from the seventh session follows:

Mother: (tearfully, to the therapist) She feels rejected by him. He's heard me say this years back. I've pointed out all these things. I don't know if I was right or wrong, but I only said what I saw . . . Now this is the outcome . . .

Therapist: (to father) What's your reaction to your daughter? Are you inclined to find she annoys you?

Father: I'm just trying to see where my . . . if I sincerely feel that . . .

Therapist: (interrupting) No, no, you answer the question being put to you, whether or not you find your daughter created in you the need not to have her too close?

Father: (puzzled tone) I don't know why my wife feels that way . . . She says because my actions . . .

Therapist: (again interrupts) No, no. now wait. You do not feel inwardly annoyed by your daughter's attempts to get closer to you?

Father: (cautiously) No.

---

[2] My cotherapist in this and subsequent excerpts from transcripts reported here is Leon Robinson, M.D. It happens that it is Dr. Robinson making the comments reported in this excerpt. (Never favorable to the concept of cotherapy, I have not undertaken it in the several years since the original publication of the paper.)

Mother: Why has she told you that? Why has she said, "Daddy, why do you always push me away?"
Father: And what did I say to that?

In this excerpt the mother engages in go-between process when she introduces an issue—the mutual rejection of her husband and daughter—which casts them as principals in a conflict in which she moves into the role of go-between. Husband and daughter have tended to negotiate with each other through the mother frequently in the past. The excerpt simply illustrates a recurrence of this pattern and has the added effect of establishing the mother as the family go-between in the eyes of the therapist. Notice how cleverly the mother disguises her powerful position in the family: Her bitter accusation of her husband, her tears, and her voiced despair over the lack of change all testify to her apparent discomfort in acting as go-between, thus to be free to make key decisions affecting the lives of her daughter and husband. Incidentally, the excerpt illustrates how one may be accusatory, as was the mother to her husband, and still be a go-between in family therapy.

To be sure, her children and husband from time to time did attempt to oust the mother from the go-between role, but not very successfully. Coaxed by the therapist, the daughter, for example, would begin to describe an area of conflict between her mother and herself only to have her mother, and then even her father and brother, deny that she had legitimate grounds for complaint. In other words, mother, father, and son allied themselves against the daughter to turn aside her challenge to her mother. One observed in this family bits of evidence of a system operating to maintain the mother as go-between with the other family members as opposing principals.

At least three therapist gambits might be applicable in family therapy with the family described above: (a) for the therapist to define the mother as a *principal* in a conflict vis à vis another family member, say the daughter, and interpret and confront her in her subsequent attempts to move back into the role of go-between; (b) for the therapist to encourage another family member to engage the mother as an opposing principal; (c) for the therapist to designate and lend consistent support to a family member other than the mother in the role of go-between and interpret and confront the mother in her expected efforts to usurp the role again for herself. In these gambits, the therapist probes the ways in which it is possible for the family to make use of go-between process. Each gambit renders it possible in some degree to expose and potentially limit the mother's control and conduct of go-between process.

Variation 2: Family Member as Go-Between with Other Family Members and Therapist Opposed as Principals

This is also a rather common interaction in family therapy, practiced by a family member who plays off another family member against the therapist, often with the effect of reducing the therapist's capacity to change the family. A common gambit is for a family member to absent himself from therapy sessions. This creates an immediate issue in which that member and the therapist are cast as principals in a conflict: The therapist demands the regular return of the absent member who, for one reason or another, refuses.

This situation occurred also in the case of the family already described. Just prior to the second therapy session, the daughter telephoned the therapist to say she had obtained a job baby-sitting which would prevent her from attending sessions regularly. If she were to attend, she said sessions would have to be scheduled to suit her. In succeeding sessions both her parents, but especially her mother, cast themselves as go-betweens in the issue of their daughter's attendance. In the seventh session, from which the daughter was absent, the following exchange was recorded:

(The therapist has just confronted the parents with the possibility that sessions would be terminated if their daughter continued to exclude herself from the sessions.)

Mother: Actually she has to work because she needs the money. She has been idle for some time now—since June.

Therapist: That's true—nobody would disagree with you there. But, nevertheless, does she completely drop this other thing from her thinking, or has she thought about both things together?

Mother: She was hoping that later on she could take time off—a day a week, but right now, when she just started on Monday . . .

Father: Well, I think what influenced her too was that Dr. Robinson and Dr. Zuk said they would be on vacation next month.

Skillfully, the parents disassociate themselves from their daughter as coprincipals. They "explain" their daughter's behavior to the therapist; they rationalize it, suggest it well may be a sign of emotional maturity. The mother implies it is important for her daughter to work to increase her sense of self-sufficiency and independence. The father reminds the therapist that he too misses sessions and for reasons that may not be actually as justifiable as his daughter's.

The episode contains a serious test of the therapist's skill and judgment. If he insists on the regular attendance of the daughter, he risks the family's using that as an excuse to leave therapy. If he accedes to her irregular attendance, he risks being "one-upped" by the family and weakens his therapeutic leverage. If he agrees to negotiate with the daughter through her parents, he risks raising them to the status of cotherapists.

What actually occurred in the course of therapy was that the daughter's regular attendance was not insisted upon by the therapist, but neither were the parents accepted as go-betweens. The therapist consistently maintained that the parents were coprincipals with the daughter in the issue of her attendance, even though they stoutly denied it. Granted that this maneuver somewhat reduced his therapeutic leverage, still the therapist was not forced into the position of appearing to reject the family for treatment because of his insistence on the daughter's presence. As time went by, however, his demand for her regular attendance increased to the point where the family was not seen in weekly sessions unless they brought their daughter with them. After about a year in which the main issue with the family was simply whether they could cooperate to attend as a unit, the family therapy was terminated. But it should be noted that during the year the daughter secured a part-time job, made a partly successful attempt to complete high school credits for college entrance, and seriously considered marriage to a boy "approved" by her parents. The year also brought a somewhat encouraging opening up of communication between the parents.

One of the difficulties in taking families with young children who have behavior problems into family therapy is that there is a tendency of the parents to cast the children as principals vis à vis the therapist. The parents then assume the role of go-between. (A variation that sometimes also happens is that the parents get cast as principals vis à vis the therapist with the children taking the role of go-between.) The parents claim that the children are unmanageable—they act up, are noisy and distractible. The parents suggest, subtly or directly, that the therapist take over the job of managing the children. This is risky business because, unless the therapist deals also with the parents' avowed secret encouragement of the children to act up, he is quite likely to get caught in a losing trap in which session after session is devoted to getting the children to pay attention. What is worse, the therapist implicitly accepts the proposition that the parents are really helpless to control their children—an almost always doubtful assumption.

In one of the writer's cases, just such a situation as described above occurred. The children were very disruptive, constantly interfering with what was being said. Vague parental efforts to control the situation were met by the children with poorly hidden contempt. The parents turned to the therapist to control the situation, openly acknowledging their ineffectiveness. But from time to time, the children were able to elicit a broad grin from their father when they succeeded in frustrating the controlling efforts of the therapist. And from time to time the children elicited further grins from their father when they questioned how seriously they were to take his admonishments.

By taking the position that they were helpless onlookers, the parents were casting themselves as go-betweens with the therapist and children as principals vis à vis each other. They hoped, it is suggested, mainly to use the children against the therapist in undermining change, but to disguise their intention by apparent helplessness. This example illustrates situations in which one may become and exert the power of a go-between simply by throwing one's hands in the air, shrugging one's shoulders, and pleading helplessness.

At least two therapist positions can be taken vis à vis this parent gambit: (1) The therapist can refuse to accept their plea of helplessness and confront them with their intention to sabotage the therapy by using the children against him; (2) he can arrange to see parents and children separately at intervals, the better to explore the nature of their secret alliance and to attempt to split the alliance.

Variation 3: Therapist as Go-Between with Family Members as Principals

In the writer's opinion this constitutes the variation of go-between process that is most advantageous to the therapist in his efforts to produce change. A major problem for the therapist is to avoid being trapped by the family into a too-rigid go-between role, such as might occur if he became for example, the "family judge" or "family counselor." The therapist loses important therapeutic leverage if the family can induce him to take the role of a certain type of go-between. Successful management of go-between process requires that the therapist reserve to himself the element of surprise; that is, the option to change from one kind of go-between to another, or to change from go-between to principal should the occasion demand.

As noted, family members will attempt to draw a therapist out of the role of go-between into the role of a principal or to trap him into being a certain kind of go-between. In the therapist's armamentarium are a number of devices to counter these efforts of the family. The therapist may simply refuse to intervene in a conflict in which he is pressed to take sides on the ground that this is not one of his proper functions. He may interpret or reflect on the conflict, thus sidestepping direct involvement. If he believes he is being trapped into the role of family judge, he may deny that he has any interest in judging or any authority to judge. If he thinks the family is maneuvering to trap him out of the role of go-between, he may undermine their intent by changing the subject.

The therapist is in a key position to take the role of go-between because of the family's ready-made perception of him as such. He can define issues in the family and endeavor to assign family members selectively as principals or go-betweens. By endeavoring to assign principals in a conflict, the therapist can project himself immediately as the go-between or endeavor to assign this role to another family member. By these means and others the therapist takes the initiative in conducting go-between process.

In the case of a married couple seen by the writer, the husband made a serious attempt to move the therapist out of the role of go-between into the role of principal. He attempted this by seeking to engage the therapist in debate. He would challenge a comment made by the therapist, break it down into parts, and question the validity of each part. The tactic of the therapist to counter the husband's was simply to define debating as not one of a therapist's functions. Whenever the husband would start to debate, the therapist would smile knowingly, shake his head, and say he could not respond because it was not his job to debate. The husband in turn smiled as if in grudging acknowledgment that he had been checked.

Much later in the therapy, this husband raged at his wife for bringing up their disagreements before the therapist. He said he resented that she would express her dissatisfaction in the therapy sessions and not wait until they were alone to do so. (He understandably overlooked the fact, of course, that one of his wife's major complaints was that she couldn't talk frankly to him.) At this point it was possible for the therapist as go-between to interpret the husband's anger and resentment as a function of his need to be the authority to whom his wife should look for guidance. In numerous ways this husband played the game of one-upmanship; most characteristic, of course, was his use of the debate. In order to remain an effective therapeutic agent with this couple, the therapist had to steer clear of engagement in debate with the husband and other such gambits of his. This couple made good progress in therapy. Although after a year and a half of treatment they still could not manage to deeply explore their relationship, they were able to cooperate in the purchase of a new home and did more things together. Their young son, for whom they were originally referred, made gains in his school work and was less "nervous."

Variation 4: Therapist as Go-Between with Family Members and an Agent of the Community as Opposing Principals

Sometimes in family therapy the family manages to organize itself as a unified principal vis à vis the therapist as an opposing principal. This presents the therapist with a serious problem, for he is prevented from exercising a subtle and critical leverage in the role of the go-between; instead he is constrained to exercise the role of one who is essentially an opponent making harsh demands. Often it is up to the therapist to reclaim the role of go-between if he is to remain as a therapeutic agent. He can do this by securing an *agent of the community* to act as a principal, thus freeing himself once more to take the role of go-between; that is, essentially by establishing an issue between the family and an agent of the community.

Recently the writer was involved in treating a family referred because one son refused to go to school. It required little time to establish a connection between the boy's failure to go to school and his mother's fear of separation from him. Intellectually, the mother could accept this explanation and in family therapy and multiple family therapy sessions she became more aware of her need to hold this particular child close to her; but neither she nor her husband could mobilize themselves sufficiently to return the son to school. He would physically resist their efforts, then they would throw up their hands in despair and dump the problem in the lap of the therapist.

In the early months of treatment, the parents tended to perceive the therapist as an ally who would spare them from the continued demands of the school. The therapist reached the conclusion that he would have to move out of the role of coprincipal with the parents against, as it were, the school authorities. He therefore stated to the parents that, in his opinion, their son was able to return to school immediately; that they should use every means at their disposal to secure his return; and that in the event they failed, he would be subject to the disciplinary action of the school and legal authorities. The therapist stated he would work with the parents *and* the school authorities to secure the boy's return to school. He thus defined himself as a "third force" operating between them and the school; in other words, he acted to remove himself as a coprincipal and assume a go-between role.

The parents as expected were in despair about the new position the therapist defined for himself. They had expected him to continue to take responsibility for "curing" their son of his refusal to go to school and had counted on him to continue indefinitely to silence the demands of the school authorities for their son's return to school. They were puzzled and angered now to think the therapist was stepping aside from an honored role of primary decision-maker and judge and offering merely to assist the parties in dispute.

The school authorities were informed by the therapist that he believed the boy was ready to return to school and that they should institute their regular procedures to secure his return. On the day the boy was due to return, as expected, he refused to leave home and his parents did follow the suggestion of the therapist to employ the services of the police. The police were called, and the boy, to be sure, struggling, was taken to school. Once in school he refused to attend class and then was taken to a local juvenile detention center. He was kept there several hours until he tearfully promised the detention officer that he would go to school the next day. The next day he did go to school by himself, but again refused to attend class and the school authorities, saying they were unable to handle such a problem, had the boy sent home.

At this point, the parents returned to the therapist in deep despair. It was obvious, they pointed out, that their boy could not be compelled to return to school. They had shown their good intentions by calling the police, but all resources had failed to secure their boy's successful return to school. The parents pleaded with the therapist to return to the former situation in which their boy was officially in treatment and thus temporarily exempt from community disciplinary action.

The therapist rejected this plea restating his wish to help the parents to fulfill their roles, but noting also that further absence of the boy from school would definitely result in his placement in a disciplinary institution. The next day the parents attempted to send their boy to school but, again experiencing difficulty, called the police who this time took him directly to the juvenile detention center. There he was confronted by the detention officer with the fact that he had not kept his promise to return to school. (It should be pointed out that the detention officer had by this time acquired a special interest in the case, had been in contact with the school and therapist, and was encouraged by therapist to use his full authority to discipline the boy.) He was detained several days at the center, whereupon he finally made an unconditional promise to return to school and was sent home. The next morning on his own initiative he got up, dressed, went to school and class. He kept his promise by attending school regularly for the past year and up until three months ago, continued in treatment in The Family Day-Hospital Program of the Family Therapy Project at EPPI once a week accompanied by his parents and brother. He has had, to be sure, several anxiety attacks and has complained of stomach pains, but these have not prevented him from regularly attending school. His school performance has not been entirely satisfactory, but according to last report he did his homework regularly and was passing most of his courses.

The case was presented as an example of the therapist's employment of go-between process to remove himself as a principal vis à vis the family and cast himself as a go-between, because as principal his therapeutic leverage had been greatly impaired. Initially the therapist was perceived by the family as an ally against the school system. Then for a time he was perceived by the family as an ally of the school system against them. Finally he was able to convince the family he was acting as a "third force," a mediator between the family and the school authorities. This case should give the reader some indication of the application of leverage to precipitate change in the face of major deep-set and deceptive resistances.

SUMMARY

This chapter attempts to develop a theory and technique of psychotherapy involving the concept of go-between process as observed in family therapy. The following points are relevant:

1. Go-between process is a group process which can influence and shift

power relationships in groups and thus it has special application in family therapy, which may be defined as the treatment technique that examines and attempts to influence and shift power relationships in the family.

2. Go-between process includes both a phase of development of conflict and a subsequent phase of attempts to check the magnitude of the conflict, the latter involving mediation and the selection of a go-between.

3. The role of the go-between is simply one step of go-between process and is not synonymous with it.

4. The role of the go-between is a critical one because the person who fills the role is empowered by the principals *to secure changes in their positions vis à vis each other.*

5. The therapist tends to be perceived by the family as a likely go-between in resolving conflicts.

6. As the go-between, the therapist may employ such devices or therapeutic gambits as confrontation, reflection, advice, denial, evasion, and so on, to maintain and increase his therapeutic leverage as go-between or block efforts to undermine him in the role.

7. A major source of power of the go-between rests in his capacity to introduce initiatives or alternatives not introduced by the principals themselves and which may even run contrary to their apparent interests.

8. The family will attempt to limit the capacity of the therapist to act as go-between, either by trapping him into playing a too-rigid type, such as the "family judge," or by trapping him *out* of the role into that of a coprincipal or opposing principal.

9. In family therapy, families will make attempts to control go-between process to their advantage, that is, as a means usually to resist the therapist's attempts to change them.

Four variations of go-between process occurring in family therapy are described and documented with case material in this chapter, two in which the initiative lies with the family, two in which it lies with the therapist.

REFERENCES

Boszormenyi-Nagy, I., & Framo, J. L. Family concept of hospital treatment of schizophrenia. In J. Masserman (Ed.), *Current psychiatric therapies. Vol. II.* New York: Grune and Stratton, 1963, pp. 159-166.

Haley, J. *Strategies of psychotherapy.* New York: Grune and Stratton, 1963.

Meissner, W. W. Thinking about the family—psychiatric aspects. *Family Process,* 1964, 3, 1-40.

Wynne, L. C. The study of intrafamilial alignments and splits in exploratory family therapy. In N. W. Ackerman, Frances L. Beatman, & S. N. Sherman (Eds.), *Exploring the base for family therapy.* New York: Family Service Association of America, 1961, pp. 95-115.

Zuk, G. H. Preliminary study of go-between process in family therapy. In *Proceedings of the 73rd annual meeting.* Washington, D.C.: American Psychological Association, 1965, pp. 291-292.

Zuk, G. H., & Rubinstein, D. A review of concepts in the study and treatment of families of schizophrenics. In I. Boszormenyi-Nagy and J. Framo (Eds.), *Intensive family therapy.* New York: Hoeber, Harper and Row, 1965, pp. 1-31.

Chapter 4 / FAMILY THERAPY:
FORMULATION OF A TECHNIQUE
AND ITS THEORY

· ·

Family therapy studies of the past dozen years, as a recent review establishes (Zuk and Rubinstein, 1965), have predominantly reflected the psychoanalytic viewpoint, even though striking departures from psychoanalytic theory and technique have been made by family therapists. For the most part writers on technique (among others, see the papers by Ackerman, 1960; Bell, 1961; Bowen, 1961; Jackson and Weakland, 1961; Whitaker, Felder, and Warkentin, 1965; and Wynne, 1965) have essentially adhered to the view that to promote beneficial change in patients the therapist must formulate and communicate insights and work through unconscious resistances. Even such departures from psychoanalytic technique as those described by Satir (1964) and Minuchin (1965) recently seem to this writer fundamentally insight-centered.

Among major contributors to family therapy theory and practice today, only Haley (1963a) has offered a clear alternative to the "insight-centered model," although he is joined to an extent by Jackson (1967) and Brodey (1967) using somewhat different approaches. Haley maintains that the therapist secures beneficial change when he enforces a dominant position vis à vis patient; that is, to the extent he controls the relationship, decides what its goals shall be, and parries the patient's attempts to undermine his control. The therapist is skillful at setting up paradoxical situations in which the patient thinks he can "win" against

This chapter was originally entitled "Family Therapy" when published in the *Archives of General Psychiatry*, 1967, **16**, 71-79. It was reprinted in the *International Journal of Group Psychotherapy*, 1968, **18**, 42-58, under the title indicated here.

the therapist, but loses. In the losing, the patient comes to accept the therapist's control and direction and changes accordingly.

As a result of experience in family therapy over the past five years, I am convinced that beneficial change, as Haley suggests, is a creative outcome of a struggle for control between the therapist and family members, but I believe that the skillful setting-up of paradoxical situations is not sufficient as an explanation of change in family therapy, although it does provide a useful basis to consider what does bring about change. The chapter will attempt to describe a technique which uses sources of therapeutic leverage believed unique to family therapy, although applications are possible in marital and to a lesser extent in group therapy. The technique arises specifically from the fact that family therapy is the transaction of a therapist with at least two or more persons who have had an extensive history of relating to one another.

Preliminary descriptions of the writer's technique and theoretical framework have been given elsewhere (Zuk, 1965, 1966). A corner-stone of the technique is a definition of family therapy as follows: *It is the technique that explores and attempts to shift the balance of pathogenic relating among family members so that new forms of relating become possible.* This definition presumes Jackson's notion (1957) that the family is a homeostatic system in which change in one part is likely to effect changes in other parts.

Another cornerstone of the technique that will be described in this paper is the fact that the expression of conflict in family therapy is like that in no other form of therapy, and that conflict generates the energy required to shift fixed patterns of relating among family members. The therapist must be an expert in searching out the main issues in the family, in keeping these issues in focus, and in exploring the sources and intensity of disagreement. Family therapy is the only therapy in which patients come with an established history of conflict and with well-developed means for expressing or disguising it.

In the more comprehensive of the preliminary papers (Zuk, 1966), I described go-between process in family therapy in four variations rather commonly encountered. In two of the variations, the initiative in conducting go-between process lay with the therapist. In the other two variations, the initiative lay with the family members; that is, they conducted go-between process "against" the therapist as a means to forestall his attempts to control and direct the treatment. In this chapter I hope to take up in much greater detail the terms of go-between process and describe the theoretical structure in which the process is grounded.

GO-BETWEEN PROCESS: ITS TERMS AND SOME DIMENSIONS

In the sections to follow terms and some dimensions of go-between process will be elaborated: (1) from the point of view of the therapist vis à vis family; (2) in the context of the family's defensive tactics; and (3) in the context of "phases" of treatment, specifically onset and termination.

From the Viewpoint of Therapist Vis à Vis Family

The therapist conducts go-between process when:
Term 1. (a) He probes issues in the family, establishes the existence of conflict by eliciting expressions of disagreement, and encourages the open expression of disagreement. (b) He exposes and otherwise resists the family's efforts to deny or disguise disagreement. (c) He encourages the expression of recent or current disagreement rather than rehashes of old. (d) He encourages expression of conflict between members who are *present* rather than absent from the treatment session.

Term 1 sets conditions for the therapist's encouragement of expression of conflict. Families differ greatly in the extent to which they will express it: Some appear only too eager to do so; others are most reluctant. The therapist must be as wary of the first type of these families as the second, for the first type often generates a lot of superficial "noisy" disagreement and frequently deeper sources of disagreement are disguised. In these families members will engage in a great deal of mutual recrimination—bitterness, anger, and hostility are openly expressed. But the process might be labeled a "pseudohostility." Wynne (1961) has used this term and means by it a shared defense against recognizing feelings of tenderness, affection, or sexual attraction; but the writer uses it here to mean the expression of hostility which serves as a mask for a more pervasive, deeper-lying hostility. A "pseudohostility" may be directed by one family member against another toward whom the first does not really feel the greatest animosity, but the latter is a convenient scapegoat.

A second and contrasting group of families will deny disagreements and even develop elaborate means for disguising them. Some of these families will appear genuinely puzzled when the therapist calls attention to sources of conflict. Family members appear confused, pained, even deeply hurt if the therapist persists in pointing out conflict. The members pride themselves on their rational approach to the solution of family problems, on their ability to find answers acceptable to all. Even from themselves they skillfully hide the fact that they simply have failed to deal with major problem areas—have swept them under the rug, as it were.

Because memory for detail is likely to be still fresh and emotions running high, the therapist conducting go-between process encourages families to talk about recent conflicts as opposed to old ones. Sometimes therapists will encounter families whose members prefer to talk about their past problems, but this may be a skillful gambit to introduce doubt and uncertainty into the treatment situation—i.e., members have difficulty recalling precisely what was said, who was present, and so on. The therapist will have to judge how much of this "recollection" to allow, and in general will tend to discourage its expression.

Therapists will also encounter family members who prefer to talk about their conflict with a family member, relative, or friend who is not present in the treatment session. Since this process also tends to introduce doubt and uncertainty, the therapist conducting go-between process will in general tend to discourage its expression. Too much control is left in the hands of the member who presents his side of the disagreement. There will be times, to be sure, when the therapist will allow this expression, but only if he thinks it will "open up" sources of conflict between family members who are present.

The therapist conducts go-between process when:

Term 2. (a) He selects specific disagreements as especially worthy of discussion, rejects others as unworthy, and resists the family's expected efforts to establish its own rules of priority. (b) This selection is part of his move into the role of the go-between. He then seeks to establish his authority in the role and resists the family's expected efforts to displace him.

In a previous paper (Zuk, 1966) it was stated that, "In family therapy the go-between may be very active, intrusive and confronting, or inactive and passive. He may move into the role of go-between by the device of attacking two parties he hopes to make into principals; or he may move into the role by calmly pointing out a difference between two parties. On the other hand, he may become a go-between by refusing to take sides in a dispute that has erupted; or he may become one by presenting a new point of view in a dispute" (p. 165). The point here is that in the role of go-between the therapist is constantly structuring the treatment situation, constantly directing it.

A case will be presented to illustrate the terms of go-between process, especially Term 2.

A family was referred for therapy on the basis that a young daughter's poor school performance seemed to have origins in disturbed family living. The family was composed of the daughter, 9 years old, her brother, 13 years old, her 40-year-old mother, and 56-year-old father. The family was of Catholic, Irish-German and upper-lower religious, ethnic, and social status origins. The mother had completed high school, but the father only the fourth grade and the difference in educational level was a serious source of conflict between them. The father was a steady job holder who was married previously and had from time to time been involved in sexual misconduct with other women in his marriages. He considered his main problem to be his explosive temper and the fact that he couldn't get his children to be respectful to him. The mother took to drinking heavily in her late teens and referred to herself as an alcoholic up until 5 years ago when she gave up drinking and joined Alcoholics Anonymous. There was also evidence of some sexual promiscuity on her part before her marriage to her husband 14 years ago, but none since.

The mother reported that at times she believed she was losing her mind. She expressed bitterness toward her husband who she said deserted her for another woman about the time she was pregnant with her now 13-year-old son. She believed the marriage started to deteriorate since that time. She expressed fear of her husband's quick temper, as did the children. Her son openly expressed bitter resentment of his father and hoped that his mother would separate.

A special source of resentment of the father was that his wife had taken their son into their bedroom, avowedly to attend to him more effectively during an illness and had not moved him out in several months. She asked her husband to sleep in another room and he complied. Another source of the father's resentment was the chaotic condition of the home, although as it turned out he contributed to the chaos by bringing and storing in the house all sorts of odd, useless objects.

The therapist had little difficulty getting family members to verbalize conflict. (This was one of the "noisy" type families referred to earlier which seem only too eager to express their feelings.) But the conflict didn't seem to go anywhere for the first few sessions: Each member expressed opposition to another in such a way as to put the other in a bad light and each seemed to know the means to put the other on the defensive. However, in the fourth session there was a break which the therapist was quick to take advantage of and which will illustrate how the therapist conducting go-between process selects certain types of disagreements as especially worthy of discussion and rejects other types.

A week or so prior to the fourth session the father brought home a bicycle that was given to him by a friend. He told his daughter the bike was hers, that he had bought it from his friend for 10 dollars, and that he had had it repaired at an additional cost. His daughter accepted the bike and rode it but it soon broke down. She took the bike for repair but it broke down again and again she returned the bike for repair, threatening the repairman that if he did not fix it properly this time or if he refused to fix it she would start screaming at the top of her voice right there in the shop. The man fixed the bike. But later it broke down again and the girl decided to give it to her brother. Her brother repaired the bike and rode it for awhile before it again broke down and was put away in storage. In the meantime, the daughter got her mother to promise to buy her a new bike as a Christmas present.

As this incident was related mainly by the daughter to the therapist, it was apparent that it met the criteria of Term 1 of go-between process in that disagreement was expressed about how the bike was purchased and who was to use it; all members involved were present and capable of telling their versions; and the incident had occurred recently and was still fresh in the memory. Because these criteria were met and because the incident seemed to epitomize so well the way conflict was handled (or rather mishandled) in the family, the therapist selected it for special attention. (A not insignificant factor influencing his decision was that the incident was one about which the father could talk with some show of control; that is, without such excitement or emotion that he would frighten other family members into quiet submission.)

The therapist specifically moved into the role of go-between by stating that he was puzzled by what actually happened in the bike incident, and that in order to clear up the confusion he would ask each member to tell his version of the story. The therapist then acted to establish his authority as the go-between by indicating that he would not allow interference in the telling of stories. He was thus introducing an unusual structure for the family: They were not used to letting each talk without frequent interruption, for one thing, and without efforts at intimidation, for another.

First, the fuller details of the daughter's story were elicited. When she came to the point at which she threatened the bike repairman with screaming if he did not agree to fix the bike again, the therapist said he thought she was using a favorite tactic of intimidation of her father's. Then the son was directed to relate his story. (He countersuggested that his father should speak next, but this was disallowed since it was believed by the therapist that it would have helped to subtly undermine the type of procedure he had established.) The son voiced his resentment that the bike was not given to him originally. He said he knew he would get it eventually because it was bound to break down, his sister would come to him to fix it, and then he would be able to claim at least part ownership. He complained that his father never gave him anything. Giving the bike to his sister was just another example of the father's stinginess toward him.

In telling his story, the father stressed his good intentions and expressed resentment that they were doubted. He told how he had bargained skillfully with the original owner of the bike to get it for the lowest price, if possible for nothing. He told how he had taken the bike for renovation to a place he knew would do it for little money. He said he fully supported his daughter when she insisted the bike should be repaired properly by the repairman.

When it came the mother's turn to tell her story, she ruefully stated it was incidents such as this one that sometimes made her doubt her sanity. She said she actually felt relieved and reassured that the therapist had also expressed doubt and uncertainty about what really happened. In the following excerpt from the fourth session, the mother related how her husband and children frequently befuddled her:

Therapist: You've said that two or three times . . . that you were losing your sanity. What do you mean by that?
Mother: I told you when I first came here I had questions about my own sanity. When you live under these conditions and you hear it morning, noon, and night, after a while you do question your own sanity. Am I hearing this, or am I imagining it?
Therapist: What's the worst part of the whole thing? A lot is going on. A lot of it looks to be kind of harmless.
Daughter: (referring to her brother) He teases me . . . with the cat.
Therapist: Teasing is teasing. I'm asking your mother.
Mother: You mean of this bickering back and forth?
Therapist: Whatever it is that drives you crazy.
Mother: Well, they'll tell me one thing and then there's a twist to the story. You saw it yourself. Each one told a slightly different version. After a while you just can't follow it. All these thoughts get in my head and I think "Oh my God, am I imagining this or is this so?" I find that the three of them—my husband and the children—are very much alike in this bit. Like even the interruptions! I don't think you could say I interrupted here today, but they do and it's constant. Nobody shows each other courtesy enough to hear each other out . . . . They all have to get heard and they all consider their own feelings more important than anybody else's.

This excerpt and the description of the bike incident should show how the therapist as go-between provides the family with a new context in which to express and examine its conflicts. As go-between he acts as the "broker" in the context—for example, he insures that all parties understand his rules for examining the conflict and he insures that all parties are fairly dealt with. He aims to fashion a context that is different from the established pathogenic pattern of relating among family members. Temporarily freed by the therapist's action from a vicious repetitive pattern, the family may experience the good feeling of more positive and productive relating and explore the possibility of new means to relate in the future.

In his excellent paper on marriage therapy, Haley (1963b) notes that the therapist is unavoidably a go-between or "broker." He states that the mere presence of the therapist as a third party requires that the spouses deal differently with each other than they have in the past—particularly because the therapist is a third party who is a presumed expert in unraveling the meaning of human interaction. He points out that the marriage therapist may relabel or redefine the activities of the spouses with each other, and he may label the treatment situation as unique in other respects—for example, as having rules which would not hold in ordinary situations.

The therapist conducts go-between process when:

Term 3. (a) He sides, either by implication or intentionally, with one family member against another in a particular disagreement. *Siding is unavoidable,* for even if the therapist thinks he is maintaining a strictly neutral or objective position, the family still judges him to be siding. The problem of the therapist is to decide when and with whom to side *intentionally* (i.e., as a therapeutic tactic), also to decide with whom the family believes him to be siding. (b) He may side with or against the entire family unit in a particular disagreement, as well as with or against single family members.

Haley, in his paper on marriage therapy, notes that a therapist cannot make a neutral statement: ". . . his voice, his expression, the context, or the mere act of choosing a particular statement to inquire about introduces a directiveness into the situation" (p. 225). He continues, "When the therapist is being directive, coalition patterns are being defined and redefined, and a crucial aspect of this type of therapy is continually changing coalition patterns between therapist and each spouse." This statement is equally true of family therapy: The therapist's most innocuous-sounding comment will be judged by family members as clear evidence that he favors the position of one member as against another. Family members will *act* toward the therapist as if he were siding and even *interpret* him as siding, however he may choose to deny that such was his intention. (It is also true, to be sure, that therapists are rarely fully aware of all the ways in which they *actually may be siding* with one member against another and may become defensive when this is *fairly* brought to their attention.)

In the writer's opinion, not only is siding unavoidable in family therapy, it is a legitimate tactic of therapeutic value in shifting the balance of pathogenic relating among family members. *By judicious siding, the therapist can tip the balance in favor of more productive relating, or at least disrupt a chronic pattern of pathogenic relating.* By siding with one family member in a disagreement with another, the therapist throws weight to the position of the former. The effect of the therapist siding *against* all members often is for the members to minimize the extent of the disagreement, but it also moves them to examine more carefully the bases of the disagreement. The effect of the therapist siding *with* all members is often subtly disorganizing, for then they become confused as to what their own position should be vis à vis the therapist—in other words, it tends to undermine any stubborn shared family resistance to the therapist's interventions.

It is probably unwise for the therapist to give the message that he consistently sides with one member against others. It is advantageous for him to keep the family guessing as to *whether* he will engage in siding and *what* the tactics of his siding will be. The therapist must retain flexibility in the face of strenuous efforts by the family to get him to side in a systematic manner so that he will become more predictable—and therefore, in the writer's opinion, a less effective therapeutic person.

In the fourth treatment session with the family that has been described here, there were several instances of intentional siding by the therapist. For instance, he engaged in siding when enforcing his rule that family members could not interrupt each other in telling the story of the bike incident, for he did not enforce the rule *with equal vigor* for all members. For example, the therapist tended to halt the attempted interruptions of the father with considerably more vigor than such attempts of other family members, particularly when his attempts were directed against his son. In this the therapist showed an inclination to side against the father. One reason for this type of siding was that it seemed necessary to the therapist to guard against the danger that the father would undermine the therapist's rules of procedure by means of an outburst of temper. A related reason was to encourage other family members to speak their feelings more freely, especially the son who was furious at his father for being continually browbeaten by him. In brief, the therapist was intentionally siding *against* the father and *with* other family members in enforcing his rules of procedure for the exposition of the bike incident.

In the fifth treatment session with the family, there was a good example of the therapist siding first with one member and then another in a disagreement as a therapeutic tactic to tip the balance of pathogenic relating. The father had accused his wife, in a typically inferential manner, of sexual misconduct with other men in the course of her attendance at Alcoholics Anonymous. The therapist encouraged the father to talk about his feelings of anger and jealousy which he, again characteristically, strenuously denied having. Turning then to the wife, the therapist asked her to respond to her husband's feelings of anger and jealousy based on his suspicions. In confirming the husband's *feelings,* despite his lack of confirmation of actual promiscuity by the wife, the therapist was implicitly siding with the husband against his wife. He was suggesting, in effect, that the husband's feelings were genuine and valid and that the wife was bound to consider and respond to them. The following excerpt from the fifth session is relevant to this point:

Therapist: The question is . . . your husband is showing jealousy.
Mother: Right. I've said this from the beginning.
Therapist: And you are responding in a funny kind of way. I don't know whether you're encouraging it or discouraging it.
Mother: You would have to understand AA. I don't know if you do. But each and every one of us help each other out in maintaining sobriety.

Father: But a man don't help no woman, and the woman don't help no man! A man helps a man and a woman helps a woman!

Therapist: Yes. Your husband is raising the question of men in particular; jealousy of the men. And you are not responding to that. You're putting it in terms of humanity . . .

Mother: I've given in to every whim about jealousy. I've stopped kissing my kids and stopped hugging them.

Therapist: But you're still sleeping with your son.

Mother: He's in my bedroom, yes . . .

Therapist: Maybe you've stopped kissing him, but you haven't stopped sleeping with him.

Father: Her son is not sleeping with her; he's sleeping in a twin bed.

Therapist: Are you defending her too now? (laughs) Whose side are you on? I'm not implying anything . . . . This has been something that you brought up here today.

Father: That's right.

Therapist: You're angry about it.

Father: I'm not angry about it.

Therapist: You say you're not and I say you are.

Shortly after this exchange in which, by encouraging the husband to express his jealousy and by confronting the wife with her evasiveness, the therapist appears to side with the husband, the therapist then turns the tables: He now confronts the husband in such a way as to appear to side with the wife.

Therapist: . . . Is that what you're saying to him: "I need companionship. I need somebody?"

Mother: I certainly do need somebody . . .

Therapist: "I need my son close to me because I get something from him that I don't get from somebody else." This I think is what your wife seems to me to say. She says, "I need something too. And whether you're jealous about it—well, that's just too bad. I need those things." That's what she's saying . . .

Father: Well, I understand that and I want to try my best to give her what she wants!

By siding alternately with father and then mother, the therapist believed he shook up their relationship and facilitated open expression of a bitter conflict between them that had been raging for some time but in a rather devious form. In the case of the father, the therapist insisted that he acknowledge his anger and jealousy in the presence of his family. In the case of the mother, the therapist insisted she express her yearning for warmth and emotional closeness. The therapist made it difficult for the parents to employ their usual techniques to avoid confronting each other with their actual feelings and attitudes. He promoted a more direct confrontation than was typical for them in their relationship; i.e., forced them to put aside the usual means both had developed to keep each other at a distance and opened up the possibility of their relating in a new way.

This discussion of siding and the illustrations should make it quite evident how complex an issue it is in family therapy. Certainly related to it, for example, are the issues of transference and counter-transference, although siding is not simply to be explained by either or both of these concepts, because as conceived of here it means an *intentional* alignment of the therapist with the position of one family member against another for the purpose of tipping the balance of the relationship between them.

The Family's Defensive Tactics Vis à Vis Therapist

Families exhibit a marvelous array of tactics which serve to forestall the therapist in his conduct of go-between process. The therapist must be alert to these tactics and act to circumvent them. Three major defensive tactics may be listed. In the first, family members seek to lead the therapist astray by subtle denials or evasions of his allegations of conflict. For example, the therapist may call attention to an issue between two members on which there seems to be latent conflict. The members deny the allegation. They say they have never disagreed on the issue. (Technically they may be telling the truth, in the sense that they may never have actually *openly* disagreed on the issue.) The therapist is called on to either hit on some device to split the team or give up the issue he introduced with an often not insignificant loss of face. As a face-saving device, I sometimes return to the issue introduced when it seems less anxiety-provoking. This is a kind of therapeutic one-upmanship in that it defines the fact that the members have formed a coalition against the therapist, informs them of his awareness of the fact, and implies a sympathetic understanding of the needs that caused them to join forces against him.

A second defensive tactic of the family vis à vis therapist is encountered when a member assumes the role of spokesman and consistently comments on or explains the meaning of the family to the therapist. This role seems most often assumed in families by the mother, but sometimes it is assumed by the father and infrequently by one of the children. In effect, the family spokesman is in the role of a go-between and as long as he occupies a go-between role, the therapist's capacity to assume it is impaired. Sometimes the therapist will decide early in treatment to prohibit a member from taking the role of family spokesman; sometimes, however, he will temporize and permit the member to be the spokesman in the hope of learning more about the key dynamics of the family. In either case, it is necessary for the therapist to identify the family spokesman early and restrain or check him at some time in the course of treatment.

A third defensive tactic is encountered when family members act toward the therapist as if he were a particular type of go-between, or when they act toward him as if he were consistently siding with a particular member against others. As an example of this type of tactic, the father in the family whose case has been presented in this paper would accuse his wife of some misconduct, then turn to the therapist and ask, "Am I right or am I wrong?" He addressed the therapist as he might a judge who would decide a case, of course somewhat rigging his question to get the answer he wanted, which was to be in effect, "Yes, Mr. X, you are perfectly right."

My practice, as therapist, was to respond to the father in one of three ways: (a) State that I was not a judge and that the purpose of family therapy was not to decide who in the family was right and who wrong; (b) ignore the father's question and change the subject; (c) not answer the question directly but turn to the wife and ask her to comment on the husband's accusation. By means of these responses the therapist took steps to turn aside the father's attempt to cast him in the role of the family judge, a particularly inflexible type of go-between in family therapy. In the third response, in which I asked the wife to comment on her husband's accusation, there was an implicit message given to the effect: "There may be something to your husband's accusation and I would like you to defend yourself." The message could be interpreted as evidence that I was mildly siding with the husband against the wife, but evidence not nearly so strong as that initially desired by the husband in his aim to cast me as the family judge.

Change at Onset and Termination of Family Therapy

Go-between process constitutes, in the writer's opinion, an alternative to the psychoanalytical insight-centered model to explain the beneficial changes that may occur in family therapy. Onset and termination are key phases in relation to the issue of change. At onset two points at issue between the family and therapist are the questions: "Is there something wrong with us?" and "If there is something wrong, how will you treat us as a family?" The family and therapist may be viewed as opponents on these questions. The therapist begins to conduct go-between process when he explores them with the family for areas of expected disagreement.

Some families, in their eagerness to convince the therapist at the onset that there is nothing wrong with them, will actually bring about some improvement. The change need not be perceived as the result of insight but as a function of the "bargaining" transaction between family and therapist on the question, "Is there something wrong with us?" The family changes *in order to get a change in the therapist's expected position.* The change is calculated to be the least necessary to secure a change in the expected position of the therapist. By means of judicious siding, by taking the role of go-between, or by shifting between these two positions, the therapist hopes to control the "bargaining" transaction in accordance with his therapeutic goals.

By the tenth therapy session in the case of the family described in this paper, beneficial symptomatic changes had already begun to occur. In the tenth session, the mother reported she had begun to clean up the mess in her house and had requested the cooperation of her husband and children in doing so. In this session the mother reported that she had moved her son back into his own bedroom and that her husband was once again occupying the bed that adjoined hers. It also became evident that her husband had been less verbally abusive to her and her children during the preceding couple of weeks.

I suggest that these beneficial changes in the onset phase constituted moves to try to budge the therapist from a position the family members believed he was occupying, and that the mother conceived of the therapy as a means to punish her husband for his past misdeeds and as a means to persuade the therapist of the righteousness of her cause vis à vis her husband. When in the early sessions it became apparent that the therapist was not easily being sold on her viewpoint, she was compelled to introduce a more subtle means of persuasion. She would show the therapist that *she* could change but her husband could not, and thus the lack of a true foundation for the marriage would become even more apparent. It did not quite enter into her calculations that her husband *would* change in relation to (or as a result of) her own change and that his change would also be of a positive nature.

It has been my experience that sometimes dramatic improvement may follow upon *the therapist's notice of intention to terminate treatment because there has been no significant progress.* When the therapist puts the family on such notice he is using go-between process in the sense that he is siding against the family as a whole. He employs this powerful confrontation because he is convinced that only by means of it can he undercut a powerful family resistance to change.

The writer has had the privilege of seeing, both in cases of his own and in cases of colleagues, dramatic improvement—even including the clearing-up of bizarre schizophrenic symptomatology—following upon the therapist's notice of intention to terminate. It may be speculated here also that *what has produced the change is actually the family's strenuous effort to prevent change;* that is, a strenuous effort by the family to frustrate the therapist's avowed intention to withdraw from treatment. In confronting the family with his intention to terminate, the therapist conducts go-between process in accordance with Term 3 stated in this paper; that is, he is siding against the whole family as a means to shake up the status quo.

SUMMARY

Family therapy is defined in this chapter as the treatment that examines and attempts to shift the balance of pathogenic relating among members so that new forms of relating become possible. Go-between process is described as a technique that may be employed in family therapy to promote the shift of pathogenic relating. This process is grounded in the fact that the unique aspect of family therapy is that the so-called patients have had an extensive history of relating to one another.

The three terms of go-between process as conducted by the therapist are: (a) His definition of issues on which the family is in serious conflict and the expression of that conflict; (b) his taking the role of go-between or "broker" in conflicts; (c) his siding with or against the family members in conflicts. As the therapist moves from one step to the next, and back again, he exerts a critical leverage on the fixed patterns of relating among family members.

Families display a number of tactics which seem aimed at forestalling the therapist in his conduct of go-between process—in effect, they are a kind of counter go-between process conducted by the family. Three such tactics are: (a) The family denies or is evasive about the therapist's allegation of conflict; (b) with the complicity of other family members, one becomes the family spokesman and thus a kind of go-between who blocks the therapist's access to this critical role; and (c) the family attempts to trap the therapist into becoming an over-rigid type of go-between, such as the family judge, or else accuses him of siding unfairly with one family member against others.

It is a main hypothesis of the chapter that families change in order to forestall the therapist's expected demands for much greater change or in order to foil his other attempts to control the relationship. Illustrations of such change are given in which the *phase* of treatment seemed also a critical factor; that is, whether treatment was at the onset phase or at point of termination. The notion of change entertained here is believed consonant with Haley's (1963a, 1963b) which was designed to contrast with the insight-centered psychoanalytic model.

REFERENCES

Ackerman, N. W. Family-focused therapy of schizophrenia. In S. C. Scher and H. R. Davis (Eds.), *Out-patient treatment of schizophrenia.* New York: Grune and Stratton, 1960, pp. 156-173.

Bell, J. E. *Family group therapy.* Washington, D.C.: Public Health Monograph No. 64, Dept. of Health, Education and Welfare, 1961.

Bowen, M. Family psychotherapy. *American Journal of Orthopsychiatry,* 1961, 31, 42-60.

Brodey, W. M. A cybernetic approach to family therapy. in G. H. Zuk and I. Boszormenyi-Nagy (Eds.), *Family therapy and disturbed families.* Palo Alto, Calif.: Science and Behavior Books, Inc., 1967, pp. 74-84.

Haley, J. *Strategies of psychotherapy.* New York: Grune and Stratton, 1963a.

Haley, J. Marriage therapy. *Archives of General Psychiatry,* 1963b, 8, 213-234.

Jackson, D. D. The question of family homeostasis, *Psychiatric Quarterly Supplement* 1957, 31, 79-90.

Jackson, D. D. & Weakland, J. H. Conjoint family therapy: Some considerations on theory, technique and results. *Psychiatry,* 1961, 24, 30-45.

Jackson, D. D. Aspects of conjoint family therapy. In G. H. Zuk and I. Boszormenyi-Nagy (Eds.), *Family therapy and disturbed families.* Palo Alto, Calif.: Science and Behavior Books, Inc., 1967, pp. 28-40.

Minuchin. A. Conflict-resolution family therapy. *Psychiatry,* 28, 278-286.

Satir, Virginia *Conjoint family therapy.* Palo Alto, Calif.: Science and Behavior Books, Inc., 1964.

Whitaker, C. A., Felder, R. E. & Warkentin, J. Countertransference in the family treatment of schizophrenia. In I. Boszormenyi-Nagy and J. L. Framo (Eds.), *Intensive family therapy.* New York: Hoeber, Harper and Row, 1965, pp. 323-341.

Wynne, L. C. The study of intrafamilial alignments and splits in exploratory family therapy. In N. W. Ackerman, F. Beatman, and

S. N. Sherman (Eds.), *Exploring the base for family therapy*. New York: Family Service Association of America, 1961, pp. 95-115.

Wynne, L. C. Some indications and contraindications for exploratory family therapy. In I. Boszormenyi-Nagy and J. L. Framo (Eds.) *Intensive family therapy*. New York: Hoeber, Harper and Row, 1965, pp. 289-322.

Zuk, G. H. Preliminary study of the go-between process in family therapy. In *Proceedings of the 73rd annual meeting*. Washington, D.C.: American Psychological Association, 1965, pp. 291-292.

Zuk, G. H. The go-between process in family therapy. *Family Process*, 1966, 5, 162-178.

Zuk, G. H. & Rubinstein D. A review of concepts in the study and treatment of families of schizophrenics. In I. Boszormenyi-Nagy and J. L. Framo (Eds.), *Intensive family therapy*. New York: Hoeber, Harper and Row, 1965, pp. 1-31.

Chapter 5 / PROMPTING CHANGE IN FAMILY THERAPY

. . . .

One reason I think families change in therapy is because, in wishing the good regard of the therapist, they follow his direction. Thus it is important that the therapist seek to guard and enhance his prestige when he can in order that families will have the greatest desire for his approval and be amenable to his direction.

Families, however, tend to oppose any direction of the therapist that raises the specter of change in the status quo. Thus, paradoxically, while wishing to please the therapist and follow his direction, families will balk when his direction involves what they perceive as a clearcut threat to the status quo. One of the great problems for the therapist is to find means to bypass this resistive tendency of families.

From the perspective of the family therapist, I find that a useful definition of family status quo may be given as follows: It is the members' conviction that they are *not* causally implicated in the current condition of the "identified patient." The therapist must take steps to dislodge this conviction and hopefully replace it with one more favorable to a successful outcome of treatment, i.e., one in which the members become convinced they *are* causally implicated. In a number of papers (Zuk, 1965a, 1966, 1967a, 1968a and 1968b), I have described go-between process in family therapy which is a method I have found useful in bypassing the resistive tendency.

This chapter was published in the *Archives of General Psychiatry,* 1968, **19,** 727-736. The impetus for it derives from my exchange with Dutch mental health professionals attending an intensive training course in family therapy which I conducted during October-November, 1967, in Leiden, Holland. I want to thank the participants in the course for helping me clarify my thinking expressed in this paper. My special thanks go to Miss Ammerentia Van Heusden, the course coordinator; and to Dr. J. A. C. de Kock van Leeuwen, director of the agency that funded it, the Dutch National Institute for Preventive Medicine.

I have suggested elsewhere that the aim of family therapy is to reduce pathogenic relating—for example, to reduce acute conflict which might engender violence, silencing strategies, scapegoating, inappropriate labeling, and promotion of inappropriate family myths. The family therapist defines his treatment differently to his patients than either the individual or group therapist. One difference is in his definition that the family is the unit of treatment, and that family members, who have an extensive history of relating to one another, must meet together regularly for as long as the therapist deems necessary. Another difference is in the definition that *family* relationships are and have been pathogenic, that is, have given rise to symptoms in members and other disturbances, and that family therapy is directed toward identification and reduction of pathogenic relating which in turn may lead to reduction of symptoms in members.

One of the important accomplishments of the therapist is to get the family committed to treatment. It is my experience that the family's decision to be treated may itself reduce pathogenic relating and promote symptom-reduction. The commitment actually is an acknowledgment that help has been needed and there is a definite intention to secure it, which has the effect of reducing tensions, and is also the beginning of a subtle process of admission by the family that it is causally implicated in the current condition of the "identified patient." The value of the family's commitment is often overlooked by therapists who regard this step not as an integral part of treatment, but rather as one of its preconditions. Achieving the commitment is a difficult operation that often requires great skill and tact on the part of the therapist.

The first section of this chapter shall deal with the issue of the family's commitment to treatment, the therapist's function in establishing a climate to promote commitment, and some characteristic resistive efforts of the family. The commitment is a negotiation between therapist and family in which the therapist recognizes that, although the family wishes to follow his direction because it wishes his good regard, the family will resist serious threats to the status quo. Thus the family will make efforts to enter treatment on terms which limit the likelihood of significant change in the status quo. The problem of the therapist is to get the family committed to treatment on terms which are most favorable for the kind of outcome he envisions.

In the second section I hope to illustrate how the therapist formulates pathogenic relating, and then how he utilizes his formulation as a lever to promote change. In my experience there is a tendency for families to discount the therapist's formulation, particularly if it is perceived in some manner to seriously threaten the status quo. Thus the therapist must couch his formulation in terms that are difficult to challenge and find means constantly to affirm the validity of his formulation. The therapist utilizes his formulation not only as an objective assessment of the family, but also as a means to bring pressure to change in a direction he deems advisable. Using the formulation, the therapist may attach positive and negative values to actions taken by the family during the course of treatment, thus encouraging certain types of actions while discouraging others. Because of the natural tendency of families to seek the therapist's approval, they will be inclined to engage in actions he approves of, but will tend to avoid those actions he has disapproved.

Two themes underlie the two sections of this chapter: (1) The partial paradox that families will tend to follow the therapist's direction but resist that direction which appears to challenge the family status quo; (2) the partial paradox that while families wish the improvement of the "identified patient," they resist the notion that improvement in the "identified patient's" condition rests in their acceptance of their own causal involvement in the condition.

ISSUE 1: THE FAMILY'S COMMITMENT TO BE TREATED

Coming for the first interview, a family is naturally beset by anxieties about what it will encounter. Does the therapist consider the family to be the agent producing the symptoms that have erupted in a member? Does he consider the family rather as a supportive agent, an assistant therapist, helpful in carrying out his therapeutic plan?

The family weighs carefully the therapist's demand that it meet regularly together. It also notes carefully his requirements concerning the frequency of sessions, their length, and the terms he sets for reimbursement of services. These are important details whose settlement can provide important clues as to the "treatability" of the family.

Characteristically families will challenge the therapist's terms or procedures for the way therapy is to be conducted. Consider the case of the Ludwig family (the names given are, of course, fictitious) which was referred to me by a school counselor because of emotional disturbance in several children. Mrs. Ludwig had spoken to a staff member over the telephone who directed her to bring to the first interview all of the members of her family living in her home. Mrs. Ludwig interpreted the directions as follows: she brought her husband (her second husband) and the five children who were products of her first marriage. Left at home were her two youngest children, products of her current marriage, and her mother, a woman reported by Mrs. Ludwig to have had at least two prior hospitalizations for a mental illness.

Mrs. Ludwig and her husband claimed that the two youngest children were left at home because they were too young and would be noisy and distractible. They did not think I would be interested in seeing Mrs. Ludwig's mother; besides, they remarked, someone had to stay with the youngest children as a babysitter. I inquired whether the whole family would agree to participate regularly in sessions. Mrs. Ludwig thought her mother might be persuaded to come in a time or two, and, if I was sure I could handle the two youngest children, she would bring them, but she was not sure that her older children would cooperate. Mr. Ludwig remarked that he would have difficulty taking time off from his job, but he might manage to make a session every other week.

About midway through the first interview, three of the Ludwig children suddenly stood up and walked rapidly from the session. Mr. and Mrs. Ludwig made no effort to stop them. I asked the parents why they thought the children left, and they mentioned the fears the children expressed about having to visit a "nut house," and embarrassment about explaining their absence from school to their teachers and schoolmates. After a few minutes I directed Mr. Ludwig to try to return the children to the session. He did bring back one of them, but failed to bring back the other two.

On the basis of the family's selection of members to attend the first session, the parents' rationale for leaving certain members out, and the chaotic condition of the family generally, securing their commitment to therapy seemed to me unlikely. The Ludwigs did not return for a second session, stating that they would try to work out their problems by themselves. It seemed to me that a stronger disciplinary threat, such as a requirement to enter treatment by a court or school system, was necessary to act as a stimulus to keep the family in treatment until the treatment process itself had had time to "take."

While families may enter treatment as a result of pressure applied by a court or school system, some may successfully resist commitment to treatment even then by regarding the treatment as a punishment, a sentence pronounced by the court or school system on the family. On the other hand, pressure from a court or school system may be the only way to expose some families to this mode of treatment which they might otherwise be inclined to avoid and which eventually proves to be productive for them despite their initial resistance.

Some families will not contest the therapist's attempt to get them initially committed to treatment, but will contest some elements in his definition later on. A family may agree to attend sessions regularly, but after a while may raise a question whether all of the members designated by the therapist have to attend regularly. In the case of the Tracy family, which I had been treating for about two months during a summer period, Mrs. Tracy raised a question at the beginning of the autumn school term whether it was necessary for three of her children (aside from her child who was labeled the "identified patient") to attend sessions and thus miss classes. I pointed out to Mrs. Tracy, admittedly simplistically, that family therapy meant treating the family as a whole, and that this rule would be followed until I felt it could be relaxed. Fortunately Mrs. Tracy accepted my definition without more than minor resistance. Had she been able to redefine the structure of the treatment—which, after all, does occur when a family member is excluded from sessions—it might have constituted a serious handicap to therapeutic progress because the therapist would have handed over to the family an important decision-making authority.

In order to pursue a specific therapeutic goal, the *therapist himself* may suggest that a family member be included who has not been present before in sessions, or he may suggest that a member be excused from attending further sessions. This may be a particularly critical step when the member the therapist "selects out" has been the "identified patient." In the case of the Steinberg family, composed of parents and a nine-year-old son, I stated, after the family had been in treatment for about ten months, that the boy should not miss his classes and should be excused from attending further sessions. The parents were somewhat surprised by my statement of this position, but accepted it. The son, whose behavior had been immature for his age, was not yet symptom-free, although he was moderately improved.

I made my decision regarding the son because I presumed the following consequences: (a) The son would not now consider himself the central object of treatment, as he had been inevitably up until the time of the decision; (b) the parents would no longer be able to hold onto the fiction that they were my "assistant therapists." In other words, by "selecting out" the son from the sessions, the parents became the main objects of treatment. By redefining the structure of treatment, I illustrated to the parents, somewhat dramatically, that they were involved as patients; that they were causal agents in a process of pathogenic relating which only included their son as one other member of the process. In the case of the Steinberg family, the parents continued in sessions with me for about eight months. An improvement in their son's maturity level was maintained during this period, and they made a moderate improvement in their own relationship.

Sometimes a family member, often with the covert aid of other family members, will exclude himself from sessions. This is also a tactic designed to limit the commitment of the family to treatment and, in my opinion, the therapist is required to oppose this limitation. In the Zelig family, Joan, a 19-year-old daughter, was the "identified patient." She was markedly immature in behavior, probably more accurately described as a borderline character disorder than a psychotic. Joan attended half a dozen sessions with her parents and her younger brother, but then refused to attend more, claiming she could see no possible benefit for herself. Over the next 12 months of sessions with her family, Joan returned perhaps three or four times. I continued to see the Zeligs without Joan in the hope of eventually securing her return on a regular basis. It could not be said that Joan was completely outside the treatment context, since she would hear about the sessions from her family. Interestingly enough, Joan made some minor symptomatic improvement during the period in which her family was seen.

I finally concluded, however, that Joan's continued absence from sessions constituted a key block to significant change in the family even though certain changes could occur in her absence. I increased the pressure on her family to secure her return, but Joan still was not induced to return. Finally treatment was terminated on the grounds I expressed to the family, namely that significant change seemed unlikely in face of Joan's absence from sessions. By this point, however, it should be noted that the family had already had the benefit of over a year of sessions.

My experience with the Zelig family brings to mind examples of the absent-member maneuver described in the useful paper by Sonne, Speck, and Jungreis (1962), although in contrast to the material provided in this paper the authors restricted their descriptions to families containing a schizophrenic member in which "well" members absented themselves from sessions conducted in the families' homes. In one case the authors concluded that, by means of a brother of a schizophrenic girl absenting himself from sessions," . . . the family had put up a very subtle smoke screen to prevent us from really doing family therapy and to effect major changes in the family" (p. 56). I quite agree with this and the other conclusions of the authors, although I find absenting a rather more general phenomenon in family therapy than they describe. For example, I find it occurring in symptomatic as well as nonsymptomatic family members; in families with problems other than schizophrenia; in families treated in the office as well as at home.

Furthermore, I have suggested that absenting may be initiated by the *therapist* rather than the family as a means to stimulate change. In one case described here I suggested, after months of sessions, that the "identified patient" be permitted to attend school while his parents attended sessions. Elsewhere I have also suggested (Zuk, 1967a, pp.

78-79) that it can have a powerful therapeutic value for the therapist, from time to time, to challenge the family's commitment to treatment by introducing the question of terminating treatment.

Although I have tended to focus on absenting techniques in this section, families may use other means to attempt to limit their commitment to treatment. Other devices are those in which the family: (a) Seeks to change the day(s) of the week on which sessions are to be held, or their location, or their length; (b) seeks to challenge the fee set by the therapist; (c) seeks the therapist's agreement to have family members treated individually by another therapist concurrently with family therapy; (d) seeks the therapist's agreement to hospitalize a seriously disturbed family member.

The purpose of the examples given in this section is to draw attention to the complexity and significance of the issue of getting the family committed to treatment on terms satisfactory to the therapist. Jackson (in Haley and Hoffman, 1967) refers to the importance of the therapist "setting the ground rules," by which he means issues such as those discussed in this section; Whitaker (also in the Haley-Hoffman book) uses the term "contract" which overlaps with and complements Jackson's phrase. Families demonstrate characteristic challenges to the therapist's terms: If they perceive his terms for commitment as a serious threat to the status quo, they will often find a means to avoid treatment. On the other hand, the therapist must not so compromise himself by accepting conditions set by the family that he seriously jeopardizes his chance to promote the family welfare.

The family maneuvers described in this section may be viewed as resistance to the notion of members' causal involvement in the condition of the "identified patient." As the family acquiesces to the therapist's *plan* of treatment, it acquiesces also to the therapist's definition that illness resides not within any one member but between members. The therapist's employment of group process reinforces his definition, even though "consciously" the members reject or resist his definition. Previously in a paper (Zuk, 1968b) I stressed the importance of definitions and labels which maintain and promote pathogenic relating in families, and the responsibility of the therapist to identify and if possible alter these definitions or labels primarily by means of applying group pressure.

ISSUE 2: THE FORMULATION OF PATHOGENIC RELATING

Pathogenic relating refers to formulations of the therapist about the distortions in patterns of relating among family members which may be important in a causal sense in producing symptoms in members. Silencing strategies (Zuk, 1965b, 1965c, 1967b) are an example of pathogenic relating, as is scapegoating, which may also be a form of silencing strategy. Inappropriate labeling of a family member's behavior may constitute pathogenic relating, as may the promotion of inappropriate family myths. In inappropriate labeling, family members have given a name to a member's behavior which stamps it as indicative of disturbance, badness, or wrongdoing. In a recent paper (Zuk, 1968b) I described a case in which parents agreed that the behavior of their son was "silly," a label that turned out upon examination to be inappropriate. I suggested that the term used by the parents was a key link in a chain of pathogenic relating involving the parents and child, and that it was necessary for the therapist to attack the link as a means eventually to undermine the pathogenic relating in the family.

I define family therapy as the therapist's employment of go-between process to reduce pathogenic relating. The therapist needs to formulate what is "wrong" with the family, that is, the nature of its pathogenic relating, and then is required to make some kind of communication of his appraisal to the family. No miracles should be expected from this communication, since the family is not likely to accept or use constructively insights about itself without a period of testing. In this testing period, useful change can occur if the therapist negotiates skillfully with the family.

Families may react differently to the therapist's initial formulation of pathogenic relating. Some may appear to accept the therapist's formulation outrightly, and only later do their reservations become apparent. Some appear to ignore or disregard the therapist's formulation. Some will deny the accuracy of his formulation from the beginning and protest the therapist's lack of fairness.

Characteristically among the first questions I ask myself when beginning to treat a family are those having to do with silencing strategies, for these phenomena can usually be observed fairly early in sessions. (It is also observable, however, that families may practice various silencing strategies, and this may not become apparent until some time after sessions have begun.) I ask myself if I can observe a coalition among members to shut another member up and also the nature of the particular technique to shut the member up employed by the coalition. What is the member's response to being shut up? What is the coalition's response when the therapist labels their behavior a silencing strategy? The therapist may find also a subtle intermeshing of types of pathogenic relating; for example, he may find silencing, inappropriate labeling, scapegoating, and promotion of inappropriate family myths to be intermeshed in such a manner as to be unable to describe one without describing the others; to be unable to challenge one without also challenging the others.

My experience with the Tracy[1] family may serve to illustrate how various types of pathogenic relating are identified in families, and then how the therapist's communication about the pathogenic relating in a family can be used as a therapeutic lever to promote beneficial change. The therapist can employ his communication as a source of support or punishment, encouragement or discouragement, confirmation or disconfirmation of the family. Predictably, families will make some efforts to contest the therapist's formulation, and to undermine it, particularly if it is perceived as a threat to the family status quo. Thus it is important for the therapist to couch his formulation in terms that are difficult to attack and possibly disprove—of course, his formulation should also be a "true" (in the sense of valid) assessment of family interaction insofar as he is able to gauge it.

The Tracys are a white family, at the upper range of the lower class socially and economically, and of Irish-Catholic origins. The parents were born and reared in Philadelphia. The "identified patient" in the family at the time of referral was a 15-year-old son who was often truant from school, engaged in petty stealing,

[1] The presentation of the Tracy family is an extensive elaboration of a "critical incident" included in the volume on family therapy for the "International Psychiatry Clinics Series" edited by N. W. Ackerman. Entitled *Family Therapy in Transition,* the book was published by Little, Brown, and Company in 1970. The "critical incident" is on pages 273-281.

and sniffed glue. The family as it appeared for the first session was composed of the parents, both in their early fifties, son M (the "identified patient"), son F, 12 years old, daughter T, 18 years old, and daughter R, 16. A married daughter and two married sons did not attend sessions.

Mr. Tracy has been a bartender for 20 years. Both parents reported that they had alcoholic fathers, and both came from homes in which there was separation or divorce. Mrs. Tracy stated that her mother warned her repeatedly not to trust men. The Tracys married after knowing each other for just a couple of weeks. Mr. Tracy nearly completed the 12th grade of high school, whereas his wife completed the 11th grade.

Toward the end of the initial evaluation session, Mrs. Tracy revealed that she had used the problem presented by her 15-year-old son as a means to coax her *husband* to enter treatment. Her children confirmed her view that her husband was the main problem in the family. Mr. Tracy had been drinking increasingly heavily during the past five years and had become withdrawn from his family. He acknowledged that he drank heavily and felt "outside" the family. In talking about her husband, Mrs. Tracy betrayed anger, resentment, and contempt. She was told by her priest that she had become "hard," but she explained that she had been driven to it by years of irresponsible behavior on her husband's part.

I noted silencing and engagement in a possibly inappropriate labeling in the first evaluation session. Mr. Tracy was treated by his family as if he were not present; as if he really were an "outsider." Mrs. Tracy also seemed interested in having the label "alcoholic" applied to her husband and confirmed by me, as if the label constituted a kind of appropriately damning symbol of Mr. Tracy's years of irresponsibility.

I tried to encourage Mr. Tracy to speak out, even interrupting his wife's complaints about him as a means to encourage him, and declined to use the term "alcoholic" or "alcoholism" in reference to him. Under my prodding, he did begin to talk about himself. In a nutshell his attitude could be described as follows: "I know I have done wrong. I am sorry for it and will try to do better. But my family, especially my wife, does not give me a fair chance. I get frustrated by the demands of wife and children. So I turn to heavy drinking as a means to isolate myself from them."

Mr. Tracy avoided making decisions, made skillful use of evasion almost as a life style, and characteristically turned over to his wife the decision-making function that might rightfully be said to have belonged to him as the head of the household. In the first few session, I concentrated on Mr. Tracy, explored his evasiveness in making decisions, and confronted him with his evasiveness. However, after about six sessions it became apparent to me that while Mr. Tracy practiced one type of evasiveness, his wife practiced another. Mrs. Tracy would announce a decision, often in a threatening manner, and then simply not abide by it. She would allow herself to be dissuaded from action by emotional appeals from her husband and children.

By the eighth session it seemed clear to me that the Tracys played a dangerous game: They made promises to each other and then did not keep them. They announced intentions or decisions to act and then did not carry them out. Everybody in the family seemed to understand this and derive what personal benefit they could from the process, although the cost in terms of raised tension levels in the members and lack of productivity was enormous.

I told the Tracys I thought they often did not mean what they said to each other, and that from that point on, that is, from the eighth session onward, I would examine what they said to each other and then what they *did* to each other in order to determine if the gap between word and action had diminished. I told them I thought the gap was dangerous because it created doubt, uncertainty, and anxiety in the children about the parents' capacity to give direction to the family; indeed it encouraged the children to provide their own brand of leadership. I realized that my statements to the family would be received as a challenge, and that I would provoke a certain antagonism and possible attempts to prove that my formulation was unjustified.

The challenge was not long in being answered. Mr. and Mrs. Tracy arrived separately for the tenth session, Mr. Tracy bringing his daughters with him, Mrs. Tracy bringing her sons. Mrs. Tracy reported that she had separated from her husband during the previous week, moving to the nearby home of a married daughter. Her decision to leave her husband was made after he returned home in a drunken condition.

Mr. Tracy did manage, although still drunk, to get to his job that evening, there announcing to his employer his intention to quit. He returned home earlier than usual to find his wife and sons gone. His daughters told him that his wife had decided to leave him, taking her sons but leaving her daughters to care for the house.

In the tenth session Mr. Tracy appeared contrite and expressed hope that his wife would return to him. His daughters were angry at their mother for what they considered her desertion, but the sons were noncommittal on the issue. I recognized that Mrs. Tracy not only presented her husband a challenge, but also challenged me in that I would be expected to take sides on the issue of her separation—siding with it, against it, or remaining neutral. My choice was to side with Mrs. Tracy on the grounds that (a) I had encouraged family members to take steps they believed to be in the interest of the family, and (b) I would be able to examine how responsibly she acted during the separation and possibly also influence the outcome by the type of examination I conducted. I told Mrs. Tracy I thought she acted out of a genuine desire to promote the family welfare and that it remained to be seen whether there was a good outcome to the separation. I did not praise the separation itself as a good solution, but only as a step which seemed to me to reflect good intention.

In the eleventh and twelfth sessions, Mr. and Mrs. Tracy continued to come separately. There was an interesting change in Mrs. Tracy's emotional response to her husband during these two sessions: Instead of anger, coldness, and contempt she showed previously, she now evinced warmth and affection. She commented favorably on his attempt to take care of things in the home. Predictably, there was a lot of pressure applied by Mr. Tracy and his daughters to induce Mrs. Tracy to return home. In the twelfth session, it was necessary for me to tell the Tracys that I would not be able to meet with them for a period of four weeks while I would be out of town. The family would, however, continue to attend sessions which would be supervised during my absence by qualified nursing personnel who regularly sat in on the sessions I conducted and lent valuable assistance.

There was some acting-up during my absence. First the youngest Tracy son, a boy who had not been in trouble before, was picked up by the police while allegedly glue-sniffing with other boys. His older brother may have been involved in this incident and have encouraged him, although the older brother was not apprehended. Then the older brother was truant from school several times, ran away from home for several days at a time, and was finally picked up by the police with two other youngsters for breaking into a market. The disturbance created by the boys followed Mrs. Tracy's decision to end her separation and return to her husband which occurred a day or two after my departure. She later rationalized her action by saying to me that it was her husband's pleas and the complaints of her daughters that caused her to return home. She suggested also that my absence contributed to a weakening of her resolve, although I countered with the opinion that it provided the loophole for her to undercut her original decision.

The family's acting-up during my absence—I think the term acting-up is applicable here—followed the familiar pattern but, from my point of view, it was especially advantageous in that it was a fresh example of the deep-set pattern of pathogenic relating in the family, and constituted a dramatic illustration of Mrs. Tracy's acquiescence in and maintenance of the pattern. I reacted sharply to her failure to advise me in advance of her decision to end her separation and stated my opinion that the acting-up of her sons was a consequence of her decision.

In confronting Mrs. Tracy with the meaning of her action in terms of my formulation of pathogenic relating in the family, I was attempting to accomplish two objectives: To disconfirm her action; and at the same time, reaffirm the validity of my formulation. The timing and intensity of the disconfirmation are certainly relevant technical features of my procedure, but in this context I wish simply to point out that the therapist does confirm or disconfirm family actions by means of shading and restating his definition of pathogenic relating. The formulation itself is a sometimes not so subtle demand for change. The family can be expected to challenge the formulation because it is a demand for change. To the extent it is subtle enough to bypass the family's fear of change, change may actually be secured. The experienced therapist takes pains to disguise his means to secure change and is disinclined to inform the family of what type of change he expects, especially when the family asks him to be specific about what change he wants.

Not all the activities in the Tracys that occurred during my absence could be termed undesirable. For the first time in two years, Mr. and Mrs. Tracy had sexual relations. It was apparent to me on my return that the parents were exhibiting more warmth and affection toward each other in sessions. Mr. Tracy began to taper off in his drinking and expressed less unhappiness with his job.

I resumed sessions with the family on November 15, 1967, the Tracys by then having been in treatment a period of approximately four months. My notes for the record covering my contact with the family during the latter part of November and December contain the following observations:

> There was some reduction in symptomatic behavior in the family this month. In particular, M stopped being truant and running away from home. On the other hand, Mr. T acted-up some by not showing up for the first two sessions this month. His wife said she was unable to get him up in the morning to come to the session. But Mr. T returned to the third and fourth sessions of the month. . . .
> There is an improved emotional climate in the family. Mrs. T is kinder toward her husband, more affectionate. The children seem less restless. Both parents note that the children seem happier. There is apparently more discussion between the parents about how to handle problems that arise at home. Mr. T notes that he feels less an outsider in the affairs of the family.

During January, 1968, three of the five meetings scheduled were canceled due to illness reported in various family members. On January 9 Mr. Tracy telephoned to say that his wife had taken ill and was diagnosed as having a peptic ulcer. (Mrs. Tracy had been treated some years previously for an ulcer.) On January 24, Mrs. Tracy returned to sessions, having been treated conservatively for her condition with success. On January 31 all of the members of the family but Mr. Tracy appeared for the session; the reason for his absence presented was his having been changed from nighttime to daytime working hours.

My notes for the record during February and March contain the following comments:

> During the period described above, Mr. T did not return to sessions. The reasoning he used was that his daytime job did not

now permit him to attend, but the family denied that this was the real reason. Mr. T's failure to participate raised a serious question about whether it would be possible and feasible to see the family without him present.

On February 21, just the children appeared for the session. Mrs. T was in the hospital for tests in connection with a possible stomach ulcer. On February 28, Mrs. T returned. By this time I had decided to tell her that a plan I thought feasible would be to see the children by themselves weekly, and her from time to time as indicated. I told her that I thought her presence without her husband acted as a restraint on the children and made for a restricted interaction, and that I expected the children "to open up" in her absence. . . .

There were some disturbing events in the family during the last week in March. Mrs. Tracy was operated on for her ulcer. The children reported that their father had returned home one evening with bruises on his face and said he had been involved as a passenger in an auto accident. To top it off, both boys were apprehended by the police and charged with taking coins from a parking meter.

During April Mrs. Tracy made an uneventful recovery from her surgery. The charge of stealing against the boys was dismissed. Unexpectedly and on his own initiative, the older son obtained a job delivering newspapers that required him to get up very early in the morning. Shortly thereafter, his brother also started delivering newspapers. In a session conducted on April 24, the older son looked depressed and reported that he had done more poorly than he had anticipated on his report card at school, and it was unlikely he would be passed to his next grade. From his school counselor I obtained accounts from his teachers of M's performance in his different subjects, and requested Mrs. Tracy to discuss seriously with the counselor M's school status and what if anything might be done to improve it.

My notes for sessions held in May and June are as follows:

On May 22, quite unexpectedly, Mr. T returned to participate in the session, accompanied by his wife. There had been some indication from the children in previous weeks that their father was expressing some interest in coming to a session, but his actual appearance was unexpected and there was no prior telephone call to inform me of his intention.

Mr. T has obtained a new job and expressed relative satisfaction with it. On May 27, I received information from Mrs. S, counselor at the school M attends, to the effect that if M attends summer classes and does well in them, he will be passed on to the next grade despite his poor school performance this year. . . .

Mr. T did not attend the sessions on May 29 and June 5, but reasonable explanations for his absence were offered. On June 12, he did return for the session. The whole family was present on this day. There was a good amount of liveliness in the family; the members seemed reasonably happy with themselves. . . . I raised a question about the further expectations of the family from treatment. Mr. T said he profited from the experience and wanted to continue, and the children agreed. Mrs. T, however, said that maybe the family had profited as much as possible for the present time, and perhaps a termination would be appropriate now.

On June 24, Mr. T telephoned me to say that the family had had a conference and concluded that they would not need to attend further sessions now. Mr. T thanked me for the help his family had received. He mentioned that his daughter T was obtaining a job with the help of her older brother, and she was now less anxious about what to do when she left high school. I wished Mr. T well and told him to call if further help was needed.

At the point of termination, it was my information that both boys were continuing in their newspaper delivery jobs and that M had agreed to attend summer school classes in order to pass to his next school grade. The parents noted that M's truancy and running away from home were no longer problems. According to Mrs. Tracy, her husband's drinking was within bounds and he was participating in a more helpful way in the affairs of the family.

My formulation of pathogenic relating in the Tracy family, and my use of it to create pressure for change, illustrate what I have done now with a number of families and with some success. That is, I have utilized a number of times a similar formulation because it is applicable to many types of families, and because it creates pressure for change but avoids arousing intense fear of change. The simpler the therapist's formulation of pathogenic relating, the better. The simpler his communication of it to the family, the better. The formulation should be couched in terms that are difficult to challenge. I described how members of the Tracy family constantly disqualified their decisions by failing to act upon them; and how members tried to "con" each other into compliance or acquiescence. I stated that actions taken by the family would be examined in the light of their "genuineness," their "sincerity"—that is, whether they really were consistent with the decisions members *said* were intended to promote the family welfare. Of course, I failed to give support to the silencing strategy directed against Mr. Tracy by his wife and children, and sought to expose it, and I failed to support Mrs. Tracy's interest in having her husband labeled an alcoholic. These were two other dimensions of pathogenic relating and were intermeshed with the more pervasive source that I have been describing.

SUMMARY

In treating families over the past seven years it has been my experience that symptom-reduction can occur early, resulting from the therapist's skill in committing the family to treatment because in the commitment process itself there rests a possibility to reduce the level of pathogenic relating in the family. It is my experience also that symptom-reduction can occur later in treatment when the therapist uses his formulation of pathogenic relating to create pressure for change rather than simply as a diagnostic exercise. The chapter provides examples in support of these observations.

In establishing the conditions which prompt change in families, the therapist must be mindful of the two partial paradoxes which seem true of his work. One of these is that families will tend to follow the therapist's direction, but will resist that direction which appears to threaten the family status quo. From the therapist's point of view, an operational definition of family status quo is the conviction of the family that it is *not* implicated causally in the condition of the "identified patient." The therapist must find means to counter this conviction of the family. The second paradox, which is interrelated with the first, is that while families wish the "identified patient" to get better and will tend to follow the therapist's direction as to how to get the member better, they will resist the notion that the member's improvement depends on their acceptance of their involvement as a cause of the member's condition. The therapist must employ indirect means to influence families to accept the proposition.

REFERENCES

Haley, J., & Hoffman, L. *Techniques of family therapy.* New York: Basic Books, 1967.

Sonne, J. C., Speck, R. V., & Jungreis, J. The absent member maneuver as a resistance in family therapy of schizophrenia. *Family Process,* 1962, 1, 44-62.

Zuk, G. H. Preliminary study of the go-between process in family therapy, in *Proceedings of the 73rd annual meeting.* Washington, D.C.: American Psychological Association, 1965a, pp. 291-292.

Zuk, G. H. On the pathology of silencing strategies. *Family Process,* 1965b, 5, 32-49.

Zuk, G. H. On silence and babbling in family psychotherapy with schizophrenics. *Confinia Psychiatrica,* 1965c, 8, 49-56.

Zuk, G. H. The go-between process in family therapy. *Family Process,* 1966, 5, 162-178.

Zuk, G. H. Family therapy. *Archives of General Psychiatry,* 1967a 16, 71-79.

Zuk, G. H. The victim and his silencers: Some pathogenic strategies against being silenced. In G. H. Zuk and I. Boszormenyi-Nagy (Eds.), *Family therapy and disturbed families.* Palo Alto, Calif.: Science and Behavior Books, Inc., 1967b, pp. 106-116.

Zuk, G. H. The side-taking function in family therapy. *American Journal of Orthopsychiatry,* 1968a, 38, 553-559.

Zuk, G. H. When the family therapist takes sides: A case study. *Psychotherapy: Theory, research and practice,* 1968b, 5, 24-28.

Chapter 6 / ENGAGING FAMILIES IN THERAPY; WITH SOME OBSERVATIONS ON AMERICAN FAMILIES

. . . .

One can discern two powerful trends in psychiatry in the United States during the past decade: One in which chemical agents in increasing number and sophistication have successfully been applied to the control of symptoms such as anxiety and depression; another in which psychiatric expertise has been called upon—with uncertain success—to deal with behavior that is at odds with the society. The behavior may result from the use of alcohol or drugs; it may be delinquency or rebelliousness in youth; it may be other kinds of antisocial behavior or criminality in adults. There is little doubt that mental health professionals are increasingly being called upon to help manage problems that were not traditionally considered basically psychiatric.

The community mental health centers have been the primary settings in which the latter dominant theme is being played out. In many quarters there is concern that psychiatry has bitten off more than it can chew. Still it is apparent that a sanction has been granted psychiatry to involve itself in the solution of a variety of social ills, and despite growing doubts and opposition, it is unlikely that the sanction will be withdrawn.

In part because many are functioning on the staffs of the mental health centers, in part for other reasons, family therapists during the past five or more years have been engaged in an effort to adapt their concepts and methods to the problems of patients seen at the centers. A decade ago a main focus of family therapists was the schizophrenic patient and his family—typically a white, middle class family—but in the past five years the range of problems seen by family therapists has broadened considerably, as has the range of family backgrounds and characteristics.

As family therapists have begun to work more extensively with poor minority families, a central problem has been how to engage these families that are so often splintered and in whom the motivation for therapy may be tenuous. As one descends the socioeconomic ladder, the dropout rate for all prospective therapy patients increases. In their New Haven study, Hollingshead and Redlich (1958) noted that practically all lower class patients were antagonistic toward psychiatric treatment and were less likely to be accepted for psychotherapy than middle class patients. A recent report by Salzman et al. (1970) showed a greater percentage of psychotherapy dropouts in lower class and non-Caucasian patients. In their report Rosenthal and Frank (1958) stated a figure of 50% as the dropout rate typical of their psychiatric clinic and others. They also found that at the Phipps Clinic in Baltimore the dropout rate for blacks was twice the rate for whites.

A high dropout rate is especially true of family therapy which requires the presence at meetings of more than a single "patient," also requiring one or more of his family members. A number of techniques are presently being applied to deal with the high dropout rate characteristic especially of poor minority families. Among these are crisis-oriented family therapy (Auerswald, 1968; Sager et al. 1968); therapy sessions held at families' homes, short-term therapy geared to specific goals, and the use of indigenous nonprofessionals to assist in family therapy. There are several centers actively using these techniques with poor minority families today, especially black families, although very little published material yet exists that describes the results of their experience.

In a previous paper (Zuk, 1968), I discussed some of the factors involved in establishing the commitment of families to therapy. In this paper I plan to develop this theme at more length, although I will use the term *engagement* rather than commitment because I will be focusing on the events in the first half-dozen sessions in which a family is seen. (Commitment seems to me a more general term than engagement, describing the emotional bond or loyalty a patient may feel toward the therapy and/or therapist.) I interview families in an outpatient-type setting in which a family member has telephoned for an appointment on the advice of a referring professional agent. I will try to describe some factors here also that limit the applicability of family therapy, or rather limit the likelihood that a course of therapy, if undertaken, will have a successful outcome.

The issue of engagement is important for two reasons in particular: (a) Therapists have found it difficult to engage poor minority families, which is the group receiving a focus of attention in the community mental health centers; and (b) it is frequently the case with families that successful engagement is not simply a precondition for the conduct of therapy, but is also often tantamount to successful outcome. It is possible to obtain good results in a few sessions focused on the issue of engagement alone, which is fortunate because especially in poor minority families, a few sessions may be all the contact the therapist will have. Even when the engagement is not successful, it has been my experience that families will report more than occasionally after a session or two that members are functioning better, or that a relationship has improved, or that a symptom in a member has subsided. Crisis-oriented and short-term psychotherapy are both grounded in the common experience of therapists that many patients do report improvement after one session or only a few. Even psychoanalytic workers have observed the beneficial effect of a single interview. Lief et al. (1961) reported that their clinic encouraged more than a single interview by psychiatric residents in screening prospective patients for intensive psychotherapy, because ". . . in our experience there is often a striking change in behavior from the first to the second interview" (p. 201).

I wish to spell out in the first part of this paper the main contraindication for family therapy. There are numerous limitations on the method which, to be sure, restrict the scope of its applicability. But these limitations are not in themselves contraindications because they do not signify that if a course of family therapy is undertaken, it will have a harmful side-effect. There have not been many papers in the literature on contraindications but in those that do exist (for instance, Ackerman, 1966, and Wynne, 1965), writers have frequently confused some practical *limitations* of family therapy with contraindications. As I see it, family therapy is contraindicated *when it appears it can only serve to support the status quo,* such as when there is a fixed family attitude that the therapist is serving as an agent for another source and other than as an independent authority or expert. I believe it is undesirable and may be harmful for therapy to serve this purpose because it undermines confidence in the method and evokes false expectations.

In the latter half of this paper I wish to discuss some characteristics of families that seem to me influential in whether they will become engaged in therapy, and whether also there will be a successful outcome of the therapy. One of the central "facts" about the family is that it is an institution in which women, in their roles as mother and wives, exercise influence at least on a par with men in their roles of fathers and husbands. In other institutions men are dominant, and their concepts, procedures, and methods prevail. In the nuclear family, the influence of the mother, particularly when her children are adolescents or younger, predominates over that of her husband. The emotional loyalty of children to their mother usually greatly exceeds that which is attached to their father.

Parsons (1955), among others, has contended that the nuclear family has become more segregated from its larger kinship system and that differentiation between the parental roles has become more significant in connection with the socializing of children. Within the nuclear family I believe that the power exercised by wives and mothers is increasing at the expense of power exercised by husbands and fathers. The interest and energy of husbands and fathers are being increasingly diverted from their roles in the nuclear family by the demands, attractions, and distractions of their jobs and the technology. The vacuum left by the men is being filled by the women.

What I have observed and have been impressed by as a family therapist is simply the *centrality* of wives and mothers in the nuclear family, and I hope to discuss some consequences of this observation and how it may affect the engagement of families in therapy.

Finally in the latter part of the paper I wish to discuss implications of certain characteristics of families in relation to the problem of engaging them in therapy. It is generally recognized that of the different types of families encountered, the Jewish family is the easiest to engage, the black family the most difficult. Traditionally Jews have been "good" psychotherapy patients despite the general trend that patients from minorities are not. (By "good" I mean motivated to engage in therapy and to adhere to the format spelled out by the therapist.)

TECHNIQUES FOR ENGAGING FAMILIES

I mentioned already that I see families in an outpatient-type setting, and so the remarks to follow are limited by that fact. When I see a family for the first time, I usually know only their name and that the family has been referred for an evaluation. I do not review records before I see the family because I find that it often sets up false biases, dispositions, or attitudes that take too much time to dispel later. I prefer to let the members tell me why they are present for the evaluation, and then afterwards check records that may be available.

It is of interest to me who attempts to answer the question I first pose: "What is the problem?" Usually it will be the mother who answers first, in part reflecting the fact that perhaps I look first in her direction, but also because in American families mothers *are* the spokesmen. Husbands typically hang back; one finds them hesitant to talk. They seem to listen closely to their wives for cues that will guide them to decide how much to reveal to the therapist.

I am of course interested in whether the family has followed the direction to bring along to the first evaluation as many as possible of the members living at home. One finds significant departures from this request: A child may be left in school on the ground that an important test was being given the same day; or one of the children may be reported ill; or it was not thought that a grandmother living at home would be considered a member of the family; or a husband simply could not get time off from his job.

If members are missing, I instruct the family that for at least the first few sessions, I wish to see the entire group living at home, but that later it may be different. If a father complains that he cannot continue to take time away from his job, I tell him to make arrangements with his employer to be away for the four or five times I will require to make a full evaluation. I say it will take me that long to decide if the family can benefit from a course of therapy, or whether some other procedure is indicated. This instruction, because it is perceived as a relatively small demand and because it suggests that the therapist may find there is nothing wrong with the family, tends to enlist cooperation.

When, as particularly in the case of lower class or minority families, a family has concluded that therapy has been recommended basically to serve as a punishment or discipline for the misbehavior of a member, the members may be very antagonistic to the therapy. They may form a tight bond of loyalty to resist the efforts of the therapist to explore problems. They may even demand—often quite courteously—that the therapist *prove* the need for therapy. In these cases it is my practice to state my impression that the family and I are engaged in a game of "Hide and Seek." I state directly that I am not obligated to prove a need for therapy; that I simply assume that a family comes to me for help; and that if that assumption is incorrect, perhaps it would be best to suspend further evalaution until the time that this is the family's belief. I find that this rejoinder, once interest has been piqued by attendance at a few meetings, often produces a more receptive attitude in ambivalent families. Some families are lost in the aftermath of this type of confrontation, but I think they would be lost anyhow.

Once in a while after therapy has been under way for some time, one finds family members threatening *each other* to discontinue on the ground that a desired response on the part of the other family member has not been forthcoming. Of course this may also be a not very subtle ploy to enlist the therapist's help in securing the desired response from the other member. Frequently before I have had an opportunity to respond, the threatened member declares his wish also to discontinue in order to avoid a feared concession. In this case, my usual response is to say that the matter is settled; that since both parties are for discontinuation and thus appear not receptive to my guidance but to have made their own plans, I will agree to a discontinuation. I may launch into a little speech about how I had hoped for better cooperation from the family members, but how I feel I have at least offered them the opportunity to air their grievances and have therefore fulfilled at least a minimal responsibility. Frequently I find this response sufficient to undercut the contest between the members. Usually one, then the other, decides then or a bit later that he will try to carry on in the therapy. Rapid progress can sometimes be made in therapy in the aftermath of these little encounters.

The presence of young children, let us say under the age of 8 or 10, seems to me to have the effect of impeding the successful engagement of families in therapy, so I follow a policy of ordinarily seeing young children through a basic evaluation period of four or five sessions, and then excusing them from further attendance. Naturally when a young child is the so-called primary patient, that is, the member who is showing symptoms or whose behavior has caused the family to be referred for therapy, the policy is changed. Then the child is included for a longer period, although after 10 or 15 sessions I again consider the advisability of having the child remain in school or at home.

The reason for my reluctance to include young children in more than the first few therapy sessions is not primarily that they should not be burdened by hearing confidences of the parents—although I feel that this is an issue too many family therapists pass over too lightly—but rather that the loyalty of the children to the parents, especially the mother, is ordinarily so strong in children under 10 years of age that it is difficult to elicit conflict with the parents. Children of this age span ordinarily clam up tightly when examined about their relation with their parents. Also of course the language they have available for the expression of conflict is still limited. And they tend to be very sensitive to and compliant with the many subtle silencing signals sent out by the parents.

One factor that drives families from engagement is the anxiety that the therapist will press them for secrets and confidences. Parents may be especially fearful that their children may learn of a peccadillo; or that some serious blunder or even criminal activity may be revealed of which they believed the children ignorant. As early as in the first session with the family, I explain that it is *not* my primary aim to elicit secrets, and that I will respect signals that a topic is too sensitive to discuss openly. Of course I will also state that it is hard to tell about secrets; that sometimes they are known by more persons than it was thought, even known by relatively young children in the family. I also state that I hope family members will signal me *clearly* their intention not to reveal certain information; but that I may then ask to be given a general notion of the subject matter to be avoided, although not specific details whose nature I have agreed to avoid exploring. I have found that after giving this type of reassurance, family members frequently do go into detail about topics or issues that they have had genuine intentions of avoiding. The reassurance has served to undercut the contest between therapist and family as to *how much* the therapist can force the family to reveal.

In one case I recall, during the evaluation period I specifically asked a young couple to stop talking about their sexual relationship in the presence of their children. Naturally the couple was surprised, for husband and wife had had experience in individual psychotherapy, and assumed that I, like their other therapists, would be interested in their sexual incompatibility. I replied that I was, but that I was more interested in their failure to recognize the *separateness* of their marital relationship from the relationship they had as parents with their children. The wife in particular exhibited a strong need to "include in" in her relationship with her husband and children all sorts of friends. By taking a stand against the failure to differentiate between the parent and child generation, I hoped to focus on this issue which I considered an important form of pathogenic relating in the family. The family stopped coming to sessions after four or five times, because I do not think the parents could accept the only terms I thought offered real hope for change and because of their ambivalent motivation for family therapy.

In the first few sessions I seek to discover what the family's preconditions for therapy are, and then either try to neutralize them (should, in my opinion, they be of the kind to foreclose change), or divert them into channels consistent with my aims. Quite frequently parents enter therapy with the preconception that the therapist will side with them vis à vis their children, or in particular a child who has been troublesome. Unable to effectively administer discipline themselves, they expect the therapist to be able to do it.

When I sense that parents have such preconceptions as noted above, I characteristically state that I am neither a judge nor a lawyer, and that I am certainly not a policeman. I say that it is my main function to understand what has been happening in the family, and that I studiously avoid taking sides, at least until I do understand what is destructive in the family relations.

In one case, it became apparent shortly after a family entered therapy that the mother had the notion that I should accept her judgment that her son, a 19-year-old who had been taking drugs, should be hospitalized for his habit. She wanted me to have him hospitalized at the institution to which I was attached. When I resisted the idea, she expressed disappointment and said it was obvious her son needed to be in a hospital. I said that might be so, and that she and her husband might decide to hospitalize him, but I would not initiate the procedure and certainly not try to secure his hospitalization at my own institution. Upon hearing my position, the mother backed off somewhat and decided to bide her time. She was convinced that eventually I would be persuaded of the soundness of her position. Of course she knew that she and her husband could have had the son hospitalized elsewhere, but she wanted *me* to accept her judgment. It came to be very important to her to persuade me that she was right, almost as important as accomplishing the actual hospitalization. Launching herself on a campaign of persuasion, the mother found herself engaged in a course of therapy under my direction that lasted about seven months. Unfortunately, I cannot report that this case had a successful outcome (the prognosis of this type of problem must be considered ordinarily poor), but I have to consider it something of an achievement to have successfully engaged the family at all, and it may be that the seeds I planted during the seven-month period of therapy may bloom at a later date.

Another preconception sometimes encountered is that therapy is a punishment meted out to the family itself, and at times there is a realistic basis for this notion. I recall a case where a family was led to believe that the length of a child's probationary period would be substantially reduced by accepting the recommendation of a court that the family enter therapy. The family followed the recommendation but proved quite "unworkable," as the effect of the judge's recommendation was to cause the family to form a solid front against the therapist who was perceived as an agent of the court. This is the kind of case in which family therapy is actually contraindicated, for the condition under which it is undertaken severely limits the capacity of the therapist to introduce change because it tends to engender resentment of the therapy. I recall telling the family in question after two or three sessions that although I felt there might be some benefit to the members in the future in a course of therapy, the timing then was unfavorable. I indicated my position to the child's probation officer and suggested that the probation period be shortened as much as possible. As it turned out, the probation officer did not think highly of the need for a probationary period for the boy in the first place. His offense was setting a fire with another boy near a garage of a neighbor. A section of the garage caught fire and some slight damage was done. The neighbor, apparently a crotchety lady previously irritated by pranks of children in the neighborhood, refused an offer of payment by the boy's parents and brought charges. Ordinarily the police in the locale, as I later learned, would have tried to discourage the lady, especially as it was a first offense, but as it happened there had recently been several episodes of fire-setting that had sensitized them.

There would probably be a consensus now among therapists that it is undesirable to provide families an extensive rationale for why they are being seen as units. Some therapists used to spend a good deal of time during early sessions explaining in detail that the labeled patient was merely a symptom of a disturbed family system, suggesting that when the system improved, the symptom would likely disappear. A frequent result of the rationale was to frighten families away, for they concluded that they were being held directly responsible for the condition of the labeled patient. However accurate this conclusion may be in theory and in fact, it is undesirable to stress it to families, particularly during the engagement phase. Having accepted the therapist's requirement to meet regularly with him, families are already struggling *by implication* with the knowledge that somehow they have been judged causally involved. While many can tolerate the anxiety and guilt associated with this implication, others cannot and these may prematurely disengage. Providing an extensive rationale is particularly undesirable in the case of lower class families, which tend to react to it with greater confusion and resentment than middle class families.

The therapist's requirement that family members meet together with him regularly *is* a strong contextual statement regarding his view of psychological causation, and it tends to be perceived as a kind of condemnation by the family; therefore, it is desirable that he temper it by avoiding verbal reinforcement of the idea. As a means to mute verbally the powerful contextual message, in early sessions I frequently repeat that I am neither judge nor jury; that faultfinding is not a goal of the therapy; and that the goal is to check and if possible replace destructive interactions that are discovered during the course of therapy.

In the first few sessions, it is important for the therapist to distinguish whether he is dealing with a "talk" or a "non-talk" family; then, if it is a "non-talk" family, to take steps to reduce the anxiety of such a family generated by the therapy session itself with its heavy emphasis on verbal exchange. The "talk" family is one in which verbal exchange among members appears to have been systematically encouraged. In this family, a rich verbal exchange has been deemed necessary to the maintenance of family solidarity. In the "non-talk" family, verbal exchange among members has been discouraged, as if such expressiveness were judged a threat to family solidarity.

The lower the social or educational standing of a family, the more likely is it to be of the "non-talk" variety. Jewish families are more than likely "talk" families, while black families are more than likely "non-talk." Families of southern European origin tend to be "talk," while northern European families tend to be "non-talk."

The "non-talk" family does not especially prize an opportunity for long-term participation in an enterprise which requires a high level of verbal exchange, so will be inclined to disengage from therapy if it extends beyond a few sessions or once painful symptoms have subsided. Thus with this family, I pointedly de-emphasize the need for a long-term commitment. I stress that the evaluation will last for only a *few* sessions. Once a symptomatic improvement occurs, knowing that the "non-talk" family is inclined to disengage at this point, I may take the initiative to decrease the frequency of visits, or stop further visits while maintaining telephone contact, or allow certain members to discontinue attendance at sessions in order for them to meet other obligations. By these devices I hope to forestall a complete disengagement for which I believe the family may not yet be ready.

An experienced therapist who believes that family therapy is necessarily a long-term intensive affair will be inclined to misjudge "non-talk" families as ones who lack sufficient motivation for change and avoid them. A beginning therapist may be inclined to attribute it to some personal deficiency if a "non-talk" family drops out, when the problem may really be a simple failure to adapt his approach to one of the many sets of *limits* families impose on therapy or any other change process to which they are exposed.

THE CONTRAINDICATION FOR FAMILY THERAPY

In my judgment, family therapy is contraindicated only when the family appears to have a fixed attitude that the therapist is serving as an agent of some other person or institution to carry out disciplinary procedures with a family member or with the family as a whole. The therapist may be perceived as an agent of the courts, of the schools, of a welfare department, or, by children, as an agent of the *parents*. In such a situation the therapist is not free to introduce change of a type he envisions as necessary and useful, but rather must be an agent of change decided by someone other than himself, or be an agent of the status quo. The situation is one in which the purpose of psychotherapy is essentially compromised and subverted.

Elsewhere I have defined the task of the family therapist (Zuk, 1967, 1969) as the identification of pathogenic relating among family members, that is, of the living process he sees erupt in his presence, that he judges destructive to the family functioning as a whole and to the functioning of the individual members. The therapist's application of means to subvert and replace pathogenic relating I have referred to in previous papers as go-between process, in which the therapist takes sides and shifts positions vis à vis family members. In the situation referred to in the previous paragraph, the situation defined as contraindicating family therapy, the pathogenic relating in the family cannot be attacked unless the therapist is able to get the family to discard its attitude. Sometimes this is possible, sometimes not. For example, in a recent case, I conveyed to a young couple my impression that they perceived me as carrying out the will of authorities at the school their children attended, and who had judged the children emotionally disturbed as well as educationally underachieving. The parents were frightened by the school's judgment and deeply resented it. They were anxious also because both had lived through some bad experiences in their lives and feared their children would discover these in the course of the therapy.

I told both parents, beginning in the second meeting, that I doubted there was a basis to continue in the face of their attitude, which I tried to define. They expressed surprise at my position, stating they wanted to do what was best for their children, but acknowledged that they resented the pressure applied by the school. During the second meeting I dismissed the children after about a half-hour, telling them that they should use some toys and games provided for them elsewhere in the clinic area. I realized that taking this step would reassure the parents that I respected their fear of revealing secrets to the children. In the third session, I asked the couple to come alone. In it the father, after an initial period in which again he criticized me for not accepting his and his wife's cooperativeness, began to recount several past episodes in which he had been convicted of criminal activity. From his description it was clear he was making an effort to describe himself as he was rather than as he wished to appear. Had the parents hung onto an attitude in which, in effect, they required me to *prove* the school's assumption that the children needed therapy, I would have suspended work with them for I would have been trapped in the role of an agent of the school. I took steps I thought would budge them from their position, and the steps had a temporarily promising effect. But I have also encountered parents who successfully circumvented my efforts to budge them from a fixed attitude, and whom I terminated for that reason.

A fixed attitude on the part of children toward their parents, or vice versa, can also be a condition signifying that a course of therapy should not be undertaken. Parents may be so resourceful and command such loyalty among their children, that the therapist is unable to act against the pathogenic relating he may recognize. Indeed, it may be the expectation of the parents that the therapist will join their side against one of the children in order to help bring the child into line.

An example of this type of situation is the case of a white, middle-class, Protestant family in which the father was a naval officer. There were two teenage children in the family, one of whom was a bright girl about 16 years of age. Some months before I saw the family, the parents were made very anxious as a result of discovering that the girl had smoked marijuana. In contrast with her quite conservative parents, the girl dressed in the flamboyant fashion of many teenagers today, but upon talking with her it hardly seemed as if she departed much from the norm of children of her background and age.

I met with the family three times, after which I suggested that sessions be suspended but that the parents could telephone me again if they felt the need for an evaluation. I took this step for several reasons. For one, although there were a number of signs of tension and friction in the family, it was clear that all of the members had resources to cope with these tensions. It had been some time since the discovery of the daughter's drug experimentation and the anxiety about it had largely subsided by the time I saw the family. For another reason, I was greatly impressed with the skill of the naval commander father to monitor communication between myself and the family. In the absence of a fresh incident, I doubted that it would be possible to bypass his skillful obstructiveness. One of the things the father did especially skillfully was to place himself in the role of my "assistant therapist," interpreting the family's behavior to me and suggesting the motivation of members. He also had the ability to silence his wife and children quite subtly and effectively.

In the absence of a "hot" crisis in the family, it seemed to me inopportune to embark on a course of therapy. I believe it could only have served at that time to reinforce the status quo, and as such was contraindicated. With this family, it was *not* a question of whether the family would become engaged. This family was used to abiding by orders, and had I ordered a course of therapy for a year or two, it would have been obeyed. But the key question was: As therapist, was I free to introduce what I believed was needed change in the family? Or were conditions such as to compel me to accept the parents', especially the father's, definition of needed change? After an evaluation period consisting of three sessions, I concluded that the latter was the case.

The example above illustrates that while engagement is a desirable goal of the therapist and may frequently be tantamount to a successful outcome of therapy, it is not always so. Indeed, in certain cases it is inadvisable for the therapist to accept a family for a course of therapy.

Earlier in this paper I suggested a distinction between factors that *limited* the applicability of family therapy and conditions that *contraindicated* it. There are a number of limiting factors which should be mentioned. They limit the likelihood that families will become successfully engaged, or if successfully engaged will experience a successful outcome of therapy. These factors do not appear to me to carry a risk that a course of therapy, if decided upon, will have an undesirable side effect, as would be the case in those circumstances I have described as contraindicating therapy.

The major limiting factor is grounded in the rule that as one descends the socioeconomic ladder, the level of family disorganization increases. Lower class families do not especially prize an opportunity for an extended relationship with a therapist. Job demands on lower class fathers and mothers tend to be disruptive to schedules for meetings set by the therapist. And lower class families are often impaired in ability to speak skillfully in the language, which increases their sense of inadequacy in therapy.

In certain instances, a limitation of family therapy may consist in the refusal of a family member to attend or in the sudden absence of a member who has attended previous sessions. I do bring pressure on families to secure the presence of a member who refuses to attend, but the pressure varies with the identity of the member. If it is a husband or father, I bring considerable pressure to bear and will usually require the man's presence as a basis for continuation. If it is a child who has been labeled the patient in the family, I will also usually require his presence as a basis for continuation. If it is a child who is not symptomatic, then I will express the hope that he can be persuaded to attend but will not suspend sessions until he does. If it is a grandmother living in the home, then I also express the hope she will attend. If a woman is separated or divorced from her husband, then I inquire if she believes he would be willing to attend, but I would not require his attendance as a basis for continuation.

In the case of one-parent families (usually, of course, families in which the mother is the remaining parent), I usually try to find a relatively concrete, practical, short-term goal toward which I direct my efforts. The therapist, if male, is unavoidably cast as a father-substitute in these situations, and must be concerned lest he build up too much dependency as a substitute father. My inclination is to direct my efforts to achieve a short-term goal and suspend regular sessions with the one-parent family, offering to be available to the mother for further consultation.

WIFE-MOTHER CENTRALITY IN THE AMERICAN FAMILY

Although there are exceptions, it seems to me the rule in American families that the woman, in the role of wife and mother, is the spokesman for the family. This certainly seems the case in my interviews with families of widely varying backgrounds. Although one encounters exceptions, it is usually the wife or mother who describes and explains the family in depth to the therapist. She *knows* her children as her husband does not seem to; she *knows* her husband as her husband does not seem to know her.

In general, husbands cannot lay claim to the same amount of emotional loyalty enjoyed by wives in relation to their children. This intense loyalty to the mother can be observed in therapy sessions in the way in which children, especially young children, tend to cluster around her and not her husband. The children are also prone to look more to her than to her husband for the cues they naturally seek from their parents in responding to inquiries made by the therapist.

The American family seems to me clearly female-dominated, quite in contrast to other institutions which are substantially male-dominated; that is, essentially managed by men and utilizing concepts and procedures devised by men. Only the family stands as an exception to the rule. The dominance of females in the family, in their roles as

wives and mothers, is evident in the relative absence of key characteristics of institutions dominated by men; for example, paying close
attention to orderly procedure, regulation, and process; establishing a
clearcut chain of command; developing codes of acceptable behavior or
performance, with rewards defined; and establishing concrete goals and
delineating steps necessary to achieve them. Although it is obviously
not true that these characteristics are absent from family life, it is
recognizable that they tend to characterize family life not nearly so
much as other institutions, agencies or organizations—all of which are
dominated by male concepts and procedures. In my opinion, the
relatively lower value placed on these characteristics in families is due in
part to the relatively high control there exercised by women.

Differences between the functions of husbands and wives in the
family have been recognized. Parsons (1955) has described the
wife-mother as dominant in the "expressive" function in the family, the
husband-father as dominant in the "instrumental" function. He
recognized that in the American family the management of the children
has become increasingly the wife-mother's affair, with the husband-
father spending a great deal of his time away from his family on the
job. Parsons was writing about this state of affairs in the American
family in the early 1950's, and was already stating, in effect, that the
balance of power had passed from the hands of the husband-father to
the wife-mother in terms of the management of children.

Presently I see the control and management of children as
centralized in the hands of the wife-mother, with the husband-father
actually occupying a quite peripheral role in the American family. I
think the ascendancy of the wife-mother role in the nuclear family has
had one special kind of harmful effect on children, a consequence of
the *type* of control and management exercised by the wife-mother. To
use Parsons' terms, children are modeling their behavior, in my opinion,
too much in accordance with the "expressive" function, consequently
not enough with the "instrumental" function, because the wife-mother
is the predominant teaching agent in the nuclear family.

Many of the common conflicts between husbands and wives reflect
basic differences in the manner in which they exercise control and
management in life, differences not quite captured by the terms

"expressive" and "instrumental." Consider the common complaint of husbands that their wives are poor handlers of money; or that they do not use their time wisely; or that their discipline of the children is erratic when it should be rational and systematic. One reason these complaints are so widespread is that they reflect a competition between the different modes by which men and women maintain and expand their power in different situations in life. Women are capable of handling money, paying attention to schedules, and administering discipline systematically; but money, schedules, and discipline are *men's* games, and to become too adept at them would cause a woman to forfeit—or believe she has forfeited—her uniqueness, her special contribution to society. Indeed if a woman were to become too skillful at applying men's games in the family, for instance, she would run the risk of destroying the very foundation on which is built the enormous emotional loyalty of her children to her, for men's games encourage distance, differentiation, and perspective, as opposed to the intimacy, warmth, and closeness which are the objectives of women's games.

The novelist Philip Wylie, in *Generation of Vipers,* brutally depicted the deleterious influence of "momism" on American youth, particularly sons. More recently, especially in the last decade, the "Jewish mother" has become a popular if somewhat ambivalent symbol of the power of the mother in the American family. Sons of varied racial, religious, and ethnic backgrounds have recognized in Mrs. Portnoy some of the characteristics of their own mothers. For some time now it has been recognized that the family is fulfilling a more specialized function than it did in times past, due in part to an increasing isolation of the nuclear family from its kinship network. The relatively great mobility that exists in American society, associated with the relative economic affluence of the United States and a rapidly expanding technology, seem to be important causes of the emergence and primacy of the nuclear family, in a sense at the expense of the extended family.

It is generally accepted that changes have occurred in American family structure during the past quarter-century that are at least in part responsible for the high incidence of rebelliousness in present-day youth, and the high incidence of mental disturbance and lawlessness among the youth that has been widely reported. The solidarity of the extended family system has been eroded as a result of high social mobility, economic pressure, and technological advances. The nuclear family has emerged as the dominant family system with increased pressure on parents to provide guidance for their children. But the guidance process has been increasingly dominated by mothers.

I have posed as a major source of the problem facing the young, that there has been an overabundancy of the mother as a teaching agent and a deficiency of the father. Children develop distrust of the father because he is a peripheral figure in the family, and they tend to distrust what he stands for. As the children move into adolescence and young adulthood, they experience a special difficulty and confusion handling their encounters with institutions, agencies, and organizations because these social units reflect in large measure—and certainly in a symbolic sense—the thinking of their *fathers.*

It has been a popular psychoanalytic explanation for the high level of mental disturbance, rebelliousness, and lawlessness of present-day American youth, to attribute it, especially in the case of sons, to a kind of delayed or reactivated expression of the Oedipus Complex. The supposition is that sons oppose their fathers—and the institutions of their fathers—for the sake of the sexual conquest of their mothers. My main criticism of it is that it doesn't take sufficient account of factors and shifts in the social and cultural climate. A sexual competitiveness between sons and their fathers perhaps is one of the motives underlying adolescent rebelliousness; but another consists in the fact that the father, as a result of continuing economic-technological pressure, has become estranged from his wife and children, and therefore is judged with suspiciousness by them. The father, as the primary teacher of children about male-dominated institutions, agencies, and organizations, has, as it were, lost his credibility.

Children, having overlearned from their mothers—husbands not being available to balance their wives' teaching of the children—are thus bound in adolescence to begin to challenge the credibility of those institutions with which their fathers are identified. The simple *unavailability* of fathers to serve as a bridge between the family and other institutions sets the stage in my opinion, for the high level and unique form of rebelliousness presently observed during adolescence and young adulthood, with offshoots of the turbulence being a high incidence of mental disturbance and lawlessness.

One finds in the turmoil of youth today not just the wish to abnegate the father and his institutions, but also the wish to create new institutions or social forms that derive from the values expressed by their mothers in family life. The extreme case in point is the hippie "community" but this trend exists much more widely in an attenuated form. In their effort to relax *boundaries* (for example, in the more flamboyant mode of dress and the decreased sexual differentiation in dress; in the looser language and terminology; in the increased emphasis on people "doing their own thing" rather than following prescribed formulas for behaving), youth seems to me testing out in the larger society what has been learned from mothers as the main transmitters of values within the family.

Replying to the question, "How does the United States look to the rest of the world these days?" the eminent British historian Arnold Toynbee—published in the *New York Times* (coincidentally I presume) on Mothers Day, May 10, 1970—concluded:

> Is there, then, no hope of reconciliation on America's home front? I catch a gleam of hope when I recall some words that I heard an American officer let fall two years ago in a discussion on the international situation. "There are going to be many more Vietnams," this officer said, "though the mothers of America won't like it."
>
> The mothers of America: This representative of the Pentagon had detected the great power that was going to be the Pentagon's most formidable adversary. The Pentagon versus the mothers of America . . . .
>
> The mothers of America have still to go into action, and I believe this is a battle that the Pentagon cannot win. In the mothers of America I do still see some hope for the world.

His rhetoric aside, I think Toynbee does capture the profound conflict that does exist between the value systems of men and women in the United States and does take notice of the growing power of women in the conflict, particularly as regards the future of their children.

After formulating the view of the American family expressed in this section, and approximately three months after writing it here, I became aware of Keniston's book (1965) on alienated youth, in which he formulated a strikingly similar picture of the family. On the issue of the centrality of the wife-mother, Keniston observed that, "American boys are increasingly brought up by women—mothers and teachers—who have the greatest power and authority over them. This 'matriarchal' situation tends to encourage identification with women, their functions, and their activities" (p. 305). Keniston argues that there is a developmental discontinuity presented children, in that their enormous dependency on their mothers ill prepares them for the independence required in adulthood. Particularly in the case of sons, their intense mother-dependency interferes with the establishment of a masculine identity.

I happily acknowledge the prior authorship of Keniston, who interestingly enough, drew his conclusions regarding the American family from extensive observations of very bright, privileged young men whom he described as alienated. My similar deductions were based on a very different sample: extensive contact in therapy with mostly lower class families with children in whom very high intelligence was the exception rather than the rule. The "alienation" of the group of children and adolescents I saw consisted largely in aggressive behavior or stealing, poor school achievement, truancy, drug dependency, and sexual promiscuity. One might speculate that very high intelligence and affluence are necessary ingredients to produce the kind of alienation of which Keniston speaks; otherwise, different "solutions" are found by youngsters whose estrangement from their fathers and overdependency on their mothers have poorly prepared them for adult society.

The material in this section is admittedly speculative, but I have presented it because it seems to me to provide significant background in connection with the problem of engaging families in therapy. In hoping to attract them it is necessary that therapists give proper recognition to the different *stakes* of husbands and wives in regard to their children. The central role of the mother means to me that her decisions regarding the engagement will tend to have greater weight than those of her husband. If a husband is opposed to therapy but his wife favors it, my experience has been that the chances of the family entering treatment are even or better. But if a wife is opposed, even if her husband favors it, then the chances are well below even.

The wife-mother is generally the spokesman for the American family, and the therapist should be aware that he will have to deal with her in that powerful role which contains some special prerogatives. Inevitably, in my opinion, he is confronted with the task of neutralizing the undesirable effects of the mother's centrality with her children. Inevitably, he is a father figure to the children and a husband figure to the mother; and he will confront the same means developed by mother and children which originally encouraged the estrangement of the biological father-husband. Out of the confrontation may come a reduction in the pathogenic relating which presumably led to the development of symptomatic behavior in children or parents.

CHARACTERISTICS OF JEWISH AND BLACK FAMILIES IN THERAPY

In this section I wish to make the following point, which may appear so obvious as to be naive: racial, religious, and ethnic characteristics have a bearing on the ease or difficulty with which families will engage in therapy, and also on the likelihood of a successful outcome. The point will be illustrated through describing certain characteristics of Jewish and black families, for these appear to be polar opposite types in regard to the question of engagement. (Readers wishing an extensive description of black families in therapy should refer to the report by Minuchin et al. 1967.)

It is only in the last few years that therapists have begun to have extensive contact with black families. The experience has been dramatic, if for no other reason than that this type of family has posed the most severe test of the limits of applicability of family therapy. The black family has proved the most difficult to engage (there is little published material to document this personal observation, but the reader may find some support for it in the paper noted earlier by Sager et al.), and it also is apparent that even when engaged, there is less likelihood of a successful outcome in black families as compared with white. On the brighter side, because many therapists have viewed work with black families as a special challenge, a number of innovative techniques have been tried; for example, family therapy conducted at times of crisis, short-term family therapy oriented about concrete goals, family therapy conducted at the homes of the families, and using indigenous nonprofessionals to assist in family therapy. While family therapy is not a panacea for poor black families, there has been an interesting development of innovative technical means to deal with the problems they present.

Experience with Jewish families, on the other hand, and perhaps ironically, has tended to maintain the status quo in regard to practice, for Jews tend to be well-motivated for therapy, whether as individuals or as families, and thus tend to respond favorably to the well-established techniques. While black families tend to be fearful of the prospect of a long-term contact with a therapist, Jewish families find the prospect appealing. While black families are slow to express themselves in words, indeed often seem to distrust words and those that use them well, Jewish families are verbally facile. While black families tend to keep the therapist "at arm's length," and are likely to be suspicious of his motives and frightened of his power, Jewish families pressure him to act "like one of the family," and if rebuffed in the invitation can be sarcastic and even contemptuous. Invariably I find that Jewish families tend to cast me in the role of "Judge"; invariably poor black families cast me in the role of "Ward Politician." In other words, there are sharp differences between these groups in the kind of expert the therapist is expected to be.

Some results in a study by Aronson and Overall (1966) are relevant to my observations in the previous paragraph. Responding to a questionnaire which sought to tap expectations of patients about their therapists, they found 67% of lower class blacks (the lower class N was 39, of which 27 were black; and the middle class N was 40) agreeing that therapists would "Avoid subjects which might upset you"; whereas 17% of lower class whites and 16% of middle class whites agreed. As a whole the lower class group more often expected the therapist to be direct, supportive, and active. An interesting if ambiguous finding was that Jews, of whom there were eight in the middle class group, tended to respond in a strong manner negatively to the 35 items in the questionnaire. The authors speculated that this result was due to a tendency of Jews to, "When in doubt, say no."

The reader should keep in mind that characteristics I have ascribed here to poor black families tend also to be characteristic of poor white families, although perhaps the number of exceptions would be greater in the poor whites. Also the characteristics ascribed to the Jewish families tend to describe the non-Jewish middle class, though perhaps again the number of exceptions is greater in the latter group.

Prejudice and bias are natural, perhaps even normal, phenomena in families. Parents train their children very early to distinguish between family members and outsiders and to be wary of outsiders. Families quickly try to identify the racial, religious, or ethnic background of the therapist, for this is consistent with their interest in being able to predict the behavior or attitudes of outsiders. Therefore, the following revision of the statement that opened this section seems in order: racial, religious, and ethnic characteristics of the *therapist* have a bearing on the ease or difficulty of engaging families and also on the likelihood of successful outcome. With reference to Jewish and black families, for example, I would say that the chances of a Jewish family becoming engaged, all other factors held equal, are greater when the therapist is Jewish; and in the case of black families, when the therapist is black. Midelfort (1957) suggested some years ago, based on his experience largely with families of Scandinavian descent, that a matching-up of ethnic background between therapist and family enhances communication and facilitates therapy. This seems a common sense viewpoint and is also consistent with my experience, although it would obviously be absurd and quite impractical to carry the rule to its logical extreme and insist on a strict matching-up of background.

The difficult paradox of being a therapist to lower class families, particularly from the poor minority groups, is that while the therapist must somehow narrow the "social distance" between the families and himself, he must not abdicate his position as an authority and expert. Martin Buber, some years ago while in the United States and in a discussion with Carl Rogers held on a university campus in the Middle West, commented that there could never be full equality between patient and therapist, because one always seeks the help of the other. Although therapist and patient share many experiences, and can relate in many respects as equals, they can never be fully equal, for their relationship *requires* a special type of dependency of one upon the other. Once that special dependency ceases, therapy ceases. To be able to "speak the language" of the lower class or poor minority family, or to become "one of the family" is a valuable asset for a therapist, but he must not so submerge his differences from the family that the members fail to perceive him as having a special authority or expertise.

Therapists of Jewish background seem to me to have an advantage in dealing with the paradox I posed in the preceding paragraph. Not only does the Jew grow up in a culture that places enormous value on membership in a family, but it is a culture which has traditionally de-emphasized the maintenance of "social distance" between groups that can be distinguished on the basis of such characteristics as social standing, income, or education. While Jewish culture honors the expert, it also expects that he shall know and practice the means to de-emphasize his separateness from those of lower standing.

Jewish family structure has taken quite a beating in the psychiatric literature in recent years. The Jewish mother is described as "aggressive, demanding"; the Jewish father, as "passive, ineffectual." The work of such novelists as Saul Bellow and Philip Roth has been like painful surgery. Yet the observant family therapist cannot help but become aware that the Jewish family is both a singular and remarkable agency for encouraging talent and achievement in offspring. In part I think it contributes to high achievement by, paradoxically, managing to encourage individuation in children while at the same time inculcating a sense of identity with the family and ethnic community. In families of other origin, individuation is often purchased at the price of a painful dislocation from the family unit. This is not nearly so true of the Jewish family, which de-emphasizes (or perhaps disguises to a greater degree) the incompatibility between individuation and loyal membership in the family. The Jewish child's special solution of the dilemma of individuation versus family loyalty seems to me worthy of further study, if for no other reason than that high achievement is so often a derivative of the solution.

SUMMARY

This paper is directed toward a discussion of the process of engaging families in outpatient therapy and describes a technique that seems to encourage engagement. Successful engagement is important because it is not simply a precondition for the conduct of the therapy, but often it is tantamount to a successful *outcome* of therapy. Not infrequently a favorable therapeutic result will flow from a successful resolution of the engagement at the end of a few sessions. For a variety of reasons, some practical and some psychodynamic, poor minority families often abruptly suspend their contact with the therapist after a few sessions, so it is especially critical in the case of this group to use techniques that maximize the possibility of successful engagement or maximize the possibility of a successful result in a few sessions.

A number of factors are described that tend to limit the broad applicability of family therapy, with particular reference to limitations imposed by poor minority families, especially black families, because there is a high dropout rate of poor minority families. A principle describing the basis for contraindicating family therapy is also stated.

The paper considers some implications of the increasing centrality of the wife-mother in the American nuclear family, with particular reference to the impact of this centrality on the level of rebelliousness currently observed in youth, especially male youth. Therapists can hardly avoid making the observation that in the American family the wife-mother is typically the spokesman, and she tends also to have heavier decision-making authority than her husband with respect to crucial issues in therapy; for example, whether the family shall become engaged.

Racial, religious, and ethnic background are important considerations in whether families will become engaged in therapy, and whether the outcome will be successful. Some characteristics of Jewish and black families in therapy are contrasted as a means to cast light on the common experience that Jewish families are easier to engage than black families.

REFERENCES

Ackerman, N. W. Family psychotherapy today: Some areas of controversy, *Comprehensive Psychiatry*, 1966, **7**, 375-388.

Aronson, H., & Overall, Betty. Treatment expectations of patients in two social classes, *Social Work*, 1966, **11**, 35-41.

Auerswald, E. A. Interdisciplinary versus ecological approach. *Family Process*, 1968, **7**, 202-215.

Hollingshead, A. B., & Redlich, F. C. *Social class and mental illness*. New York: John Wiley and Sons, 1958.

Keniston, K. *The uncommitted: Alienated youth in American society*. New York: Harcourt, Brace and World, 1965.

Lief, H. I., Lief, V. F., Warren, C. O., & Heath, R. G. Low dropout rate in a psychiatric clinic. *Archives of General Psychiatry*, 1961, **5**, 200-211.

Midelfort, C. *The family in psychotherapy*. New York: McGraw-Hill, 1957.

Minuchin, S., Montalvo, B., Guerney, B. C., Jr., Rosman, Bernice L., & Shumer, Florence. *Families of the slums*. New York: Basic Books, 1967.

Parsons, T. The American family: Its relation to personality and social structure. In T. Parsons, R. F. Bales, et al., *Family, socialization and interaction process*. Glencoe, Ill.: Free Press, 1955, pp. 3-33.

Rosenthal, D., & Frank, J. D. The fate of psychiatric outpatients assigned to psychotherapy. *Journal of Nervous and Mental Diseases*, 1958, **127**, 330-343.

Sager, C. J., Masters, Yvonne J., Bonall, Ruth E., & Normand, W. C. Selection and engagement of patients in family therapy. *American Journal of Orthopsychiatry*, 1968, **38**, 715-723.

Salzman, C., Shader, R. I., Scott, Dorothy A., & Binstock, W. Interviewer anger and patient dropout in walk-in clinic. *Comprehensive Psychiatry*, 1970, **2**, 267-273.

Wynne, L. C. Some indications and contraindications for exploratory family therapy. In I. Boszormenyi-Nagy and J. L. Framo (Eds.), *Intensive family therapy: Theoretical and practical aspects*. New York: Hoeber, Harper and Row, 1965, pp. 289-322.

Zuk, G. H. Family therapy. *Archives of General Psychiatry*, 1967, **16**, 71-79.

Zuk, G. H. Prompting change in family therapy. *Archives of General Psychiatry*, 1968, **19**, 727-736.

Zuk, G. H. Triadic-based family therapy. *International Journal of Psychiatry*, 1969, **8**, 539-548.

. . . .

PART III:: PATHOGENIC RELATING

. . . .

Chapter 7 / ON THE PATHOLOGY
OF SILENCING STRATEGIES

. . . .

In the limited literature dealing with silence in psychotherapy, emphasis is usually placed on the motivation of the silent patient (Zeligs, 1961; and Arlow, 1961). The patient is often said to be using his silence to defend against the intrusive efforts of the therapist. This chapter suggests that there is a rich learning history determining a patient's resort to silence in psychotherapy or in other human situations. Individuals are exposed early to a wide variety of silencing strategies which aim to impose silence on them. How can such silence be imposed? By means of a process as crude as a mother saying to her child, "Now shut up or you'll get a beating!" to a process so subtle as one who says, "Do be quiet, child, for mother has such a headache." It should be clear that in imposed silence the motive originally exists primarily outside of the person who actually engages in silence—that is, in another person or group who might be labeled the silencer(s).

A number of silencing strategies which have been observed in psychotherapy, primarily in family psychotherapy, will be illustrated here and an attempt made to assess some aspects of their structure and dynamics. It is hoped to provide evidence for a general theory that silencing strategies, insofar as they successfully accomplish their aim, are important determinants of thought and affect disturbances.

The definition of silencing strategies is as follows: those maneuvers designed to punish an individual for some transgression by isolating him in silence. The motivation for silencing strategies is complex, but an effort will be made to describe at least two levels. A number of

This chapter was published in *Family Process,* 1965, **4**, 32-48. From the perspective of 1970, the division of "public" and "private" level motives made in this article strikes me as rather artificial and arbitrary. The choice was probably based in my interest at the time in correlating analytic and group process concepts.

descriptive statements and hypotheses have been deduced for which evidence will be presented. They are as follows:

1. Silencing strategies may be conducted primarily by verbal or nonverbal means;
2. They may be conducted by one person primarily or an alliance of persons;
3. They may be directed primarily at an area of communication or at a person;
4. A primary "public" level motive for them is to induce compliance or conformity;
5. A primary "private" level motive for them is to possess the victim as an object for the needed projection of feelings of being bad or inanimate;
6. There is a causal relation between silencing strategies and pathogenic silence and babbling which may themselves be used as powerful silencing strategies.

SILENCING STRATEGIES CONDUCTED PRIMARILY BY VERBAL OR NONVERBAL MEANS

An example of a mainly verbal and very subtle silencing strategy is contained in the everyday greeting: "Good morning, how are you?" Taken quite literally, this response seems to be a rather direct inquiry into the state of physical and mental well-being of another person. But it is understood that the greeter ordinarily expects that his statement will not be taken literally; that is, that the person greeted will respond primarily to the form and not the substance of the greeting. The result is that, for all practical purposes, a person is silenced on the subject of his well-being, in actual contradiction to the stated inquiry. Telling a person to be sure to "speak up clearly" may also be a subtle and quite effective silencing strategy.

One of the most common ways of conducting a silencing strategy by mainly verbal means is through the procedure known as "changing the subject." This may be done crudely or with remarkable subtlety. It may be done crudely, for example, by the child who does not want to answer the question put to him by his mother, or subtly by the wife who wishes to hide from her husband her unauthorized purchase of a new hat. Crude and subtle changing of the subject is frequently observed in family psychotherapy. A therapist may confront or put a sensitive question to a family member only to have that person or another family member interrupt with a statement on an unrelated issue. Or the person so challenged may erupt in an outburst of temper with the object of diverting the therapist from his inquiry.

Two mothers seen in family psychotherapy were masters at changing the subject by mainly verbal devices. In the case of one, statements by the therapist were simply reflected back to him. The mother would say, for example: "Oh yes, I see, you mean I'm the type of mother who is too close to her daughter and I shouldn't be—is that it?" She made repeated use of this maneuver to sidestep a defense or explanation of her behavior. She *seemed* to accept the statement; in reality, she merely reflected it. By reflecting it, she maneuvered the therapist out of his role of therapist into the role of teacher or counselor. Thus she arranged for her behavior to appear simply a "mistake" which she would surely correct in the future now that it had been brought to her attention. That she actually regarded the behavior as justified and that she was emotionally deeply committed to it became only too clear in later sessions. In the case of the second mother, the question put to her: "How do you feel about that?" was frequently sidestepped by referring it on to her schizophrenic daughter or husband for an answer. If the therapist again put the question to her, she would simply deny its relevance. She would say: "Well, how do you suppose any mother would feel?"

Another mainly verbal silencing strategy observed in family psychotherapy is the practice of family members to refer to the hospitalized member as being the central problem when other family problems have been raised. This maneuver is part of an attempt to deny involvement in the dynamics of the primary patient's illness. Family members may point out strenuously that they are present not to discuss their difficulties but those of the primary—that is, hospitalized—patient.

On the other hand, silencing strategies may be conducted mainly by nonverbal means. For example, laughter may be used as a signal for family members to change the subject to one that is less "sensitive" (Zuk, 1964). Clearing the throat or coughing may also serve this purpose, or yawning or shifting about restlessly in a chair. As an example from everyday life, the mother who hands her nagging child a piece of candy is practicing a rather crude but effective silencing strategy by primarily nonverbal means. Clever children sometimes brazenly countermanipulate their parents who employ this device.

A mainly nonverbal silencing strategy was observed in family psychotherapy in one mother who grimaced as if in pain when her schizophrenic daughter began to criticize her. Observing this, the daughter broke off her comments and asked her mother what the matter was. The mother denied anything was the matter, but continued her facial expression of physical pain. The daughter halted her criticism, saying that now she couldn't remember what it was she had to say and perhaps it really wasn't justified after all. Another mother was observed to accomplish the same effect by raising her hand toward the offending child, then bringing it to rest on her bosom, as if the child's words of criticism were causing chest pain or discomfort.

STRATEGIES CONDUCTED PRIMARILY BY ONE PERSON OR AN ALLIANCE OF PERSONS

Silencing strategies that have been discussed up to this point may be conducted mainly by one person or persons in alliance. Persons may cooperate in the conduct of a silencing strategy with either a clear or vague awareness of their "policy."

A person may even be an unintended victim of a silencing process. Consider the situation of the child who hurries to tell his parents some bit of news only to find them engaged in a heated argument. He tries to interrupt but to his dismay finds that first one, then the other parent ignores his presence. In this case the parents, as a result of their interaction but not as part of any premeditated policy, have silenced the child.

A similar situation may sometimes redound to the benefit of the so-called victim. Consider the situation of an oral examination in which the examinee fervently hopes that two or more of his examiners may become embroiled in discussing a fine point, thus forgetting him in the process. The examinee may even go to some length to provoke such a hostile interaction, despite some risk that his strategy might backfire against him.

The so-called "silent treatment" is an interesting maneuver engaged in by a group against a member who has violated its code. The members agree not to speak to the victim as a punishment for his violation. The process is unique because it uses silence to induce silence.

In family psychotherapy parents may ally themselves in silencing strategies directed against a child. Parents will also ally themselves in silencing strategies against the therapist. It has even been observed that children, when they perceive their parents to be under attack, will support them against the therapist in various evasive tactics. Thus one schizophrenic daughter, in whom babbling was an important symptom, simply babbled more at a point in a session in which her mother was being confronted with some unpleasant interpretation.

The so-called "absent member maneuver," which has been described by Sonne, Speck, and Jungreis (1962), may be considered a silencing strategy directed by one member of an alliance of family members against the goals of family psychotherapy. In the absent member maneuver, a family member who is usually relatively healthy permanently or intermittently absents himself from treatment sessions. The authors regard this as one means by which family members resist the uncovering of certain secrets.

It has come to be a rule of thumb in family psychotherapy to regard the person who is silent in a session, whether primary patient or not, as an individual of special significance for the family system. This is either the person who is powerful enough to get other family members to speak his thoughts and feelings for him, or the person who threatens to betray the system and agrees or is compelled to keep quiet. In an example of the first type of person, it became clear that a mother who was a very rigidly controlled and controlling person, could get her children to express her violent emotions for her, thus preserving her exterior picture of control. In an example of the second type of person, a mother was observed to struggle desperately to have her daughter excused from sessions on grounds of "immaturity," but actually it appeared more to be because the daughter might expose and undermine the strong family defensive structure vis à vis the therapist.

STRATEGIES DIRECTED AT AN AREA OF COMMUNICATION OR AT A PERSON

"Changing the subject" may be considered the silencing strategy par excellence directed primarily at an area of communication, whereas the "silent treatment" is the strategy par excellence directed primarily at a person.

Large social systems have well-recognized means for isolating in silence certain types of communication. Book-banning has from time to time been used as a silencing strategy directed against an area of communication, and insofar as it prevents an author from being read, it is also directed against an individual. In the realm of power politics, economic blockades are strategies directed by one state, or a group of states, against another. They are sanctions taken against the offending state to punish it for certain transgressions. They seek to bring social and economic pressure on the offending state as punishment for lack of compliance and in order to insure future compliance.

The phenomenon of "scapegoating" should be mentioned here as a kind of silencing strategy directed primarily at an individual or group and also indirectly at an area of communication. Scapegoating may become a major pathological symptom of ethnic, racial, or religious strife. In "stereotyping," a subdivision of scapegoating, the offending party is isolated by caricaturing certain of his physical or mental traits.

Several writers (Boszormenyi-Nagy, 1962; Bowen, 1960; Wynne, 1961) have considered the schizophrenic offspring to be the family scapegoat. The inadequacies of the family members are heaped on the so-called victim, who for various reasons accepts them as part of his identity and way of relating to people. The schizophrenic offspring may be deeply convinced that his central role in life is to absorb and reflect the projected inadequacies of his family.

A PRIMARY "PUBLIC" LEVEL MOTIVE IS THE WISH TO INDUCE COMPLIANCE OR CONFORMITY

Many of the strategies that have already been described are obviously motivated, at least on a superficial level, by a wish to obtain compliance or conformity with a demand. Clearly, for example, the "silent treatment" is leveled against an individual both to punish him for a transgression against a group code and to bring pressure on him for future compliance with the code. In meetings of formal organizations, it is not unusual for members who seek recognition from the chairman by unorthodox means simply to be ignored. The chairman pretends not to see or hear the transgressing member. When the member finally becomes impressed with the chairman's nonverbal "message" and does comply with the formal procedures for recognition, he may suddenly be seen or heard. He is eventually rewarded for observance of the rules by the lifting of the silencing maneuver. However, it may also be the case that the member is not heard even if he should comply with formal procedures. Here the motive of the chairman may not be to punish a procedural transgression in a current situation, but to punish old transgressions. The chairman may be using his critical position to avenge some real or imagined slight done to him in the past by the member.

It sometimes occurs that a schizophrenic episode may itself be induced by a silencing strategy designed to promote compliance with a wish. In one instance a schizophrenic break seemed precipitated by the rejecting behavior of a husband who wanted to obtain a divorce from his wife—a young woman who had already experienced two hospitalizations. He gave her the "cold shoulder," a variant of the "silent treatment." He simply ignored her, acting as if she didn't exist. Leaving her alone for long periods, he rarely explained where he had been or was going. The threat of separation, with its attendant feelings of isolation, terror, and despair, resulted in increasingly disorganized thinking and behavior and finally in an outright schizophrenic episode.

In another case in family treatment, a sister of a primary patient was obviously the object of considerable effort by family members, particularly the mother, to get her to comply with their wish to restrain her verbal assaultiveness toward them and the therapist. Their problem was of course complicated by the fact that her explosiveness to some extent served their obstructive purposes; at times they obviously encouraged her to behave as she did. One method used consistently by her mother to enrage her—to be sure, the mother was perhaps only partly conscious of her intent to do so—was simply to complain in the sessions about her daughter's loudness and then to compare it with her own lifelong effort to speak softly and courteously when spoken to. By holding herself up as a model of deportment, she triggered her daughter's sense of inadequacy and subtly provoked her to an outburst. The outburst produced babbling, which is believed to be another kind of response to a silencing strategy—a response in which the person talks a lot but says little and thus in effect is silenced.

A "PRIVATE" LEVEL MOTIVE IS TO POSSESS THE VICTIM AS AN OBJECT FOR PROJECTION

This formulation about the deeper motivation for silencing strategies was suggested by a formulation given by Searles (1963) to account for his experience with a deeply regressed schizophrenic patient. He notes that, in psychotherapy with this mute, bedridden patient, he found himself saying less and less as time went by. He described this experience as follows:

> . . . I reached a point where I was simply bringing in my chair and placing it in a stereotyped location several feet from his bed, saying, "Hello, Mr. _____." . . . Then came a session in which I simply brought in my chair and sat down, as usual, but without saying anything, and at the end of the session, as I got up and was starting out with my chair, again without any words to him, suddenly he raised up on an elbow, looked at me and asked, in a loud, clear, astonished tone, "Aren't you even going to say goodbye?" (pp. 54-55).

Searles contends that this session marked a turning point in his work with the patient, "... from moving-towards-lifelessness to movement-into-living" (p. 55). He rationalizes his experience by assuming that he came to represent, in the transference situation, a projection of the patient's feelings about himself. He believes he became the "... embodiment of the patient's subjectively unalive, inanimate, personality-components, now safely externalized and susceptible to resolution in the transference-analysis" (p. 55).

The writer would contend that Searles became the object of a powerful silencing strategy being conducted by the patient—specifically, the patient's mutism. The effectiveness of this silencing strategy may be measured by the fact that Searles himself became silent in the face of it; in effect, he became a victim of it, although a positive therapeutic value of his response eventually was demonstrated. Searles apparently defined his response to the patient as a "neutral" one, in contrast to a more active, intrusive intervention with patients, but one can visualize that it was actually quite a dynamic approach in that it fitted into the need of the patient to project his unwanted feelings about himself onto another.

In the "silent treatment" demonstrated by the patient toward Searles, a primary motive was hypothesized by this writer to be the patient's need to project onto the therapist his own sense of being bad or inanimate. This particular motive was not among those mentioned in a symposium on the silent patient held at the midwinter meeting of the American Psychoanalytic Association in 1958. In the symposium, Zeligs (1961) presented in some detail a case of a female patient who used silence to master her anxiety. He noted the numerous small devices used by patients which are akin to silencing strategies: coming late to sessions, loquaciousness, procrastination or prolonged silence during the analytic hour as a reflection of a power struggle between patient and analyst. He speculated also that silence on the part of the therapist may be an effect of the countertransference. The "innocent" confrontation or interpretation of the therapist may be a silencing strategy in the service of a countertransference reaction.

Silence may also be an essential condition for an encounter between patient and therapist, as it has been suggested. Whitaker, Felder,

Malone, and Warkentin (1962) make this point with regard to the schizophrenic patient. They write:

> Silence is for us an encounter between patient and therapist with no speaking, no smiling, no movement at all. It may be eye to eye, or staring at a fixed point or into space. . . . Such a silence may include any feelings; for example, love, hate, togetherness, isolation. When it intensifies the isolation of the patient it may provoke overt psychotic responses (p. 150).

These therapists may crudely interrupt the patient's strenuous efforts to avoid silence:

> Each time the patient speaks he may be told to shut up, with increasing aggressiveness at each repetition. If the patient speaks with feeling we respect his communication (p. 150).

An example given by Whitaker et al. shows how a silencing strategy may be turned to advantage in the therapy of a schizophrenic patient. They recorded the following exchange between a patient and two therapists.

Patient: . . . Do you think I'll ever get better?

Therapist 1: (Speaking to the other therapist and completely ignoring the patient) Did you get your steps made in the backyard over the weekend?

Therapist 2: Yes, let me tell you about it.

Patient: Do you think I'll ever get better?

Therapist 1: Don't interrupt, we're talking about something important. (p. 150).

Case A

Now described in some detail will be the writer's experience as therapist in individual and family psychotherapy with a schizophrenic young woman against whom he believes powerful silencing strategies were directed by her parents—strategies deeply motivated by their wish to project onto her their own feelings of being bad or inanimate. This young woman became socially withdrawn in the face of the threat of deep emotional involvement with persons other than her mother and father. She yearned for the involvement, yet greatly feared it. One great fear was that her mother's life depended on the continuation of their attachment. She was not unpopular with boys, but when a relationship with a boy reached a certain intensity, she fled from it. She held several semiskilled jobs, but became depressed by the hopelessness of resolving her conflict and would give them up. She withdrew to her bedroom, slept much of the day, talked very little. Slowly, in her isolation, she developed ideas of persecution and fantasies. She imagined that radar was trained on her constantly to pick up her evil thoughts. One particular thought was that she was a prostitute.

During the first month of her hospitalization at Eastern Pennsylvania Psychiatric Institute she was pleasant and superficially communicative. She could accuse her mother of showing overpossessiveness and animosity toward her. At the end of the first month, the daughter experienced a full-blown schizophrenic episode with a return of the delusional ideation that she was a prostitute. The episode may have been triggered partly by a rather intense attraction toward a hospitalized young man, partly as a reaction to the developing transference to the therapist, and partly as a transference-like reaction to the hospital and ward milieu. Within a month the more acute symptoms of the episode had subsided and she settled into a state characterized by restlessness and seclusiveness. Approximately six months after her hospitalization, she became quite uncommunicative, except that she would answer appropriately simple questions put to her. It was obvious that she was still delusional, but her silence masked her delusions.

After the acute symptomatology of the psychosis subsided, the young woman would sit restlessly but silently. The silence in the sessions would be broken only by the therapist's comments, which in time became fewer and fewer. The difficulty of sustaining a one-way communication became extremely burdensome. Gradually it became clear that by her continued use of silence, the young woman exerted great control of the situation. She forced the therapist into an essentially dependent role whichever method of relating he might select: whether an intrusive or coercive strategy or a strategy of waiting watchfulness.

A formulation slowly took shape in the therapist's mind that, far from reflecting an absence of transference, the patient's silence was a sign that the patient had actually incorporated the therapist with her mother's imago. Her silence was essentially a reflection of the chronic passive-aggressive struggle with her mother for control. The therapist was re-experiencing with the young woman her lifelong impasse with her mother—her entrapment in her mother's powerful silencing strategies to which she reacted with a strong, ultimately self-defeating and pathological countermeasure, namely, her silence.

The therapist came to experience the despair, hopelessness, and deep sense of frustration that the silent patient can so easily elicit. Lack of confirmation of one in one's perceived professional role is frustrating, and the silent patient hardly confirms one in one's role. The therapist felt robbed of the very tool upon which his method seemed largely to depend: namely, upon words in a mainly verbal interaction. Under the "assault" of the patient's silence, it is the rare therapist who does not come, in time, to feel quite expendable.

The writer as therapist came to regard himself as being entrapped in a masterful silencing maneuver. The feelings aroused in him as a result of this entrapment might not have been greatly different from those of the patient in a similar entrapment with her mother. The writer was impressed that the patient was not only projecting her own feelings of being inanimate or bad onto him, but also asking him to understand her unspoken despair about the past and sense of hopelessness about the future. She was severely testing the therapist's capacity to endure within himself feelings about herself and her life situation which she found unendurable.

In early family psychotherapy sessions, when the young woman was still relatively communicative, her attempted criticisms of her parents were forever drowned by their pained denials. The mother would frequently override her daughter's complaints with the comment: "What have I done? I've tried to be a good mother." Then the mother made the implication that her daughter's criticism was causing her to become physically ill. The effect of this strategy was to effectively shut her daughter up.

The following excerpt from a family psychotherapy session will illustrate some elements in the mother's silencing strategy:

(Present are the therapists,[1] mother, father, primary patient, and patient's maternal aunt.)

Therapist 1: (to aunt) Can you criticize Mrs. A?

Aunt: In what way? (Mrs. A giggles)

Therapist 1: Well, in some of the harder things.

Mrs. A: (to her daughter) I want you to criticize me. Did I do anything wrong to you? Huh? Well, talk—you don't talk, what is it? You're keeping the doctor and everybody. Talk! Does anything bother you? Did I do anything to you as a child? Maybe—I don't remember. Talk! Tell me, I don't know!

Patient: (in a whisper) You didn't take me to the Shore.

Aunt: See, that bothers her. She always wanted to go on vacation and her parents never took her.

(Later in the session)

Therapist 1: (to daughter) Do you expect your mother to change?

Mrs. A: (interrupts) What does she want me to do?

Therapist 1: (to daughter) Do you have the courage to say so, even? Do you have the courage to tell her how you'd like to see her change?

Mrs. A: (again interrupts) What does she want me to do? Cut my hair?

Aunt: (to Mrs. A) Even if she finds the words to want to say it, you knock it right out of her. You talk, and she's bottled up again.

At the time of the session from which the above excerpt is taken, the young woman had become relatively uncommunicative. Notice that the mother pleads with her daughter to talk and explain herself; yet when the girl finds the courage to utter a single sentence in her defense, she is accused of ungratefulness. In her inability to tolerate her

---

[1] Cotherapists with the family were the writer and Mrs. Geraldine Lincoln, a psychologist. Cotherapy is a technique in which I think the liabilities greatly outweigh the advantages, but at the time this paper was written I was still exploring the technique.

daughter's criticism, the mother was joined—or rather supported—by her husband. It appeared that the husband at times really believed the complaints to be justified, but supported his wife in her denial of them.

It should not be thought that the younger woman was completely a passive victim of the mother's silencing strategies. To be sure, she complied in order to keep the family secret her mother feared to reveal: namely, the basis for her intense symbiotic tie with her daughter. But she also countermanipulated the mother in that, having assumed the silent position, she could draw her mother into a dependent, pleading role. She actually exerted considerable control over the mother, although her control was operative *within* the larger circle of control of the mother. She complied with the mother's symbiotic demand regarding her, but developed her parasitic role to a high level. For example, she would get her mother to plead with her to reply to a question. Failing to obtain a reply, the mother would then engage in a review of the possible alternative answers to the question she had put to her daughter, hoping that her daughter would select one. This greatly amused the daughter, who would graciously nod her head when the mother settled finally on an alternative that suited her. Thus she found, in her assumption of the silent position, a means of retaliation against the mother within the scope of a larger relationship which was, to be sure, dominated by the mother.

CAUSAL RELATION BETWEEN SILENCING STRATEGIES AND PATHOLOGICAL SILENCE AND BABBLING

The suggestion is made that silencing strategies, when they are conducted successfully, may have at least two types of effects: They may actually induce silence or they may induce babbling, which is also considered a type of very meaningful "noncommunication," or induce both reactions alternately. Silence or babbling are not uncommon symptoms in schizophrenia or other of the more severe mental disorders; nor are they uncommon, in more benign forms, in the neurotic conditions.

It is suggested that silence and babbling, in both their benign and pathological forms, are causally related to silencing strategies. In the case of silence, it is suggested that the primary "public" level message to the so-called victim is: "Conform; be compliant or you will be isolated in silence." The victim replies: "I will not conform or be compliant to your likes, but I will agree to a certain isolation in silence because that is better than an outright dissolution of our relationship." In the case of babbling, the primary message to the victim is the same but the response is different. The victim says: "I will not conform or be compliant to your likes, *or be isolated in silence,* but I will agree *not to make sense* because that is better than an outright dissolution of our relationship."

It is not unusual for the perpetrators of the silencing strategy to see the defiance of their victim everywhere. In this they are dominated by their "private" level motivation, which is to project their own feelings of being bad or inanimate onto him. The victim's silence or babbling are seen as outright signs of defiance, even though the perpetrators have considerably helped to determine these responses in the victim. They exert strong pressures to shut the victim up or cause him to babble, then condemn him for being stubborn or insolent or spiteful.

Case B

Another case of the writer's will be presented as evidence for a causal relationship between silencing strategies and pathological babbling. It will provide some contrast to the previous case study which focused on a suggested origin for pathological silence. The patient was a young woman whose hospitalization appeared to be precipitated by her husband's threat of divorce. She had had previous hospitalizations each associated with some stressful life situation: In the first instance, a schizophrenic episode occurred shortly after her marriage; a second break came shortly after the birth of her first child. Her major symptoms were babbling and silly, hebephrenic-like smiling. She was not delusional or hallucinatory and she could be coherent for short times, especially when a subject was raised that had little relevance to her own distressed life situation.

In individual psychotherapy, it became apparent that she "played" with the therapist by means of her babbling. By it she could control the depth of the relationship. She could refuse to respond to a certain point by talking about something else. Yet while fleeing from verbal involvement with the therapist by means of her babbling, she at the same time carried on an intense sexually seductive effort. Of course, she ignored the therapist's confrontation of her on this score. It was fascinating to observe how skillfully she conducted her campaign of seduction while fleeing from any other form of emotional involvement. Gradually the question took shape: Was she transferring into the therapy situation her own feeling that in her marriage she had been "used" as a sex object and not a person?

In family psychotherapy sessions with the young woman and her parents, it became clear to what great lengths the parents, and particularly the mother, would go to avoid answers to direct questions. The mother's answers were circuitous and, if the therapists were not cautious, subtly sidetracking. The hypothesis was developed that the daughter's babbling was an extension of a deeply held family device to avoid certain kinds of topics or communication simply by talking about other things. An excerpt from a session will illustrate the use of this device:

(Present are the therapists,[2] mother, father, and hospitalized daughter. Just prior to and during the first few moments of the exchange, the daughter was heard babbling in a low voice.)

Dr. R: (to mother, referring to her daughter's babbling) Do you feel comfortable with this kind of talk?

Mother: Well, I don't know what you call comfortable. It's just the last few weeks we have difficulty relating anything to her conversation.

Dr. R.: You haven't answered my question.

Mother: (in an irritated voice) I'm not comfortable with this kind of conversation.

Dr. R.: Is it difficult for you to answer my question?

Mother: No. In the first place, I would never think of asking you if you were comfortable if this was your daughter babbling at you.

[2] Cotherapists with the family were the writer and Dr. David Rubinstein, a psychiatrist.

Dr. R.:   Well, if you asked me, I would say "no" immediately.

Mother: (irritated) Well, how do you think I feel?

Dr. R.:   I don't know if you don't tell me. (pause) You do it by sidetracking answers or sidetracking questions.

(A few minutes later)

Dr. Z.:   I'm trying to figure out why Mrs. B does it.

Mother: It's probably a thing that's been done more or less all my life. I grew up in a very conservative family. . . . I would always say the diplomatic thing rather than the thing that would cause the situation to become worse.

Dr. Z.:   I think we can make an analogy. We can look more closely at your daughter's major symptom. What she does is to carry your pattern to the nth degree—the avoidance of answers. . . . Somehow this is a useful pattern to keep whatever emotion you might have under tabs.

It seemed confirmed by the clinical material that the young woman's babbling, as with the silence of the girl whose case was previously presented, was a pattern learned rather early in her family life. Especially from her mother, she learned that *not* to make sense—for example, by avoiding giving a direct answer—was a safe response when threatened or anxious. It was interesting to observe how, in family psychotherapy sessions, she repeatedly failed to be confirmed by her parents as an individual who made sense. For the most part, what she said was ignored; it was rather taken for granted that her utterances were meaningless. Of course, her wish to resume her marriage, quite in contradiction to their wish, merely served to confirm her parents' opinion that she could not make sense.

SUMMARY

Some of the steps in the process believed to eventuate in pathological silence or babbling can be summarized as follows:

Step 1. A forceful, consistent, subtle, and frequent resort to silencing strategies leveled against an immature, dependent personality (for example, a child) by one or more closely related personalities (for example, parents) who are multiply-motivated: at one level, by the wish to enforce compliance or conformity; but at a deeper level, by the wish to possess an object on which to project their own unwanted feelings of being bad or inanimate.

Step 2. The "public" message conveyed by the silencing strategy is: "Conform; be compliant or you will be isolated in silence." The reply is: "I will not conform or be compliant to your likes, but I will agree to a certain isolation by silence because that is better than an outright dissolution of our relationship"; or, "I will not conform or be compliant to your likes, *or be isolated in silence,* but I will agree *not to make sense* because that is better than an outright dissolution of our relationship."

Step 3. Because of their motivation on the "private" level, the perpetrators of the silencing strategies are never satisfied that their efforts have resulted in the wished-for compliance or conformity that they "publicly" claim motivates them. They are compelled by their deeper needs to see defiance everywhere.

Step 4. Having been compelled to submit to silence or babbling, the so-called victim is surprised to discover the immense power that resides in these positions. He discovers that he can use them *as most powerful silencing strategies* against his original silencers and others.

Step 5. Quite unconsciously the victim has absorbed, despite his conscious resistance, some of the negative feelings projected onto him by his silencers, and he employs these feelings as motives to justify use of his powerful new-found weapon against his silencers.

Step 6. The person comes to view himself as chronically the victim of silencing strategies against which he must continually use silence or babbling as primary means of defense; he does so less and less selectively, thus with increasing psychopathy.

Silencing strategies are interpersonal processes. They are a class of isolating techniques designed to exclude or prohibit certain areas of communication by imposing silence on individuals who have come to represent the threatening areas of communication. It is suggested that silencing strategies may be causal factors in pathological silence and babbling.

Silencing strategies may be primarily verbal or nonverbal and may be conducted primarily by one person or an alliance of persons. A primary "public" level motive for them is to induce compliance or conformity; a primary "private" level motive, to possess the victim as an object for the needed projection of feelings of being bad or inanimate.

In psychotherapy with the silent patient, the therapist is himself the object of a massive silencing strategy being conducted by the patient—namely, the patient's silence. The employment of the strategy may signify, among several possibilities, the existence of a transference situation in which silencing once played an important role in the patient's life, as Arlow (1961) has suggested. Silence may be a sign of an impasse in a therapeutic relationship, or a sign of a breakout from an impasse, or a sign of sudden deepening of a relationship.

REFERENCES

Arlow, J. A. Silence and the theory of technique. *Journal of the American Psychoanalytic Association,* 1961, **9**, 44-55.

Boszormenyi-Nagy, I. The concept of schizophrenia from the perspective of family treatment. *Family Process,* 1962, **1**, 103-113.

Bowen, M. A family concept of schizophrenia. In D. D. Jackson (Ed.), *The etiology of schizophrenia.* New York: Basic Books, 1960, pp. 346-372.

Searles, H. F. The place of neutral therapist-responses in psychotherapy with the schizophrenic patient. *International Journal of Psychoanalysis,* 1963, **44**, 42-56.

Sonne, J. C., Speck, R. V., & Jungreis, J. The absent-member maneuver as a resistance in family therapy of schizophrenia. *Family Process,* 1962, **1**, 44-62.

Whitaker, C. A., Felder, R. E., Malone, T. P., & Warkentin, J. First stage techniques in the experiential psychotherapy of chronic schizophrenic patients. In J. H. Masserman (Ed.), *Current psychiatric therapies. Vol. II.* New York: Grune and Stratton, 1962, pp. 147-158.

Wynne, L. C. The study of intrafamilial alignments and splits in exploratory family therapy. In N. W. Ackerman, F. Beatman, & S. N. Sherman (Eds.), *Exploring the base for family therapy.* New York: Family Service Association of America, 1961, pp. 95-115.

Zeligs, M. A. The psychology of silence: Its role in transference, countertransference and the psychoanalytic process. *Journal of the American Psychoanalytic Association,* 1961, **9**, 7-43.

Zuk, G. H. A further study of laughter in family therapy. *Family Process,* 1964, **3**, 77-89.

Chapter 8 / SOME DYNAMICS OF LAUGHTER
DURING FAMILY THERAPY

· ·

Laughter, a behavior that conceals as much as it reveals, has deep meaning in human affairs. One of its important functions is to disguise feelings such as anger, love, hostility, joy, shame; or it may reflect some general tension or anxiety. As a socially acceptable cloak for feelings which may be socially unacceptable, laughter warrants close psychological study.

A peculiar psychodynamic characteristic of laughter as a defensive maneuver is that it need not totally conceal underlying motivation or affect. "Smile when you say that," the maxim of the Old West, is a good example of this feature of laughter (or in this case its variant, smiling) as a socially acceptable device to check a direct hostile reaction to hostility. Laughing or smiling when expressing criticism with underlying anger often spares a critic a direct angry response in return. In the term made popular by Bateson, Jackson, Haley, and Weakland (1956), the critic thus "double-binds" the one criticized. The one criticized is put under a social obligation to play by the rule of the game and also cloak his feelings with laughs, smiles, or jokes. In this situation, laughter tempers feeling which if expressed directly might lead to an undesired outburst of anger or hostility.

An important function of laughter is to serve as a socially acceptable means of probing the motivations or feelings of various parties in communication with each other. This function is greatly exercised in sophisticated society. That laughter is a powerful device to probe, modulate, or inhibit motivation and affect is confirmed not only in everyday observation and clinical experience, but also in psychological theory (see, for example, the work of Freud, 1960, on wit and humor).

This chapter was published in *Family Process,* 1963, **2**, 302-314. My coauthors were Ivan Boszormenyi-Nagy, M.D., and Elliot Heiman, M.D. The paper was excerpted and reprinted in *Research in Family Interaction: Readings and Commentary,* edited by W. D. Winter and A. J. Ferreira, and published by Science and Behavior Books, Inc., Palo Alto, California, 1969, pp. 242-244.

The present study attempts to define a relationship in the laughter behavior of various members of a family, one of whom is a schizophrenic young woman. A symptom of the girl's illness is her bizarre laughter, which may be defined as laughter which appears unrelated in meaning to the social situation; and the question is raised whether the girl's laughter was really as inappropriate as it appeared on gross observation. This study asks the specific question: Is there a factor in the immediate, ongoing family psychotherapy situation which influences her seemingly bizarre laughter, or is the behavior strictly determined by her intrapersonal fantasies? "Embarrassed" laughter, which was frequently employed by the parents, particularly the mother, especially when a point was made or subject raised which was sensitive, was inferred to be a significant signal to others present. Some current thinking about the etiology of schizophrenia (Bowen, 1960; Boszormenyi-Nagy, 1962; Wynne, 1961) suggested the idea that the laughter of both parents might be a device they regularly employed to avoid certain kinds of communication; thus, by implication, that laughter was a symptom not only of the psychopathology of the schizophrenic daughter but to some extent also of her overtly nonschizophrenic parents. Thus the study also examines the question whether there may have been a kind of cooperation or complementarity in the transmission of tension or anxiety underlying the laughter of the parents and the daughter.

The findings of the study, finally, will bear on an important issue in personality theory originally championed by Lewin (1935) and taken up recently in the monograph of Tyler, Tyler, and Rafferty (1962). The issue has been examined in a prior monograph by one of the present writers (Zuk, 1956) and by others (Atkinson, 1958; Eriksen, 1952; Rotter, 1955). Lewin said that every behavior is a product jointly of intrapersonal characteristics and characteristics in the immediate, ongoing social situation. But it has been pointed out that psychological studies, for the most part, have considered the impact of only one of these sets at a time. It will be suggested that the findings lend support to the demand in personality research not to discount the joint impact on behavior of intrapersonal and situational variables, even in instances in which it seems most unlikely that more than one set of these variables is operating. The special relevance of the findings in increasing understanding about the range of situational determinants of apparently bizarre symptoms in psychosis should also be noted.

PROCEDURE

The data on which this study was based were derived from family psychotherapy sessions tape-recorded in 1961 and 1962. The technique of family psychotherapy has been described in several papers (cf. Bell, 1961; Ackerman, 1958; Jackson and Weakland, 1961; among others). The family in this case was composed of a mother, father, and schizophrenic daughter; a white Protestant family whose social class status would probably be described as lower-upper in level.

Twenty-three tape recordings were available to the writers. The first author joined the second as a family psychotherapist in January, 1962. The authors continued to see the family—usually at two-week intervals —over the next six months. From time to time these intervals stretched over three weeks or more because of scheduling difficulties.

The patient, now a 23-year-old girl, was admitted to Eastern Pennsylvania Psychiatric Institute (EPPI) in October, 1957. Her admission diagnosis was schizophrenic reaction, paranoid type. The following is an excerpt from the admission note on the girl: "She has become confused and disorganized in her thinking, and has active hallucinations and delusions. She states that she believes the end of the world is to be brought about through some act of the devil, that she wishes to go into retreat and think and study the Bible. She feels there is nothing wrong with her and denies any need for help."

The patient had been seen in intensive individual psychotherapy with a psychiatrist at EPPI for approximately two and a half years when this contact was broken. She was seen briefly by another psychiatrist and then transferred as a therapy case to the first author.

In the family psychotherapy sessions, the laughter of the mother could be described as of the "embarrassed" sort, a kind of quavering chuckle reflecting underlying tension or anxiety. She often tagged it on to the end of a phrase or sentence in an apparent attempt to make what she had to say as socially palatable as possible. The father's laughter was heartier. At times it was also of the "embarrassed" variety, but more frequently than his wife's, his laughter was associated with a statement —usually his own—intended to be humorous. The laughter of the schizophrenic daughter was quite bizarre. Apparently without adequate social stimulus, she would break into wild, uncontrolled laughter.

A brief description of the daughter in a "typical" family therapy session might help the reader visualize better the extreme bizarreness of her behavior. She would enter the therapy room listlessly, drop her body like dead weight into a chair and mold it to the chair's contour. Usually she did not respond directly to questions, although from time to time she would suddenly interject a startlingly direct comment. Her bizarre laughter deeply disturbed her parents, especially her father. He seemed unable to tolerate the laughter, once abruptly walking from the therapy room when she began to laugh. Both parents made some attempt to understand the possible significance of her laughter. The father said once that he thought she laughed when she intended to cry, i.e., that it was an emotional expression the very opposite of what was intended.

The basic measure employed in this study was frequency of laughter—presumably reflecting tension or anxiety—in psychotherapy sessions. On an arbitrary basis, the most recent 13 sessions were selected from 23 available tape-recorded sessions for analysis of laughter behavior. The sessions were not controlled with respect to persons present, and obviously the content of the sessions varied considerably. The schizophrenic daughter was usually silent. The parents did most of the talking.

The third author, a fourth-year medical student at Jefferson Medical College assigned for the summer for research to EPPI, made a tabulation of laughter engaged in by the family members in the 13 psychotherapy sessions. He was not made aware of the basic questions being investigated in the study until after his tabulation was completed. Because he did not personally observe any of the psychotherapy sessions, it was necessary for him to be oriented to the various voices and kinds of laughter heard on the tape recordings. In general, the laughter of the father and mother was easily identified; the laughter of the patient was more difficult to judge, sounding frequently as if she were wheezing, sniffling, or even crying.

In order to arrive at some index of reliability of ratings, frequency of laughter was rated independently in one psychotherapy session by the first and third authors. The comparatively greater difficulty in rating the laughter of the patient as compared with the laughter of the parents was revealed by a 79% agreement (27 out of 34 occasions) of the third author with the first on identifying the patient's laughter. Agreement of the third author with the first was better in the case of the mother and father's laughter: 95% agreement (18 out of 19 occasions) on the laughter of the mother; 100% agreement (4 out of 4 occasions) on the laughter of the father.

Two other pieces of information were tabulated by the third author: (a) The person whose comment occurred at the time of or appeared to precipitate the occurrence of laughter (designated in the text and Table 3 as the "trigger" person); and (b) the person toward whom the comment was directed (designated in the text and Table 3 as the "receiver" person). Agreement on the "trigger" person ranged from 56% (in the case where either of the therapists was thought to be the "trigger" person) to 75% (in the case where the mother was thought to be the "trigger" person). In about two-thirds of the cases of disagreement about the "trigger" person, the person laughing at the time of the comment was the patient. Thus, the relatively poorer agreement was a function in part of the difficulty in identifying the schizophrenic daughter's laughter.

Agreement on the "receiver" person ranged from 56% (in the case where the mother was believed to be the "receiver" person) to 83% (in the case where the patient was believed to be the "receiver" person). Here it is to be noted also that in slightly more than two-thirds of disagreements, the person doing the laughing at the time of the comment was the patient. Again the relatively poorer agreement between judges with reference to the "receiver" person was related to difficulty in identifying the daughter's laughter.

Another item of information kept by the tabulator was the time during the session at which laughter occurred. This item proved to be crucial in uncovering the clearest and probably most significant finding of the study: namely, that laughter by the family members, over the group of 13 sessions tabulated, occurred more frequently in certain 15-minute intervals than others. When this was discovered, it was decided to try to isolate specific characteristics of the intervals in which the differences were most striking.

Psychotherapists would probably accept the assumption that interaction with their patients in individual psychotherapy "deepens" (that is, becomes more intense, dynamic, emotional, or revealing of personality difficulties) as the therapy hour progresses. But in order to document this assumption in the case of family psychotherapy, as opposed to individual psychotherapy, five experienced family psycho-therapists—unaware of the basis for requesting their views—were asked to characterize the first and third 15-minute intervals of family psychotherapy sessions. These were the intervals in which the most striking differences in frequency of laughter occurred between the patient and her parents. Four of the five agreed that the first 15 minutes of the session was an interval for structuring the entire situation and testing the capacities of the participants to be responsive. The same four therapists agreed that by the third 15-minute interval, the period from minutes 30 to 45 of the psychotherapy session, the capacities of the participants to express deeper feelings and thoughts had been explored. As one therapist put it: "There is a tendency for that interval to be the one in which things are popping—things are really happening by then."

RESULTS

Shown in Figure 1 are mean amounts of laughter made by the parents and patient in successive 15-minute intervals of the 13 conjoint family psychotherapy sessions. In the first 15-minute interval, the mean amount of laughter of the mother was 9.2 (for 13 psychotherapy sessions in which the range of frequency of laughter in the first interval was 1 to 25). The mean amount of laughter of the father in this interval was 3.5 (for 12 sessions in which the range in this interval was 0 to 11). The mean amount of laughter of the patient in this interval was 2.7 (for 13 sessions in which the range was 0 to 11).

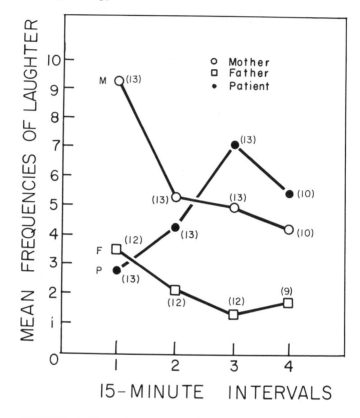

FIGURE 1. Mean frequencies of laughter by members in the intervals of therapy sessions.

Mean amount of laughter of mother in the second interval was 5.1 (for 13 sessions, range of 1 to 13); of father, 2.1 (for 12 sessions, range of 0 to 6); of patient, 4.2 (for 13 sessions, range of 1 to 6). Mean amount of laughter of the mother in the third interval was 5.0 (for 13 sessions, range of 0 to 11); for father, 1.4 (for 12 sessions, range of 0 to 5); for the patient, 7.1 (for 13 sessions, range of 0 to 24). Mean amount of laughter of the mother in the fourth interval was 4.3 (for 10 sessions, range of 1 to 11); for father, 2.9 (for 9 sessions, range of 0 to 3); for the patient, 5.5 (for 10 sessions, range of 2 to 9).

It is of interest that despite the mother's relatively high mean frequency of laughter in the first interval of the psychotherapy sessions, there were two sessions in which she laughed only once and one in which she laughed only twice in this interval. Conversely, despite the patient's relatively high mean frequency of laughter in the third interval, there was one such session in which she did not laugh at all in this interval, two in which she laughed only once, and one in which she laughed only twice. These findings testify that whatever the factor was tending to elevate the laughter levels of the patient and her mother in particular intervals, it was not always operating or else other effects sometimes counterbalanced the weight of the factor.

Figure 1 compares the mean frequency of laughter in the second, third, and fourth 15-minute intervals with the first, thus establishing a "laughter pattern" for each family member. The numbers in parentheses represent the number of psychotherapy sessions on which the means are based.

Table 1 shows the raw frequencies of laughter in the successive 15-minute intervals. This table served as the basis for the chi square analyses shown in Table 2 and is to be read specifically in conjunction with Table 2 since it will establish more clearly the nature of the trends in the data. Table 2 describes five hypotheses which are examined. Chi

TABLE 1. Raw frequencies of laughter of family members at 15-minute intervals in therapy sessions

Family member	15-minute intervals			
	1	2	3	4
Mother	120 (13)	66 (13)	65 (13)	43 (10)
Patient	35 (13)	55 (13)	92 (13)	55 (10)
Father	46 (12)	25 (12)	17 (12)	17 (9)

Note: Numbers in parentheses are numbers of sessions on which raw frequencies are based.

TABLE 2. Chi square analyses of raw frequencies of laughter by family members in 15-minute intervals of therapy sessions

Hypothesis	Occasions of Laughter	Chi Square	P	Hypothesis Accepted?
Mother's laughter is equally distributed in the first three 15-minute intervals of 13 therapy sessions.	251	23.5	<.001	No. (More laughter in first 15-minute interval than later intervals.)
Patient's laughter is equally distributed in the first three 15-minute intervals of 13 therapy sessions.	182	27.5	<.001	No. (More laughter in third 15-minute interval than earlier intervals.)
Father's laughter is equally distributed in the first three 15-minute intervals of 12 therapy sessions.	88	15.6	<.001	No. (More laughter in first 15-minute interval than later intervals.)
Mother and father's laughter in the first three 15-minute intervals of 12 therapy sessions is similarly distributed.	326	.9	>.05	Yes.
Mother and patient's laughter in the first three 15-minute intervals of 13 therapy sessions is similarly distributed.	433	42.3	<.001	No. (Patient's laughter more frequent in the third 15-minute interval; mother's more frequent in the first 15-minute interval.)

square test of the mother's laughter revealed that it was *not* equally distributed in the various intervals ($\chi^2 = 23.5$; $P < .001$). Reference to Table 1 indicates that the mother laughed almost twice as frequently in the first 15-minute interval as in the second and third.

Chi square test of the patient's laughter revealed that it was *not* equally distributed in the various intervals ($\chi^2 = 27.5$; $P < .001$). Reference to Table 1 indicates that the greatest frequency of laughter

TABLE 3. Percentages family members and therapists were "trigger" or "receiver" persons (see text for explanation of terms) in 12 therapy sessions of 706 occasions of laughter by family members

Family member laughing	"Trigger" Person				"Receiver" Person			
	Mo.	Fa.	Ther.	Pt.	Mo.	Fa.	Ther.	Pt.
Mother (293 cases)	35	47	15	3	27	15	50	8
Father (107 cases)	12	78	9	1	18	14	57	11
Patient (306 cases)	22	27	50	1	24	25	28	23

by the patient occurred in the third 15-minute interval. Chi square test of the father's laughter showed that it also was *not* equally distributed in the various intervals ($\chi^2 = 15.6$; $P < .001$). Reference to Table 1 indicates that the father's greatest frequency of laughter occurred (in an overall pattern that is similar to that of the mother) in the first 15-minute interval.

A chi square test reported in Table 2 comparing the patterns of laughter of the mother and father showed the patterns to be *similar* ($\chi^2 = .9$; $P > .05$). Both mother and father tended to laugh most frequently in the first 15-minute interval of sessions analyzed and markedly less thereafter. A chi square test comparing the patterns of laughter of the mother and patient showed the patterns to be different ($\chi^2 = 42.3$; $P < .001$). Reference to Table 1 indicates that whereas the mother tended to laugh most frequently in the first 15-minute interval of the sessions, the patient tended to laugh most frequently in the third 15-minute interval.

Table 3 reports information about the "trigger" person and the "receiver" person. Table 3 shows the percentages of time a family member or therapist was the "trigger" or "receiver" person and also the person doing the laughing at the time of remarks made by the "trigger" person to the "receiver" person.

Table 3 reveals that much of the mother's laughter (47% of the 293 separate occasions of her laughter) occurred in the context of a comment made by her husband to one of the other participants. Mother also laughed more frequently in the context of comments she or her husband directed at the therapists than in the reverse situation (146 versus 40 such occasions of her laughter). The father, on the other hand, appeared much less responsive, in terms of his laughter behavior, to comments made by his wife to other participants. He laughed little (12% of 107 occasions of his laughter) in the context of comments made by his wife to others. On the other hand, his laughter frequently (78% of the 107 occasions of his laughter) accompanied a comment which he himself made to others present in the therapy sessions.

In the case of the patient, her laughter occurred about as frequently in the context of comments originated by one of her parents (49% of 306 occasions of her laughter) as in the context of comments originated by one of the therapists (50% of 306 occasions of her laughter). Interestingly, however, 49% of the patient's laughter occurred in a context in which one of the parents was being addressed, usually by the therapist. Only about half as much of her laughter (28%) occurred in a context in which one of the therapists was being addressed, usually by the parent.

Despite the relatively poorer agreement on the designation of "trigger" and "receiver" persons, the results reported in Table 3 are suggestive that frequency of laughter was influenced in some degree by the direction of communication between the participants in the psychotherapy sessions. The incidence of the mother's laughter, in particular, seemed markedly affected by comments which her husband directed to the therapists. He was not nearly as responsive to comments made by his wife to others.

SUMMARY

This study examined laughter behavior in family members, one of whom was overtly schizophrenic, in numerous conjoint psychotherapy sessions covering a very wide range of discourse. The significant finding was that the laughter of the schizophrenic daughter, a symptom of her illness, was not wholly unrelated and inappropriate. Her bizarre laughter was a reaction at some level to the immediate, ongoing psychotherapy sessions. Assuming that laughter is a socially acceptable device to mask tension or anxiety, the finding suggests that the schizophrenic daughter was particularly tense or anxious in the third 15-minute interval of psychotherapy sessions; that is, in about minutes 30 to 45. By contrast, the findings suggest that the parents, especially the mother, were particularly tense or anxious in the first 15-minute interval. It is striking that in the interval in which laughter occurred most frequently in the parents (the first), laughter occurred least frequently in the schizophrenic daughter; conversely, in the interval in which laughter occurred most frequently in the daughter (the third), laughter tended to occur least frequently in the parents.

This reversal of patterns of laughter between the parents and daughter suggests at least the possibility of a factor of complementarity influencing the laughter behavior; that is, that the frequency of laughter in one family member was to some degree dynamically determined or affected by the frequency of laughter in another. One can infer that laughter was employed as a device by which the family members monitored each other's tension or anxiety states. An alternative explanation, one not involving the assumption of complementarity, would be that the daughter was merely least tense or anxious in the first 15-minute interval which was given over primarily to structuring the psychotherapy session, but she became much more tense in the later interval given over to deeper probing of feelings. It is possible, in other words, to explain the daughter's low frequency of laughter in one interval and high frequency in another by reference to some other process than ascribing a dynamic interaction between the laughter behaviors of the family members.

The results infer that certain characteristics of the intervals, particularly the first and third, affected the frequency of the parents' laughter and the daughter's laughter differently or, perhaps more significantly, in opposite directions. At some psychodynamic level, the laughter of the parents and bizarre laughter of the daughter apparently constituted signals or communications to each other. But the full intent or effectiveness of the signals is not clear, although one possible interpretation of them is that they did serve as some kind of check on or monitoring of each other's laughter behavior and at another level on each other's tension or anxiety states. The study delineated two characteristics in the immediate, ongoing psychotherapy situation which seem to have influenced the frequency of laughter behavior of the family members: One involved a factor of time (specifically, the earliness or lateness of the interval in the psychotherapy sessions); the other, of persons (specifically, who the particular persons were being talked to and talking at the time laughter occurred). The influence of the earliness or lateness of the time interval in the psychotherapy situation was established, however, with greater reliability than the influence of the persons being talked to and talking in the context of laughter behavior.

Greater complexity of design would have been necessary to prove the operation of a factor of dynamic complementarity affecting the laughter behavior of the family members. However, the results are clear that factors within the immediate, ongoing psychotherapy situation affected the laughter behavior of the family as a whole and produced significant differences in the patterns of laughter of the family members. In a case in which it seemed that a behavior was determined strictly by intrapersonal factors—as the bizarre laughter of the schizophrenic daughter seemed to be so determined—the presence of influencing factors in the immediate, ongoing psychotherapy situation was demonstrated.

REFERENCES

Ackerman, N. W. *Psychodynamics of family life.* New York: Basic Books, 1958.

Atkinson, J. W. *Motives in fantasy, action, and society.* Princeton, N.J.: Van Nostrand, 1958.

Bateson, G., Jackson, D. D., Haley, J., & Weakland, J. Toward a theory of schizophrenia. *Behavioral Science,* 1956, 1, 251-264.

Bell, J. E. *Family group therapy.* Public Health Monograph No. 64. Washington, D.C.: Department of Health, Education and Welfare, 1961.

Boszormenyi-Nagy, I. The concept of schizophrenia from the perspective of family treatment. *Family Process,* 1962, 1, 103-113.

Bowen, M. A family concept of schizophrenia. In D. D. Jackson (Ed.), *The etiology of schizophrenia.* New York: Basic Books, 1960, pp. 346-372.

Ericksen, C. W. Defense against ego-threat in memory and perception. *Journal of Abnormal and Social Psychology,* 1952, 47, 230-235.

Freud, S. *Jokes and their relation to the unconscious.* New York: Norton, 1960.

Jackson, D. D., & Weakland, J. H. Conjoint family therapy: Some considerations on theory, technique and results. *Psychiatry,* 1961, 24, 30-45.

Lewin, K. *A dynamic theory of personality: Selected papers.* New York: McGraw-Hill, 1935.

Rotter, J. B. The role of the psychological situation in determining the direction of human behavior. In M. R. Jones (Ed.), *Nebraska symposium on motivation: 1955.* Lincoln, Neb.: University of Nebraska Press, 1955, pp. 245-268.

Tyler, F. B., Tyler, B. B., & Rafferty, J. E. A threshold conception of need value. *Psychology Monographs,* 1962, 76, No. 11 (Whole No. 530).

Wynne, L. C. The study of intrafamilial alignments and splits in exploratory family therapy. In N. W. Ackerman, F. Beatman, and S. N. Sherman (Eds.), *Exploring the base for family therapy.* New York: Family Service Association of America, 1961, pp. 95-115.

Zuk, G. H. The influence of social context in impulse and control tendencies in pre-adolescents. *Genetic Psychology Monographs,* 1956, 9, 117-166.

Chapter 9 / A FURTHER STUDY
OF LAUGHTER IN FAMILY THERAPY

. . . .

Consideration will be given in this chapter to a special function of laughter in human communication. By far the greater emphasis in the numerous theories of laughter has been on its individual or intra-personal function; its interpersonal or communicational function has not received as much attention. It is the purpose of this paper to show that laughter does serve an important communicational function. The hypothesis of the study is this: that in human situations laughter is frequently employed, consciously or unconsciously, as an important nonverbal message which qualifies meaning for the purpose of disguise. A brilliant example of this function of laughter is contained in the powerful modern drama by Albee (1962), *Who's Afraid of Virginia Woolf?* The dialogue is filled with instructions to the characters to laugh or smile as they speak their lines. Albee states explicitly that the laugh, chuckle, or smile is often made to qualify—for example, emphasize or negate—in order to disguise intent. Sometimes a character appears to have conscious awareness that by his laughter he wishes his comment to be disregarded or ignored, or that he wishes special conditions to be attached to it. At other times, the character seems quite unconscious of his laughter and its intended meaning.

As Albee's profound psychological drama unfolds, the incidence of laughter seems to decline. A recent study in which the writer was involved (Zuk, Boszormenyi-Nagy, and Heiman, 1963) showed a similar trend in laughter as family members became more involved in family psychotherapy sessions. The parents of a schizophrenic girl were observed to laugh less frequently as the psychotherapeutic "drama" progressed. The greatest incidence of their laughter occurred in the first

This chapter was published in *Family Process,* 1964, 3, 77-89.

15 minutes of psychotherapy sessions. The lowest incidence occurred in the period from the 30th to the 45th minute of the sessions. Conversely, the *greatest* incidence of bizarre laughter in the schizophrenic daughter occurred in the interval from the 30th to the 45th minute, and the *least* in the first 15-minute interval. The daughter simply reversed the pattern established by the parents. It was conjectured that the pattern of laughter in the family members was evidence of a form of complementarity among them; that laughter served to maintain a secret line of communication among the family members.

Some comments made in a recent study (Titchener, D'Zmura, Golden, and Emerson, 1963) bear on the meaning of laughter. As the members of a family were being interviewed together, the laughter of the mother took on special meaning. The writers interpreted as follows: "These laughs, which became characteristic, are an extremely important means of communication for her. They are placed throughout the record, usually in reply to her husband, indicating cynicism and doubt, in response to his communication of affect." The mother's laughter, say the authors, had a special communication function. When not laughing, she was ". . . wooden, routine and nearly apathetic." The mother used laughter to communicate a wide range of feeling ". . . including bitterness, sarcasm and doubts of sincerity."

The hypothesis has been formulated that laughter is frequently employed as an important nonverbal mechanism to qualify meaning for the purpose of disguise. Support to document the hypothesis will be sought in excerpts from family psychotherapy sessions with three families seen in intensive, long-term family psychotherapy in the Family Therapy Project at Eastern Pennsylvania Psychiatric Institute. The purpose of presenting the excerpts is specifically to illustrate laughter as a qualifier of meaning. But there is a special clinical significance to the study of the excerpts. In each case the family undergoing psychotherapy contains one member who is schizophrenic. A striking symptom of the schizophrenic person is bizarre laughter. The study also attempts to relate the bizarre laughter of the schizophrenic patients to subclinical patterns occurring in their families.

FAMILY A

The first excerpt is from a family of lower middle class, Italian-Catholic background; the therapist is the author. The excerpt centers on the question of whether it would be possible for the daughter to separate herself from the parents, even for her to move out of the parents' home in the event of her marriage.

Father: How would you feel about it?
Patient: What?
Father: If you were married—would you rather live close or far?
Mother: She wants to live close. Don't you want to live close?
Patient: I don't know, to tell you the truth. It depends.
Therapist: If she were married, where would you want her to be?
Father: Well, that wouldn't be up to us.
Therapist: Well, I know that. But would you have something to say about it?
Mother: She could live with us if she wants.
Therapist: She could live with you?
Mother: Sure. (at this point the patient begins to giggle and laugh; she continues this laughter for several seconds) If she wants to, she's welcome. She can live in the front room. I'll give her my room. (now mother joins patient's laughter briefly) They don't want to live with the parents, Doctor. They want to live alone. She's laughing, but she wouldn't want to live with me.
Therapist: Why are you laughing so much?
Patient: Your expressions! Nothing.
Mother: You want to live with us, or you want to live alone?
Patient: I don't know. Before I wanted to live in the neighborhood, you know.
Mother: Now you wouldn't want to live with us—you want to live alone?
Patient: Yeah.
Mother: It's better to live alone than to live with the mother after you're married, you know.
Patient: Everybody's different. (more laughter here from the patient)

Therapist: (to mother) But would you be able to take that big loss? (Mother begins to giggle and laugh in response to this comment; patient then joins her mother in laughter) You're laughing just like your daughter was. I don't understand why both of you are laughing.

Mother: I don't know what you mean by big loss? What am I going to do—if she gets married?

Father: Well, he means if she gets married you'll be losing her.

Mother: How about the other people that marry their children [sic]—do they lose them?

Patient: Supposing I was to go to California?

Mother: Swell. (chuckles) I wish you would—then I could come to see you.

Father: You had mentioned about going to California. You wanted to get in the movies. (patient begins to giggle) You wanted to be somebody. (patient breaks into hearty laughter)

Therapist: Who did she want to be?

Patient: The teacher told me I had dramatic ability. But after I went to dramatic school, I got disappointed.

Mother: She went to charm school. Did I tell you, Doctor?

Patient: When I used to read the Shakespeare and all that, they told me I had good dramatic ability. But then I went to that school and it was a different story.

The first instance of laughter is the patient-daughter's, followed shortly thereafter by the mother's. Notice how closely related in time is their laughter and how in the daughter it seems to act as a stimulus for it in the mother, and vice versa. The patient tells the group that she is laughing at their "expressions," but one may assume a more basic origin of the laughter. *By means of it mother and daughter "quietly" reaffirm their allegiance to one another; or rather, their allegiance to their symbiotic relationship.* Throughout the excerpt, by their laughter, mother and daughter seem to be signaling each other that the content of their dialogue is to be discounted or qualified. The laughter reassures the members of the symbiotic pair of their secret and inviolable trust in each other.

One may conjecture about the effect of the laughter on the therapists. They may be puzzled by it, at least in the immediate context of the psychotherapy session. They may rightly conclude by it that they have approached an area of "sensitivity" in the family, but it constitutes at the same time a sharp resistance against further probing. They are, in a sense, warned by the laughter of the presence of tension and anxiety. The warning is made still more ominous by qualitative differences in the laughter of the family members: its pitch, intensity, frequency, and duration.

FAMILY B

Laughter can be a very characteristic device employed by family members to maintain certain family secrets and particular alliances between members. Excerpts of family psychotherapy sessions[1] with Family B will illustrate a family in which this function of laughter is very characteristic. This family is of lower-middle class Jewish background. Excerpt 1 occurs several minutes after the family members (father, mother, brother, and daughter-patient) have gathered. It is significant that in the period before the arrival of the therapists there is no recorded instance of laughter. Laughter occurs only after the arrival of the therapists, revealing thus how it may be used by an entire family group as a defense against intrusive efforts by outsiders.

Excerpt 1

Brother: (laughs nervously) Family circle. This is like a family circle. The whole family. You're uncles! (to the therapists)
Therapist 1: That the way you see it?
Brother: It's like in a family here. (laughs)
Therapist 2: Is that a good feeling?

[1] The cotherapists in this case are Dr. Ivan Boszormenyi-Nagy and Dr. David Rubinstein.

Brother: Yeah, it's a good feeling.
Therapist 2: Well, we like to be uncles.
Brother: Yeah, well I'm just saying, a family circle, you know.
Therapist 2: I don't think you're asking too much.
Brother: Well, uncles (breaks into laughter) are just–. Oh, I'm just kidding. I'm glad to be friendly with people. But I want D [the patient-daughter] to come home. That's why I'm here, you know. (to the therapists) You're welcome to come home to play chess with me, you know. You're welcome to my house. (laughs)
Therapist 1: You play better than I do.
Brother: Yéah? No, I'm not too good at chess.
Therapist 2: At least, you know better than I do. You might teach me. But it's a good feeling–to be in a close family circle.
Brother: Yeah. (laughs) Yeah, but Doctor, we're here for D's sake, you know. I mean, that's why I'm here. I'd like to see her come home.
Patient: Yeah, I want to go home.
Brother: She's been here a year already. I don't know if it's a waste of her life.
Patient: Yeah, it's a waste of my life. That's the truth.
Brother: She ain't going to live forever. That's the truth. (chuckles) I ain't going to live forever, I know that.
Mother: (to patient) It's a waste, but you still don't cooperate. You do this; you do that.
Brother: Yeah, you're not doing what you're supposed to. We told you that last week. See (breaks into laughter)–I don't want to be the big speaker here. My father's supposed to speak up. But I got to do it, it seems like. My father just sits here.
Father: Well, you've got to speak up for yourself. D's got to speak up for herself. Nobody is supposed to speak up for anybody else. It's not normal; it's not well if I have to talk for you. If I have to console, if I have to pity you–you're being spoiled. You've got to pull yourself out of the rut. You've got to be disciplined; you've got to obey. You can't come to me for sympathy. You have to learn to obey. You're a patient here.
Patient: Yeah, I'm a patient here and I have to obey. I sit in one place all the time.

Father: Well, you have to make it yourself. Nobody can do it for you. You've got to know right from wrong.

The first instance of laughter is the brother's. It seems to occur in response to a fantasy that the therapists have actually become members of the family. He is pleased by the thought, pleased that the "uncles" permit him a larger freedom of expression in the family. He reacts positively to his new power and authority. But later in the excerpt he retreats, perhaps before some unconscious threat emanating from his father. He presses the father to speak and the father does respond but with a series of platitudes.

The brother's laughter seems to occur in the absence of jokes or humor. It is partly a reflection of his uneasiness in the situation. One may guess that the uneasiness is due to mixed feelings: fear that perhaps he should not be assuming the more authoritarian role, but also pleasure in doing so. The laughter connotes pleasure at new-found authority, however fleeting. It is a nonverbal counterpoint to remarks about his humble role in the family.

Excerpt 2 from a psychotherapy session with Family B will illustrate in particular the mother's laughter. It has a marvelous subtlety in helping her express her apparent helplessness and thus discouraging any demands that might be made of her.

Excerpt 2

Therapist 1: Her mother still does more things for D than D does for her.
Patient: What does she do for me? She gives me old clothes that my cousin wore?
Mother: I brought all your own clothes in.
Patient: She don't give me that much. She gives me hand-me-downs and everything like that.
Mother: I've been bringing you your own clothes, what are you saying?
Therapist 1: Does she ask you for thanks?

Patient: She never gives me nothing.

Therapist 2: That's Dr. N's feeling—that you sacrifice more for D than D does for you.

Mother: So, that's my make-up. (chuckles) I'd say it's my make-up, regardless.

Therapist 1: For example, if she asks you for money for a telephone call, you are ready to take a scolding from the doctors.

Mother: Well, I'm not that sick that I don't know right from wrong. When you told me it was wrong, I myself felt it was wrong and I didn't do it.

Therapist 2: That's what I mean—that you are ready to sacrifice yourself for D.

Therapist 1: What do you get in return?

Mother: I don't get too much. But then I feel, have I ever got too much in my whole life—and that's it. I feel that since she's here she's improved a lot. She was pretty sick and she's improved a lot. I would be willing to have her come home, but I do know that she'll just go back to the same—

Therapist 1: But you said you don't get anything. You are used to not getting anything.

Mother: (chuckles) Yeah, that's my point of view. I mean, I get quite a few things.

Therapist 1: But you tend to not talk about it.

Mother: Oh, I tend to not talk about it? Well. (chuckles) Maybe it's so deepseated that I don't talk about it. Maybe back in my childhood I felt rejected. It might go back far.

Therapist 2: Do you get real angry sometimes?

Mother: It's good to get angry. But I don't show it.

Therapist 2: When you came in this morning, did D kiss you?

Mother: No she didn't.

Therapist 2: How did you feel?

Mother: Well, I felt she should kiss me, but then I felt a different angle—I felt the patient should do as she pleases. If she doesn't feel like kissing, she shouldn't do it. If she feels like showing her true feelings, she should do it.

Therapist 2: This is something intellectual.

Mother: Oh, well, (chuckles) so I'm getting intellectual. (now laughs more broadly) Maybe she's becoming a person in her own right and doing what she wants to do.

Therapist 2: But do you feel angry?

Mother: Yes, I can feel angry, yes.

Therapist: Were you angry?

Mother: Yeah, I don't know how far—extreme my anger goes. I feel I would like her to kiss me. But then I feel that maybe she's taught that she should do as she darn pleases. If she's angry at her mother, she shouldn't have to kiss her mother. Those are my feelings.

Therapist 2: But then it's as Dr. N says—you avoid expressing how you feel.

Mother: Well, it's in me—(chuckles)—I feel bad—but I have to consider her feelings too.

Therapist 2: How angry do you feel?

Mother: I do feel pretty angry.

(Later in the session)

Mother: (to therapist) I mean, I know you want to bring a point out but I don't know which it is.

Therapist 2: Well, what Dr. N is trying to pinpoint is, you feel very hurt in comparison to D. You feel that maybe you have been more sacrificed. Maybe you felt angry on account of it. D, for example, has got more from her father than you.

Therapist 1: I would put it even in a more personal form. Maybe you feel like somebody raising a snake. You feed the snake and then it grows up to bite you.

Mother: Look, (chuckles) I don't know what it's all about. You mean, in other words, that the mother has hostility towards her child? That part I have accepted, and I know. But about snakes, I don't, ah—(breaks into laughter here)

In this excerpt the mother emits more chuckles than laughs. We do not easily grasp precisely what it is she is chuckling about. There are at least two psychodynamic levels at which these chuckles may be understood. One is that by them the mother hopes to reinforce the strength of her comments about her role as passive, patient, and undemanding mother of an irresponsible child. The other is that her chuckles may be a sly negation of her statements. They may be explained as an unconscious eruption of narcissism in connection with her dominant role in her symbiotic relationship with her daughter.

Excerpt 3 will illustrate some features of the father's laughter in family psychotherapy sessions. Only the father, daughter-patient, and therapists are present in the session. The strategy of the therapists was to remain silent in order to promote the fullest interaction between father and daughter.

Excerpt 3

Father.   It gives you something.
Patient: Gives mommy something.
Father: Oh, you're referring to her.
Patient: Yeah. (chuckles)
Father: Oh, her. Yeah, I agree with that. I thought you were referring to you. Well, it gives her a sense of love and security. See, her interpretation of love would be sort of—absorbing.
Patient: Yeah. (chuckles)
Father: See, absorb a person, Give them so much love that they feel you'll return that love, see. But that's (chuckles slightly) false love. That's sick love. It's sick. The idea of love is to let the other person do for themselves.
Patient: Well, mommy devours you, you know.
Father: That's right. With all that affection; with all that attention; without realizing it.
Patient: Yeah (chuckles)—it overpowers you. I mean, it's like you can't meet her on an equal level. It's like she's devouring you—draining you.
Father: You know, I just want to make an illustration. Take, for instance, a flower. You have that flower, you look at it, you love it. You take it, put it in your hands like this and crush it. I love this flower, right? (chuckles) Now, meanwhile with all the love that flower will die. (laughs throughout the latter part of the sentence) If you love that flower, you water it, put it in a pot and you let it take care of itself. (father again chuckles, then laughs and is joined in the laughter by his daughter)

Patient: Yeah, that's right.

Father: See, nature provides for life. It's got to develop.

Patient: Then, it's like I find my friends more growing, you know. Friends my age are not so kind, they're more for themselves.

Father: It's a whole human being, not a half human being.

Patient: You know, mommy didn't come on account of that, uh–yesterday. (giggles and laughs) I said it and she figures that was what it was. On account of what we were talking about yesterday. I mean, I don't feel I have a chance with mommy in these meetings. I feel she has it so much over me; as far as asserting herself and being more powerful. I don't feel–I'm much quieter than my mother.

Father: Well, I mean, uh, you see, you also got to understand that she doesn't do this intentionally. She feels she's doing good for you. But it's the wrong way. In the case of mother, if you would assert yourself, you would be doing yourself good and her good.

Patient: (to the therapists) I feel my mother and father completely devour me. That's always happening to me with my friends too. They can assert themselves over me. (giggles and laughs) I always get in that position. Maybe it's because at home I let my mother and father do it to me, and then I go out at night and my friends start doing the same thing. (begins to laugh at about the middle of the last sentence and carries it all through the sentence)

The laughter occurring in this excerpt is perhaps the most bizarre of that in any of the excerpts presented; it is more clearly disassociated from the dialogue than in previous excerpts. Why? At the psychodynamic level, it may be conjectured that the father and daughter are engaged in maintaining some information in secret from the therapists and that laughter is employed as a signal to further this process. The dialogue raises the question of the existence of incest fantasies between father and daughter. The daughter may share the father's implicit incest suggestion, but she too has need to disguise it. She changes the subject by referring to the fact that her mother did not come to see her the day before. By this maneuver she may wish to advise the father implicitly that her mother will defend her against his sexual advances; that her mother is more powerful than he. An alternative explanation is that perhaps she fantasies the wish her mother were present to demonstrate her own sexual powers and superiority over her mother.

FAMILY C

Sometimes laughter in the absence of jokes or humor serves as an attempt to create an atmosphere of gaiety or levity. The family presented in the following excerpt is from the upper socioeconomic class and is Protestant. The participants in the psychotherapy session are the father, mother, married daughter, married daughter's husband (son-in-law), patient-daughter, and the therapists.[2]

Father: Gee, the Market really collapsed. How do they feel about the steel strike?

Son-law: I didn't talk to anyone in the Market. (patient enters)

All: Hi, K, how are you?

Married Daughter: You have a pony tail. (chuckles)

Mother: How are you darling? It's good to see you, (chuckles)

Married Daughter: Yes. (chuckles)

Son-in-law: You're all decked out like Christmas. (general laughter)

Mother: That looks like your Easter Bonnet. (more laughter from the group)

Father: (to entering therapists) Good morning, doctors! Get over here in a comfortable chair. (mother chuckles)

Mother: Yes, you don't want to miss his, uh, pearls. (she laughs and there is general laughter)

Therapist 1:   There enough chairs around?

Married Daughter: K, looks like you put on a few pounds.

Mother: Yes. (chuckles)

---

[2] The cotherapists in this case are the writer and Dr. Ivan Boszormenyi-Nagy.

Father: (to patient) I'll sit next to you so I can bother you.
(mother chuckles)
Married Daughter: Well, we did our income tax until 3:30 yesterday morning. (chuckles)
Son-in-law: There's nothing like being organized.
Mother: (chuckling throughout comment) Well, we were early this year. There's something about it, you know—you just don't like to spend the money.
Father: I think that's the wrong way to feel about it. (here patient laughs "bizarrely") Everyone should feel proud to pay their income tax.
Mother: Oh, honey, you surely don't mean it.
Son-in-law: That's chauvinism! (general laughter)
Father: (to patient) Well, sweetie, how have you been? Busy? I haven't been getting any mail from you lately.
Mother: (chuckling throughout comment) Has she been getting any from you?
Father: No, come to think of it, she hasn't. (general laughter) I did send her a post card. That's about all, I guess.

The laughter in this excerpt seems part of an attempt to cover the deep anxiety and tension of the family members. They are straining to appear at their ease, flexible, able to handle any situation as it comes. But the laughter is too forced, too artificial, too inconsistent with the general purpose of the visit. They are laughing at anything, thereby signaling unconsciously their deep discomfort to each other, despite conscious intent to show sophistication, poise, and control.

DISCUSSION

This study is intended to document the view that laughter has meaning not only in the context of individual psychodynamics, but also in interpersonal communication. The excerpts illustrate the hypothesis that laughter is often employed as a nonverbal mechanism to qualify meaning for the purpose of disguise.

Freud (1960) and Bergson (1956), among others, viewed laughter as a mechanism for disguise. Freud thought that laughter reflected the displacement and freeing of energy previously used for repression. He noted that some of his neurotic patients laughed in the psychoanalytic hour when a valid interpretation was suddenly made. Bergson perceived that *any* attempt to disguise reality was potentially laughable. His theory helps to explain the phenomenon of laughter in the absence of jokes or humor as simply a function of a wish to disguise reality.

Neither Freud's theory nor Bergson's nor any of the other numerous theories of laughter, specifies its value as a unique nonverbal *communication* in human interaction; that is, as a particular message to a listener in a context of many listeners, several of whom may not be privileged parties to the message. To the casual observer, laughter may appear too weak a stimulus to play so powerful a role in human communication as ascribed to it here. But Weakland (1960) in a paper defining the nature of the double bind in communication, states that "... it is important to remember that objectively very slight signals—thus ones easily ignored—can drastically modify or even reverse the significance of much more obvious or lengthy messages" (p. 377).

The qualifying of information for the purpose of disguise is implied in the concept of the double bind described by Bateson, Jackson, Haley, and Weakland (1956). The double bind is a situation in which the person is faced with contradictory messages. The fact that the messages are contradictory is not readily apparent because of attempts at concealment, or denial, or because the messages are actually on different levels. The person for whom the complex message is intended is not permitted to evade nor can he effectively neutralize it. Schizophrenics are believed frequently to be the "victims" of double-bind communication with important family members. To be sure, they are not always passive victims, but sometimes actively participate in the maintenance of pathological double-bind communication.

Depending on the context, laughter as a signal of the wish to qualify meaning for the purpose of disguise may be an important prop in the maintenance of the pathological double-bind system, as well as other pathological systems; for example, in the pseudomutual system (Wynne, Ryckoff, Day, and Hirsch, 1958), the undifferentiated family ego mass system (Bowen, 1960), and the pathological need complementarity system (Boszormenyi-Nagy, 1962). Even the grossly bizarre and inappropriate laughter of schizophrenics may play a complementary role in the maintenance of pathological systems, as at least one study (Zuk, Boszormenyi-Nagy, and Heiman, 1963) has suggested. The excerpts from the family psychotherapy sessions are suggestive that the grossly bizarre laughter of the schizophrenic may be a dissociation from or projection magnified many times of an aspect of a pathological family communication process. One repeatedly sees an element of bizarreness in the laughter of family members of a schizophrenic whose laughter is bizarre and inappropriate.

Laughter, apparently so gross and nonspecific a signal, can exhibit a high degree of selectivity under appropriate conditions, as it was the attempt to show in the excerpts. Laughter was used as one means for family members to reaffirm their allegiance to one another, while not specifically alerting the therapists to that fact. To be sure, it also had secondary idiosyncratic meaning; e.g., as an expression of contempt, irritation, anger, submission, disgust, sadness, and so on.

It is hard to escape the conclusion that laughter of the type discussed here, even at its most bizarre, is always a sign of some degree of readiness to reveal the thoughts which it seeks to disguise. It is a communication to the listener, be he family member, stranger, or therapist, that the thoughts are under some degree of pressure for expression.

REFERENCES

Albee, E. *Who's afraid of Virginia Woolf?* New York: Atheneum, 1962.
Bateson, G., Jackson, D. D., Haley, J., & Weakland, J. H. Toward a theory of schizophrenia, *Behavioral Science, 1956,* 1, 251-264.
Bergson, H. Laughter. In W. Sypher (Ed.), *Comedy.* Garden City, New York: Doubleday, 1956.
Boszormenyi-Nagy, I. The concept of schizophrenia from the perspective of family treatment. *Family Process,* 1962,1, 103-113.
Bowen, M. A family concept of schizophrenia. In D. D. Jackson (Ed.), *The etiology of schizophrenia.* New York: Basic Books, 1960, pp. 346-372.

Freud, S. *Jokes and their relation to the unconscious.* London: Hogarth, 1960.

Titchener, J. L., D'Zmura, T., Golden, M., & Emerson, R. Family transaction and derivation of individuality. *Family Process,* 1963, 2, 95-120.

Weakland, J. H. The "double-bind" hypothesis of schizophrenia and three-party interaction. In D. D. Jackson (Ed.), *The etiology of schizophrenia.* New York: Basic Books, 1960, pp. 373-388.

Wynne, L. C., Ryckoff, I., Day, J., & Hirsch, S. I. Pseudomutuality in the family relations of schizophrenics. *Psychiatry,* 1958, 21, 205-220.

Zuk, G. H., Boszormenyi-Nagy, I., & Heiman, E. Some dynamics of laughter during family therapy. *Family Process,* 1963, 2, 302-314.

. . . .

PART IV:: INTERVIEWS

. . . .

INTRODUCTION

. . . .

There seems to be considerable interest among mental health workers in the "styles" or "personalities" of therapists. In family therapy, there is a small but growing list of transcripts in which unique characteristics of the therapist are reflected. Haley and Hoffman's *Techniques of Family Therapy* is a good presentation of a number of therapist "styles."

This section contains transcripts of two therapy sessions. Throughout the book numerous short excerpts from sessions are sprinkled, but these are usually too short for the reader to get a clear notion of how I try to develop a therapy session. The object of this section is to provide the reader that notion.

The first transcript is a section of an initial interview with a family. It stands as a contrast to the second, which is a transcript of the complete seventh interview.

Each of the transcripts has a relatively brief introductory and closing section describing the families being interviewed, the pathogenic relating observed, and some of the steps taken by the therapist toward his goals. A rather special feature of the cases is that follow-up material was available and is presented here.

Chapter 10 / AN INITIAL INTERVIEW
WITH AN ARKANSAS FAMILY

- -

In May, 1967, at the invitation of members of the Department of Psychiatry at the University of Arkansas Medical School in Little Rock, I interviewed a family living in the Little Rock vicinity. The interview was videotaped, and the transcript that follows is approximately a 25-minute excerpt from the videotape. The transcript was originally prepared as an aid to viewers of the videotape at a family therapy institute held by the American Orthopsychiatric Association during its annual meeting in Chicago on March 20, 1968. Although it is not a transcript of the complete session, which lasted approximately 50 minutes, it does contain the high points.

Shortly before I saw the family, I reviewed the medical/psychiatric chart that had been prepared. For the following information about the family, I must rely on my memory of what was in the chart and also a review of the videotape and the transcript itself. The reason for referral of the family was a suicide gesture of the daughter, Gilda, who was 16 years old. She swallowed a bottle of pills. (I do not recall what kind.) Gilda's younger brother, Tony, 11 years old, was also present in the interview. He had been involved in an auto mishap which, according to one professional report, may have left him with minimal brain injury. Mr. Masters, a man about 50 years of age, managed a gasoline service station. His wife, close in age to her husband, operated a beauty parlor. (All of the names here are, of course, fictitious.) The family was white, lower-middle class, and, I believe, Protestant.

My immediate impression was that this was not one of the "expressive" families that use words so abundantly and melodramatically. The parents appeared stoical yet tense; waiting to be asked questions rather than volunteer information. In the first 15 minutes of the session, I recall searching for a point of vulnerability in the family and shortly thereafter found it in the person of young Tony.

184

Tony resented his isolation from the main arena of the family; and he resented also the therapist's attempt to enter the arena, for he tried by resort to tears to prevent the therapist from discovering the situation in the family. Had he been able to prevent it, I think he would have felt more important to and needed by the other members. His mother explained that the family tried to spare Tony too much emotional stress, attributing the need to do so to injuries he sustained in an automobile accident which made him "nervous, high-strung." My tactic was to encourage him to express himself, and at the same time to discourage him from playing the role of the clown in the family. I wanted to subvert the conspiracy of silence that I felt was directed at him.

My encouragement of Tony probably influenced Mrs. Masters to express herself more directly than she usually liked. She revealed that she and her husband had been on the verge of a separation. It appeared from her comments that she and her husband had settled into a destructive impasse in their relationship in which both children were entrapped and in which both at times served as go-betweens to mediate between the parents. Mr. Masters confirmed the situation between himself and his wife.

Gilda's role was ticklish as a female adolescent who at one moment probably had the desire to be the savior of the marriage; and at another moment perhaps wished to have her father for herself. A suicide gesture might be an act of desperation to permit her to resolve a situation that had become unbearably stressful.

With Gilda my tactic as therapist was to encourage her to reveal the manner in which she played a go-between role between her parents. I hoped to cause her to defend her right to the role. I hoped to find out from the parents what stake they had in maintaining Gilda as a go-between.

In initial interviews with families it is the therapist's main task to determine the pattern of pathogenic relating, and then work toward engagement since overcoming the resistance to engagement is also one of the major tasks of the therapist. In the Masters family it seemed to me that engagement would prove difficult because of negative attitudes in the members with the exception of Gilda. In follow-up sessions, I would have been inclined to emphasize the gravity of Gilda's suicide gesture as a lever to hold the family in treatment.

(The session has been in progress about 15 minutes.)

Dr. Zuk: Is that clear . . . what I said?

Tony: I don't know. I guess you have to ask him. (indicating his father)

Dr. Zuk: Well, I'm asking you.

Tony: Start with him.

Dr. Zuk: No, I'm going to start with you. I'm being serious with you.

Tony: Well, I do feel about as close to him as he does to Gilda.

Dr. Zuk: Well, do you think he feels that close to you?

Tony: Well, he has been.

Dr. Zuk: What do you mean by that "has been"?

Tony: I don't know. Well, he has been ever since he opened up that station.

Dr. Zuk: Well, that's just been recently . . . since this morning . . . yesterday. (to father) When did you open the station?

Mr. Masters: . . . two or three days.

Dr. Zuk: So for the last two or three days he's been close to you then?

Tony: Yep.

(long pause)

Dr. Zuk: (to Tony) What's the matter?

Tony: (crying and sniffing) I just want to get out of here!

Dr. Zuk: (to his mother) What's he crying about?

Mrs. Masters: He's very emotional. He cries easily.

Dr. Zuk: Does he really?

Mrs. Masters: He's upset.

Dr. Zuk: What's he upset about?

Mrs. Masters: I think he's embarrassed.

Dr. Zuk: About what?

Mrs. Masters: This is so strange to him. Different.

Dr. Zuk: You mean this type of meeting?

Mrs. Masters: Uh huh.

Dr. Zuk: Why is it different?

Mrs. Masters: Well, we brought him once before . . . and . . . and he didn't like it.

Dr. Zuk: He doesn't like it? He doesn't like *me*?

Mrs. Masters: I thought that he would . . . but uh . . . because usually he enjoys talking.

Dr. Zuk: Does he?

Mrs. Masters: (inaudible)

Dr. Zuk: Well, will you tell me how he feels? What's the trouble? Well, I'm taking you at your word that you're very close. If that's true, then . . .

Mrs. Masters: Do you mean the trouble right now, or trouble in general?

Dr. Zuk: Yes, trouble now and in general.

Mrs. Masters: Well he's a highly nervous child and he always has been. I mean he has been since his accident.

Dr. Zuk: Well, I've heard that already; but tell me what's really going on with him.

Mrs. Masters: I think it all goes back to the accident.

Dr. Zuk: To the accident? He's crying now because of the accident?

Mrs. Masters: Probably the results of it, yes.

Dr. Zuk: What are the results?

Mrs. Masters: Well, the doctors told us he would be a highly nervous child.

Gilda: Can I say something?

Dr. Zuk: Yeah, it if will help me understand what the results are.

Gilda: I don't think that his problem is that he's highly nervous.

Dr. Zuk: What?

Gilda: I don't think that his problem is that he's so highly nervous. I think that it's something that . . . We're all used to shielding him . . . and I think that the main thing right now is that . . . he's very unsure of whether or not he's loved.

Dr. Zuk: Yes, that's a problem.

Gilda: Like on a trip . . . the last trip over here. We were talking about his hair, and he said: "I can't part my hair on this side because I want my daddy to love me." And he's so fussy. If you don't do everything exactly right, then no one's going to love him.

Dr. Zuk: Well, that's a problem. (to mother) Would you agree with your daughter's comments?

Mrs. Masters: I was never conscious before, until people made that remark, that he felt that way.

Dr. Zuk: Felt what way?

Mrs. Masters: That he had to do other things that everybody wanted him to.

Tony: (crying; partly inaudible), . . . your handkerchief, daddy. (sniffing) Why don't you say it: Love has nothing to do with the side you part your hair on. And I don't want you to start talking about hair styles here at the clinic! (sniffs again)

(long pause)

Dr. Zuk: Well, Tony, what's going on in your family?

Tony: Nothing that I know of that bothers anybody.

Dr. Zuk: You don't know anything that bothers anybody?

Tony: Nope.

Dr. Zuk: All right, what do you think is wrong about them then?

Tony: . . . 'cept one night very late when mommy and daddy got into an argument and mommy said daddy could get a steady job and bring home a paycheck every week. And she just wandered off into her room . . . like through the jungle all to herself . . . and even without . . . (inaudible)

Dr. Zuk: Yeah. But uh . . . what is that supposed to mean?

Mr. Masters: Everybody went off.

Dr. Zuk: What should she have done?

Tony: I don't know. I just got . . . (inaudible) . . . And when I came back in I just told mommy and daddy to start all over and . . . no arguments, no nothing . . .

(pause)

Dr. Zuk: Anybody pay attention to you in the family?

Tony: (inaudible)

Dr. Zuk: Huh?

Tony: Most of the time somebody does. Mom, Gilda, daddy.

Dr. Zuk: In that order?

Tony: Some of the times in that order. But most times daddy is the one that pays attention to me because he's the one that loves me. (inaudible comment)

Dr. Zuk: You mean that what you're talking about is silly now.

Tony: No, it's not!.

Dr. Zuk: You don't even mean that.

Tony: I do too!

Dr. Zuk: You want me to believe that?

Tony: You can believe what you want! But I know my father loves me.

Dr. Zuk: Doesn't sound to me like you really think that.

(a jumble of comments from family members)

Dr. Zuk: What do you expect to get from coming here, if you continue coming? What do you think you'll get out of this type meeting if you continue? Does anyone have any ideas what they want?

Mr. Masters: Hope to find out ... changes made to ... everybody's ...

Dr. Zuk: Now, who's unhappy? Are you unhappy?

Mr. Masters: I'm unhappy with the way it is, yes sir.

Dr. Zuk: Because why?

Mr. Masters: Because I can't figure out what it's all about.

Dr. Zuk: (to mother) What would you want to get out of it, coming here week after week? What would you want to get out of that? Taking your time ...

Mrs. Masters: Well, um, I didn't especially want to come. I think if we wanted to settle our differences then we could have a family conference around the kitchen table and settle them. If each one of us wanted the others' happiness bad enough, it could be achieved. And if we don't want it that way, then we're wasting our time coming here.

Dr. Zuk: Do you know what the disagreements are about?

Mrs. Masters: It's any number of things that's built up.

Dr. Zuk: Any number. Can you mention a couple of them? Or aren't you sure?

Mrs. Masters: I think number one is financial troubles. You can worry yourself sick over unpaid bills.

Dr. Zuk: Who worries? You, or your husband?

Mrs. Masters: I don't know how much he worries about it. I know I've worried myself sick.

Dr. Zuk: You don't know how much he worries about it?

Mrs. Masters: I . . . I say that I'm not going to speak for him.

Dr. Zuk: Well, what does he usually do with unpaid bills?

Mrs. Masters: We usually get them paid, but . . . I'm just saying I worry an awful lot.

Dr. Zuk: You don't want to talk about it.

Mrs. Masters: No. I can't speak.

Dr. Zuk: Now, so that's one of them. What's a couple of the other various tough disagreements?

Mrs. Masters: Well, I think, um . . . Gilda was right when she said him being away from home so much. We don't do anything as a family.

Dr. Zuk: Uh huh . . .

Mrs. Masters: Usually not even eat our meals together.

Dr. Zuk: Will it be that way now, by the way, with the new station? Maybe even more?

Mrs. Masters: Probably be worse.

Dr. Zuk: Be worse? Is that right, Mr. Masters?

Mr. Masters: It will.

Dr. Zuk: Well, so this is another thing. Finances and spending time together. Anything else that would be another issue for a disagreement?

Mrs. Masters: Well, we almost separated two weeks ago over . . . There's this little donut shop up there. And he goes up there an awful lot, when I think he can spend some of that time at home with the children.

Gilda: That's what I said when . . . (inaudible) . . . we could find him just about any time we wanted to by just going to the donut shop or to the cleaners . . .

Dr. Zuk: Now, what are you saying? What are you saying?

Mrs. Masters: What do you mean, "What am I saying?"

Dr. Zuk: I don't know what you mean by "going to the donut shop" or "going to the cleaners." What does that really mean?

Mrs. Masters: He was having coffee with this lady in the cleaners.

Dr. Zuk: Oh, I see. You were going to split up about this? You were going to separate about this?

Mrs. Masters: (inaudible)

Dr. Zuk: You take it seriously? Seriously enough to split up? You do take it very seriously?

Mrs. Masters: It is very serious.

Dr. Zuk: It is. And you've known about this? (to father) Your wife knows all about it: Did you know that?

Mr. Masters: Yes.

Dr. Zuk: She does know it.

Mr. Masters: You see this is not the first time that I have had . . . (inaudible),. . .That's one reason she's so unhappy. This donut shop has a big plate glass window, and people in there all the time. And when you have a coffee break you can't drive all the way home, two miles, and have coffee with the family . . . (inaudible) . . . and their imagination, and other gossip going around. Apparently there was an affair going on between me and this woman in the cleaners. Well I've had several affairs with women according to her, and . . .

Dr. Zuk: Over the years?

Mr. Masters: . . . over the years, yes.

Dr. Zuk: (inaudible)

Mr. Masters: We had a grocery store at one time, and women would come in and trade with me.

Dr. Zuk: This is in your wife's imagination. Nothing ever . . . Is there some truth to it?

Mr. Masters: No sir. Just like I said, it's being accused of it. But that's as far as it ever went.

Dr. Zuk: . . . complete imagination . . . (inaudible)

Mr. Masters: No, no. Me having coffee with this lady is true.

Dr. Zuk: It is true . . . that you do see the woman?

Mr. Masters: I don't now. But there are several women that work at the drugstore and I've had coffee with them.

Dr. Zuk: And your wife would put two and two together; that you're seeing these women, having an affair, and it's just not a sociable thing. Is that . . .

Mr. Masters: Well the thing is, there's eight stools in this donut shop where you drink coffee. And women came in and sat down and had coffee with me, and I'm talking with them while I'm drinking.

Dr. Zuk: Uh huh. But what your wife, I think, is saying is that she's taking this pretty seriously.

Mr. Masters: Yes, sir.

Dr. Zuk: She .. (to mother) Were you saying that this was the basic thing?

Mrs. Masters: I didn't say anything about him having coffee in the donut shop with the women. I'm saying he goes in the donut shop and gets two cups of coffee and goes tripping down the sidewalk with it to this woman in the cleaners. And that's where he drinks his coffee. And he has also done it when there wasn't any cleaning involved.

Dr. Zuk: Well, then, you're taking this as a serious thing. Some kind of an affair between your husband and . . .

Mrs. Masters: I did never say that it was an affair. I said it's not right for him to buy her coffee when he's been so broke he couldn't buy coffee to bring home.

Gilda: (inaudible)

Dr. Zuk: Are you very angry at your husband about this?

Mrs. Masters: I am very upset because we have been talked about, and now we're both in business in that community.

Dr. Zuk: People know about it?

Mrs. Masters: Yes. A woman came to my beauty shop, was the first I knew about it. And she had seen him taking coffee down to the cleaners.

Dr. Zuk: (to Gilda) Why are you in all this? What business is it of yours?

Gilda: They're my parents.

Dr. Zuk: Yes, but how did you get involved? You're just a kid, aren't you?

Gilda: Uh huh . . .

Dr. Zuk: Then what business is it of yours? It's their argument. What are you doing in it?

Gilda: Well, I don't think you can be close to a person and say you're close and then hear all these . . .

Dr. Zuk: Who are you close to?

Gilda: Daddy . . . And then I heard all these rumors.

Dr. Zuk: And who told you all these rumors?

Gilda: Mother told me part of them, and then . . .

Dr. Zuk: (to mother) You shared with your daughter some of these concerns you have?

Mrs. Masters: I talked to her.

Dr. Zuk: How about your son? Did you talk with him about this?

Mrs. Masters: I think he's too young.

Dr. Zuk: (to Tony) Do you know about what's going on?

Tony: No, I really don't.

Dr. Zuk: You sure? (to Gilda) Well, you are nosey! Even if your mother tried to talk with you about it, I think one of the things you could have done was say, "It's none of my business. Take it up with my father"; but you didn't do that.

Gilda: We talked about it.

Dr. Zuk: Who?

Gilda: Daddy and I.

Dr. Zuk: Oh, you talked with your father about it. What did you talk with him about?

Gilda: He asked me what was wrong with me and I said I was worried . . . (inaudible) . . . having an affair with this woman . . .

Dr. Zuk: What does that mean: "He was having an affair?" What do you mean by that?

Gilda: Well I don't think that . . . (inaudible) . . . well, I don't think it was anything more than . . . you know . . .

Dr. Zuk: You don't think so?

Gilda: No . . . in a cleaners or donut shop.

Dr. Zuk: Well, when you talked with your father about it, what kind of response did you get?

Gilda: He said that it wasn't true. And that we'd always . . . (inaudible) . . .

Dr. Zuk: Well, yeah, now is this a big thing between the two of you? Being . . . (inaudible) . . . Is Tony in this?

Tony: I never heard anything about it, so I guess I ain't.

Dr. Zuk: You're out of this too, huh?

Tony: Who else is? Everybody else is in it 'cept me. I just go up in my room and play my guitar.

Dr. Zuk: Well, what response did you get from your father when you told him that you knew about something?

Gilda: I think he acted a little shocked.

Dr. Zuk: Shocked? And what was the outcome?

Gilda: Well, we finally shut up and he keeps drinking coffee, so . . .

Dr. Zuk: We? We shut up? Who's we?

Gilda: My mother and I.

Dr. Zuk: You both said it . . .

Gilda: She was upset and I was upset . . .

Dr. Zuk: You didn't send your daughter to talk to your husband, did you?

Mrs. Masters: No.

(Mother and Gilda turn to each other and speak so low that therapist cannot hear.)

Dr. Zuk: I couldn't get it. Do you want to say something, or do you want to just talk between the two of you?

(pause)

Mrs. Masters: (to Gilda) Are you upset?

Gilda: Well, I was just going to say that you never sent me to talk to him; that you made it a point to give me the car and tell me to go to certain places to see if he was there.

Mrs. Masters: Many times I was going to use the car and I couldn't beat you to it.

Gilda: Well, I'm not denying that.

Tony: . . . (inaudible) . . .

Dr. Zuk: (to Tony) . . . you have something to gain here, because with you here at least you hear what is being said. One of the things you have to gain from being in the meeting is not being left out. At least you would be present.

Tony: I wouldn't want to be left out. I just want to get out! I don't want to leave my family or nothing like that. I just want to get out! (tearful)

Dr. Zuk: Get out from what?

Tony: From arguments and things like that!

Dr. Zuk: Oh! I see, I see. You want them to stop it? You don't want any part of it. Why?

Tony: Oh, I don't know. She don't seem very happy.

Dr. Zuk: Well, it would be better if you would stop playing "happy" all the time.

Tony: Playing! I ain't playing, mister. I'm just happy all the time . . . sometimes.

Dr. Zuk: Well, you're happy so much that you're breaking in two.

Tony: I may not be happy now, but I'll tell you one thing: when I'm happy, I'm happy. You asked me a few minutes ago if I loved my father and I sure do, brother, I certainly do. I really do, daddy . . . (crying)

(inaudible comments by therapist and father)

Dr. Zuk: I think it's real. (to father) I think he's talking to you. Well, I don't think we have too much more time. What more we gonna' talk about? (to Gilda) What were you trying to do in taking those pills? Why'd you do that?

Gilda: I can't really express it, completely.

Dr. Zuk: Well, what led you to it? What specifically? What led you to take the pills?

Gilda: We had a big argument.

Dr. Zuk: Who's we?

Gilda: Daddy and I.

Dr. Zuk: Oh, I see. About what?

Gilda: Oh, let's not bring that up. It had a lot to do with . . . (inaudible) . . .

Dr. Zuk: Well, now you're talking about the woman? Is that what you're talking about; or other things? Are you talking about the lady?

Gilda: No.

Dr. Zuk: Well, what did it have to do with?

Gilda: We were fighting about money. He was saying what all was wrong with me and I was telling him what all was wrong with him.

Dr. Zuk: And that's what led up to the pills? Is that why you took them?

(pause)

Dr. Zuk: (to mother) What conclusion did you come to? Did you raise a question with your husband about separation?

Mrs. Masters: Yes.

Dr. Zuk: What happened about that? What conclusion? Did you come to a decision about that?

Mrs. Masters: We never come to decisions . . . just . . . as far as really settling anything.

Dr. Zuk: Um hum. What do you mean, you "never come to a decision"?

Mrs. Masters: Well, I mean we never just sit down and talk the problem over and come to a conclusion where we'll both be happy.

Dr. Zuk: Um hum. (to father) How long has it been since you've talked really seriously to your wife about things?

Mr. Masters: In quite a while.

Dr. Zuk: Quite a while because you're away so much.

Mr. Masters: Yeah, and when you do try to talk something over, why, there's no deviation; just a straight line that's got to go the way that she sees it.

Dr. Zuk: . . . the way she wants it, otherwise there's no . . .

(end of excerpt)

POSTSCRIPT

The excerpt from the transcript of the session with the Arkansas family plus the introductory material were prepared in the form in which they appear here during the summer of 1969. During the summer of 1970, partly in preparation for this volume, I asked Dr. Robert F. Shannon, director of the Division of Child-Adolescent Psychiatry at the University of Arkansas Medical School, if he could supply any follow-up material on the family. Late in August, Dr. S. Otho Hesterly, the clinical psychologist in the Division, who had been closely involved in treatment of the family, replied, giving full details of what was known about the family subsequent to my interview. I am very grateful to Dr. Shannon and Dr. Hesterly for their kindness in sharing the information with me, I am including it here in a summary form.

Dr. Hesterly corrected my recollection about the ages of Gilda and Tony—she gave them as 17 and 13, respectively, in 1967. The parents had sought help in March, 1967, as a result of Gilda's suicide gesture: She had swallowed "all the pills in the house." The incident apparently followed a bitter argument with her parents.

The family had been seen in sessions twice prior to my interview. One week afterward the family returned to view the videotape of the session. During the viewing Tony became upset and had to leave the room. The next scheduled session was canceled, the reason being given that Mrs. Masters was ill. Two appointments in June were kept, but only Gilda showed up for an appointment scheduled at the end of June. She said her brother had diarrhea; that her mother had to stay with him; and that her father thought that if his son could not attend, there was not much point in his attending. Gilda expressed her discouragement with her parents; she thought the prospect of involving them in therapy was poor.

Gilda was invited to return for individual therapy sessions in December, 1967, and was seen every other week until June, 1968, when she left for a trip to Europe with a group of teenagers. During this period she was very active: She was attending a local college on scholarship; she had a part-time job; and she was active in church-affiliated affairs. Her parents expressed resentment that she was away so much and not helping with housework. Her father thought she should be working full-time to help with family finances.

Contact with Gilda was lost for about nine months, when in the spring of 1969 she telephoned the clinic to request that a letter describing her psychiatric treatment be sent to a university in Texas. She was applying to the university which had noted her psychiatric treatment and had asked for a report.

Dr. Hesterly concluded that Gilda had improved in her life adjustment but that her family relationships remained confused. My impression that the Masters family was not likely to become engaged in therapy was confirmed, although it occurs to me that the members probably benefited selectively from the few sessions they did have. Gilda made no further suicide gestures and she appeared to be living an active, productive life.

Chapter 11 / A SEVENTH INTERVIEW
WITH A PHILADELPHIA FAMILY

. . . .

PROLOGUE

The Dormeyers, a white, Protestant, upper-lower class family from the Philadelphia vicinity, were referred for therapy because of a 15-year-old son's use of drugs, mainly marijuana, and his unacceptable behavior and achievement at school.

Mrs. Dormeyer had been separated from her husband for a number of years, and during these years had worked to support her three youngest children who lived with her. Hank, the 15 year old, was in junior high school; Brenda, 14, was also in junior high school; and Randy, 11, was in the fourth grade. Brenda was doing average work in school, but Randy was a poor reader and was just barely adequate in other school subjects. Two older sons in the Dormeyer family usually lived with their father, although both boys visited their mother from time to time, and from time to time they also left home to live a hippie-like existence. Mr. and Mrs. Dormeyer split up because, as Mrs. Dormeyer acknowledged, she was not content to let him lead the family in the direction he wanted, and she objected to his harshness with the children. She was an able, intelligent woman who was the manager of a small restaurant.

It was evident from sessions prior to the one reported here that Mrs. Dormeyer was a prime mover in a process by which her sons—her daughter, surprisingly, did not appear to share in the process, or at least shared in it differently—had become skilled in provoking and scorning authority. Also, while she herself struggled to provide a home for her children, and worked regularly and was responsible in her job, she managed to convey to her children and get them to accept her distaste for what she believed was the drudgery of ordinary daily life. She encouraged them to fancy "the good life," and made a sharp distinction between it and the ordinary one most people had to live. She got the message through to her children that she would willingly endure the drudgery for their sake, if only it would allow them to be "free." Of course by this means she obtained great loyalty from her children. They were quick to defend her against criticism from others and reluctant themselves to level criticism at her.

Mrs. Dormeyer often preached moral values to her children, but then confused them in the application of these values in their daily lives. For example, she instructed them that it was their duty to learn from their teachers, but then proceeded to undermine judgments made by the teachers. She told them it was right to be respectful of authorities such as the police, then heaped contempt on the police for actions taken against the children—Hank, specifically. She preached the sanctity of marriage, but acknowledged she had often undermined her husband's authority in the family during the time they were living together.

In sessions Hank usually had a chip-on-the-shoulder attitude, but was not especially sullen and was not an unlikable youngster. Rather one got the impression of a basically gentle adolescent boy, confused by the contradictory demands made upon him by family, school, and peer group. His younger brother, Randy, tried to play the role of the clown in the family, but not very successfully. He did not have Hank's verbal facility or glibness and often blundered. Brenda, in early sessions and in the one reported here, was sexually provocative in her dress but struggled to deny that she was. She pretended to be unaware of what was happening in the family; she "played dumb," but she wasn't.

The seventh session, which is approximately 1½ hours long, had the following progression of issues: Brenda's denial of sexual provocativeness in her mode of dress; Hank's uncertainty as to why he participated in an anti-war demonstration; the acceptance by Hank of Mrs. Dormeyer's equation of independence with freedom from the routine tasks of life; Mrs. Dormeyer's recollection of how she came to make her equation regarding independence and life's routine; the therapist's challenge to the meaning of slang employed by the children; Mrs. Dormeyer's effort to rationalize the inconsistency of her emotional involvement with a man other than her husband with her personal belief in a moral code that proscribed such involvement.

The main thrust of my effort in the seventh session was to disrupt the "loyalty system" that existed among mother, son, and daughter (the youngest son, Randy, was not present in the session due to illness). By the seventh session I had concluded that a major source of pathogenic relating in the Dormeyer family was the mother's equation of independence with being freed from the routine of life's daily chores; her perception of authority, especially emanating from men, as threatening her own independence and that of her children; and her ability to engage the intense loyalty of her children in upholding her definition of independence or personal freedom. I associated Hank's symptoms with this "pathogenic" process.

There are numerous examples of the family's "loyalty system" in the transcript. As the therapist challenges one member, another steps in to defend the member. As the therapist's challenges become too forceful, he himself becomes the subject of verbal assaults by Hank and Brenda. Mrs. Dormeyer does not engage in verbal assaults on the therapist; rather she tries to become his intermediary, his go-between with the children. The therapist takes steps to prevent her access to this role, as it would inevitably be used to block his effort to disrupt the "loyalty system," which would be a first step toward establishing a new "loyalty system" in which the therapist would set the rules.

Throughout the session the therapist points out inconsistencies in the members' behavior. With Hank, it is his presence at an anti-war demonstration in which he did not share the goals of the demonstrators; with Brenda, it is her wearing of a miniskirt that she denied was sexually provocative; with Mrs. Dormeyer, it is the discrepancy between her statements about her moral beliefs and her current involvement emotionally with a man who was not her husband.

From my viewpoint, the moment of highest therapeutic value in the session occurred toward its end, when Mrs. Dormeyer was required by the therapist to make her moral code consistent with her emotion-centered activities, specifically her emotional involvement with another man. The "loyalty system" is sorely tested at this moment. While the children rally to her defense, at the same time they are closely scrutinizing her credibility. During her exposition, Mrs. Dormeyer does something she ordinarily avoids: She acknowledges she feels guilty about her emotional involvement and that she has suffered punishment because of it. I think this is an important admission, not because I believed she *should* feel guilty, but because she thereby confirms to her children that there is an unavoidable relationship between a person's affective life and the moral and ethical codes of society. I think Mrs. Dormeyer has often led her children to believe that there was no necessary relationship between these two dimensions. As one consequence of Mrs. Dormeyer's admission, we find Brenda exhibiting a surprising level of maturity in stating that she intends to learn by her mother's mistakes and that, while she likes boys and wants them to admire her, she is not yet capable of mature love for another person.

By the seventh session I was confident that the family was becoming engaged in the therapy and so was comfortable with probing vigorously some of the family defenses. My provocative, at times somewhat teasing statements—which I was comfortable making and felt quite appropriate in the session—might not have been appropriate if the engagement of the family were not clearly established. Although there are numerous instances of my bluntly confronting members of the family (or of "siding against" the family, to put it another way), there are a number of instances also of sympathy given and praise for conduct under difficult circumstances.

TRANSCRIPT OF SESSION

Dr. Zuk: Good morning.

Nurse: (this is Mrs. Carol Broderick, R.N., who is assisting the therapist in the session) Good morning.

Hank: What's so good about it?

Dr. Zuk: Somebody's missing.

Mrs. Dormeyer: Yes, Randy. He's back with a cold and temperature again.

Dr. Zuk: So he's home suffering

Mrs. Dormeyer: 'Fact I came home last night and I hear this clump, clump, clump. His sneakers are in the drier.

Dr. Zuk: James is here. (referring to noise made by a young patient in the hall)

Nurse: James is here. James is announcing his arrival.

Dr. Zuk: Yes, that's right.

Mrs. Dormeyer: We had a wonderful two weeks.

Nurse: They were telling me they had no fights for two weeks.

Dr. Zuk: No fights for two weeks. That's not always good; but the way you sounded, it sounds good.

Mrs. Dormeyer: I asked him (referring to Hank) last night: "Why is it you can't get up nice in the morning?" I get up and I'm cheerful, and I try to wake you up nice and cheerful so that the day will go well with you. And you always give me a hard time. You say, "That's nothing, mommy, it's no hassle," and we all walk out the door and it's nothing. (laughs) So even that isn't a hang-up any more. So I can holler at them in the morning; it's all right.

Hank: Just don't holler at me.

Mrs. Dormeyer: No hollering; O.K.

Dr. Zuk: Is that what you mean by fights? Mostly in the morning . . . about not getting up? (a change of subject) Hank looks a little different this morning. I don't know whether it's the combination of clothes.

Mrs. Dormeyer: Isn't it pretty.

Dr. Zuk: It is nice.

Hank: Well, thank you.

Brenda: He's beginning to (inaudible) . . .

Mrs. Dormeyer: I told her he's got Pilgrim feet.

Dr. Zuk: What does that mean?

Mrs. Dormeyer: Big silver buckles, like the Pilgrim forefathers. (Brenda laughs)

Hank: It's all mind over matter. It's all in your head.

Dr. Zuk: I think what it is, it is closer to . . .

Brenda: (interrupts) . . . the season.

Dr. Zuk: Yeah, they fit the season, but also, uh, I would have a hard time defining you as a nonconformist today from your clothes.

Hank: (inaudible)

Dr. Zuk: Well, I said I would have a hard time defining you as a nonconformist, or a . . . not that that's so good, but I'm saying that before, it was the only thing you were, uh, were kind of labeling yourself. Somebody who is outside.

Hank: Uh huh.

Dr. Zuk: By your clothes today, I'm not so impressed that you're an outsider.

Mrs. Dormeyer: Don't say that or he'll come back next week with a blue jacket on.

Dr. Zuk: Maybe I shouldn't say that. Of course I'm also wondering about this young lady. (indicating Brenda)

Mrs. Dormeyer: Isn't that a sweet smile?

Dr. Zuk: Have your skirts . . . dresses . . . gotten any longer? Stand up and let me see. It's not gotten too much . . . it can't get too much shorter.

Mrs. Dormeyer: Oh yes it can.

Dr. Zuk: Really, I don't think so any more. (Brenda, who is sitting next to Hank on the couch, leans over to whisper to him)

Mrs. Dormeyer: That's not polite. That's not polite!

Dr. Zuk: What's the private conference about?

Nurse: I think they're planning a strategic defense. (Brenda laughs)

Dr. Zuk: Well all I can say is, you'd better not come in next week wearing a dress like that. (Mrs. Dormeyer laughs)

Nurse: Well, you wouldn't bring in Brenda as a nonconformist either.

Dr. Zuk: No, that's the point, I think, with girls today . . .

Hank: The styles are so way out, it's hard to tell. Thousands of different types girls can wear.

Dr. Zuk: I don't know what it does for them. Does it make them more or less women? I'm not sure. Does this skimpy outfit (indicating Brenda's) make a girl more or less a girl? It's like these clothes they're making now. What do you call them: unisex clothes; have you heard of them?

Hank: Yeah.

Mrs. Dormeyer: Boys and girls, matched up.

Dr. Zuk: They're similar in . . .

Hank: Now in bell-bottoms they put "male" and "female."

Dr. Zuk: Where? Inside you mean?

Hank: Yeah, in the lining. Like the waists on the girls are tapered . . .

Mrs. Dormeyer: Oh, it's just the opposite, Hank. Because when I worked in (information deleted) . . . , I had to wear marine cover-alls, and the hardest place I had to fit was my hips, because the men's hips come down and the girls' . . . (inaudible, a jumble of voices)

Brenda: . . . and girls don't have hips like guys.

Dr. Zuk: Are all the girls wearing these dresses today?

Brenda: No.

Dr. Zuk: Not all of them.

Brenda: Nobody in my school wears them. Only Joan and I have them.

Dr. Zuk: Who?

Brenda: Joan.

Dr. Zuk: Two? Well, but they're that short? The other girls aren't wearing dresses that short, are they?

Hank: Sure.

Brenda: Yeah.

Dr. Zuk: It's just that they don't have that particular dress (referring to the style of dress Brenda is wearing, rather than specifically its length). But the shortness is a standard for girls now?

Brenda: Not really. Girls wear them where they like them.

Hank: It all depends on the individual.

Dr. Zuk: They can wear them longer, but they can't wear them much shorter! They do wear them shorter? *You* like yours short, right?

Brenda: Yeah.

Dr. Zuk: *Your* dresses should be short.

Brenda: No, not really. It all depends on what dress I'm wearing. What type of dress, and what it's for.

Dr. Zuk: Oh yeah?

Brenda: Like, my Easter dress is down to here.

Dr. Zuk: Did you wear your Easter dress the other day?

Brenda: On Easter, yeah.

Dr. Zuk: That one was a little longer, huh?

Brenda: Yeah, it comes down to about here. That's pretty long compared to the others. But you have to consider what it's for.

Dr. Zuk: When would you wear . . . well, you would wear your Easter dress on Easter or on some special occasion.

Brenda: No, I would wear it when I have some place to go, like on some dress-up day in school.

Dr. Zuk: That's not a new dress . . . a new suit. Your Easter suit?

Brenda: Yes.

Mrs. Dormeyer: Sure it is.

Brenda: I bought it all myself.

Dr. Zuk: What did you do on Easter?

Brenda: I went down to the Shore. (referring to New Jersey beach communities)

Dr. Zuk: In the new suit? Where did you go at the Shore?

Brenda: Summers Point.

Dr. Zuk: Did you wear your dress that day?

Brenda: No, I wore a pair of pants.

Mrs. Dormeyer: We went fishin'.

Dr. Zuk: You all went fishing? The three of you?

Mrs. Dormeyer: No, Hank was off by himself to the sit-in demonstration in New York.

Dr. Zuk: You were participating in the sit-in?

Hank: Well, like, I marched some and chanted, and stuff like that. Carried a few signs . . .

Dr. Zuk: What was that actually about?

Hank: Well . . . anti-war demonstration.

Dr. Zuk: And where was it? In Washington Square, or . . .

Hank: No, New York. Through Bryant Park to Central Park.

Dr. Zuk: Bryant Park? Where is Bryant Park?

Hank: 18th Street.

Dr. Zuk: 18th? Oh, that's around, uh . . .

Hank: You know, off Broadway. About two blocks north of Broadway.

Dr. Zuk: Did everybody walk from Bryant Park to Central Park?

Hank: Oh, they walked longer than that. There was fifty thousand people walked there.

Dr. Zuk: What'd you go for?

Hank: Why not? (slight pause) I'm not against the war in
Vietnam.
Brenda: You're not for the way they're going about it.
Dr. Zuk: (to Hank) What is your position?
Hank: Well, like I say, I'm . . . I'm for all-out victory in
Vietnam.
Dr. Zuk: Well, what'd you go up to New York for?
Hank: Why not?
Dr. Zuk: Well, it seems to me the march had the opposite
purpose.
Hank: Like, it's really neat, you know. Like, fifty thousand
people all together on one thing.
Dr. Zuk: But you say you're for an all-out victory in Vietnam.
The march, it seems to me, at least all I've been hearing about it, really
was for a withdrawal.
Hank: So, it's ironic.
Dr. Zuk: It's ironic, but you don't mind that. It's all right.
(laughs)
Hank: Look, I'm not going to get up and say, "Look, you
rotten bastards, you're wrong." I don't know; it depends where a
person stands; the way a person feels about it.
Dr. Zuk: Well, tell me how you feel about it. It's some
puzzlement as to what your view is on Vietnam; and how you
happened to be up there when you don't believe in what they . . .
Hank: Well, a friend of mine was going up, and it was a
Saturday afternoon.
Dr. Zuk: Saturday or Sunday?
Hank: It was a Saturday. Well, we were planning. We were
just going to go around to New York . . . just to go up to New York.
Dr. Zuk: Take a train or bus?
Hank: We thumbed it.
Nurse: Did you stay overnight?
Hank: No, we just stayed for the day. I was surprised at the
time we made. We got three rides all the way up to New York City.
That don't happen all the time.
Dr. Zuk: So you wanted to go with your friend. Now, *he*

wanted to go to the march?

Hank: Uh huh.

Dr. Zuk: So maybe he thinks differently about the war.

Hank: I don't know; the kid's all mixed up in his head. I don't know what the guy thinks.

Dr. Zuk: Well, what did you want to do in New York; just go up and visit for the day? Or go up for the march? Or anything that came along?

Hank: Well, I knew that there was something going on. I know that with fifty thousand people, it couldn't all end up in peace. 'Cuz like, we were on top of this maintenance building, right on the corner of Bryant Park. We were sitting up there watching the marchers go by and, you know, watching cops beat them up. Like, hippies getting into fights with the cops. Like about four hippies jumped on two cops and were beating them up; and so about twenty cops got around the hippies and then start pounding on them.

Dr. Zuk: How did you feel about that?

Hank: I was pretty mad. I was going to call them "dirty pigs."

Dr. Zuk: Who were you mad at? The cops?

Hank: The cops, yeah. Well like, the cops, they had orders not to, you know, interfere; and they were pushing, you know, just getting up against you and pushing the whole crowd back. Really, about four cops getting in a line and just keep pushing, and like, people were getting stepped on, and just packed into a corner. And they didn't like that, so they started fighting back.

Dr. Zuk: Well, what else happened in that march?

Hank: Nothing much. Just different people's opinions . . . news reporters coming up and asking what's going on. I just say, I had no opinion. My friend, he was on the New York radio. He was asked: "Why are you here in New York"? And he said: "I'm here protesting against the war in Vietnam." He started to explain, and some kid came up and said: "My brother was shot in Vietnam."

Dr. Zuk: You still haven't said what you were there for.

Brenda: I think he said it at least four times.

Hank: I think I said it. I just go up to . . .

Dr. Zuk: Not to me you didn't.

Brenda: He went up because he wanted to.

Dr. Zuk: Is that why you went?

Hank: Yeah (sarcastically). No, I wanted to go up and beat some cops. I went there because, like, I had nothing else to do and, like, why not go up to New York for the day? And we went all around in New York, not just the demonstrations. Like, I've never been up to New York by myself before without an adult with me.

Dr. Zuk: This is the first time you've been up with a friend?

Hank: Yeah. I have been up there many times before, like, with my mother and father.

Dr. Zuk: But you were participating in something there, and you didn't, uh . . . What did you believe in? It seems to me . . . I don't know what you believed in. You became a part of something, and yet you didn't have any reason to be there, really. I'm wondering what you became a part of it for. So policemen were there and they got into a fight with some hippies, and this made the policemen wrong, I suppose.

Hank: The cops had strict orders not to interfere.

Dr. Zuk: You thought they had strict orders.

Hank: Well they had.

Dr. Zuk: How do you know?

Hank: Because it was announced on the radio before I went up.

Dr. Zuk: Well, how would the radio people know such things?

Hank: How do I know where they got their information. Like, they wouldn't broadcast it on the news if it wasn't true.

Dr. Zuk: All I'm asking you, Hank, is: What did you believe in when you went up there and got into that big crowd? Do you believe in anything?

Hank: I just told you my point of view.

Dr. Zuk: You just said you happened to be there. I think . . . it may be better to stay away from such a crowd if you don't know what you're doing there.

Mrs. Dormeyer: What are you trying to do, Doctor?

Brenda: He just went along for the ride. I hate it when you start that.

Hank: Get to the point! What are you driving at?

Dr. Zuk: Well, I asked you a question . . . that's what I'm driving at. I didn't quite get what Brenda was saying there. You hate what?

Hank: You just keep rapping at the mouth . . . in circles, until you get us so confused we feel like getting up and taking off.

Dr. Zuk: What did you say, Brenda?

Brenda: I just told you what I said.

Dr. Zuk: No.

Brenda: (laughs) Forget it.

Mrs. Dormeyer: Doctor, am I wrong or are you trying to find out how much anger there is underneath all this talk.

Dr. Zuk: No, I'm not. At the moment I'm just asking what he was doing there.

Brenda: Going along for the ride.

Dr. Zuk: That's an answer. I don't really like that answer, because to me it's just a drifting sort of thing. Whatever you happen to find yourself in is what you take.

Brenda: We don't always like the truth.

Dr. Zuk: Huh?

Brenda: . . . don't always like the truth.

Dr. Zuk: Well see, I don't know what you mean by the truth there.

Mrs. Dormeyer: Do you really want to know why you went up, Hank? I think I know.

Hank: Let's hear it.

Mrs. Dormeyer: (to therapist) May I, or do you want him to bring it out?

Dr. Zuk: Well, he's the one who signed over to you the right to explain.

Hank: She don't have to explain. I told it to you. I went up there just because I wanted to go up for the day.

Mrs. Dormeyer: That isn't true, Hank. You know two more reasons why you went up?

Brenda: Oh come on, don't leave me in suspense; this I want to hear.

Mrs. Dormeyer: Don't you realize what you've been trying to show me the past month? Didn't you go up in spite of my not wanting you to go? First of all, you wanted to assert your independence, and show me that you are quite capable of taking care of yourself. And I think there was an excitement and appeal. And at your age, excitement is something you want to be in on; and there's not much of it in Philadelphia. And I think he's proven something to me, too.

Dr. Zuk: Well, what did it prove?

Mrs. Dormeyer: Well, between his jaunt to Baltimore one week and his jaunt to New York the next, I don't think I look on Hank as a little boy anymore.

Dr. Zuk: You went to Baltimore first? What'd you do there?

Mrs. Dormeyer: He was going to go to Florida for his spring vacation.

Brenda: . . . only got as far as Baltimore. (laughs)

Mrs. Dormeyer: Then he had the good sense to come home . . . which even gives me more faith in him.

Dr. Zuk: How long was he in Baltimore?

Mrs. Dormeyer: Not even overnight. Things got a bit rough for him, and he . . .

Dr. Zuk: His friend and he went down . . .

Nurse: The same buddy you went with?

Hank: Uh huh.

Mrs. Dormeyer: Maybe I'm wrong, but this is just about the right age for it.

Dr. Zuk: Right age for what?

Mrs. Dormeyer: For exploring a little bit. Putting your foot out a little bit.

Dr. Zuk: What happens when you put your foot out?

Mrs. Dormeyer: He's just trying to tell me: "Mom, I'm not a child anymore, and I'm capable of taking care of myself a little bit, and don't treat me like a little boy."

Nurse: Is that true? Does your mother treat you like a little boy?

Mrs. Dormeyer: I may have been overprotective.

Brenda: You got a right to be overprotective.

Mrs. Dormeyer: I don't think so, Brenda. Sometimes an adult, in their own fear for their children, loses sight of the natural facts of life.

Dr. Zuk: The Baltimore thing must have been rather upsetting to you. You were probably very much upset about what he was going to do.

Mrs. Dormeyer: Well, I didn't know he was going.

Dr. Zuk: Oh, you didn't. You found out when he got back?

Mrs. Dormeyer: Uh huh.

Nurse: Neither time?

Mrs. Dormeyer: I suspicioned the second time.

Brenda: Oh, you knew it!

Mrs. Dormeyer: (irritated) I just got through saying I did.

Dr. Zuk: Suspicioned a second time that, uh . . .

Mrs. Dormeyer: . . . that he was going up to New York.

Nurse: (to Hank) Did you leave a note after you left . . . where you were?

Brenda: He leaves his notes with me. (laughs) I relay the message.

Dr. Zuk: Did you relay this message?

Brenda: (to the therapist, teasingly) Go away!

Dr. Zuk: What did you say?

Brenda: "Mom, I think Hank went up to New York for the weekend."

Dr. Zuk: What did you say about the Florida trip?

Brenda: Oh, he told us about that himself.

Dr. Zuk: Oh, he told you in advance?

Brenda: No, when he came back.

Hank: I didn't even know I was going to Florida. I was downtown all week. I spent the weekend in town and I met a friend of mine in town, and we figured we was going to Washington, D.C., and explore the Capitol. 'Cuz like, I never been down there. I've been down there once when I was, like, three or four years old.

Mrs. Dormeyer: Next time you want to go, let me give you a few dollars for eating money, all right?

Hank: And so we started to talking about things, and decided to go to Florida.

Brenda: Florida popped up!

Dr. Zuk: Why didn't you go to the moon?

Hank: If I had a spaceship, I'd go.

Dr. Zuk: Do you really need one?

Hank: I don't know; maybe if I'd "trip" a couple of times, I'd fly there.

Dr. Zuk: That's right.

Hank: What are you trying to do, put me back on drugs?

Dr. Zuk: I didn't say that, did I? (Brenda laughs)

Mrs. Dormeyer: Nobody can talk you into anything, Hank. It's your own decision.

Dr. Zuk: All I'm saying, Hank, is that you have a tremendous desire for accomplishment, but you're not prepared for it. So what are you trying for? You're just going to lose, you know. (Hank laughs)

Brenda: (to Hank) Do you agree with him? No.

Hank: What gives you the idea I won't accomplish what I . . .

Dr. Zuk: You know, I can really see you on some flat plateau, and maybe you're up on a hill and, like the kids make these things . . . guns with rubber bands . . . you attach a rubber band to yourself and off you go! (Mrs. Dormeyer laughs) What do you get out of it? You get a sharp rap in the rear end, but that's about all. You wouldn't get anywhere. Not to the moon. (Mrs. Dormeyer laughs again)

Hank: (laughing) Tell me more; I want to hear this; you interest me.

Dr. Zuk: That's the most distressing thing. You have these fantastic dreams about accomplishment. Who do you want to be: the President, or a general, or God, or what?

Hank: I was thinking about being a dictator. They're pretty neat dudes.

Mrs. Dormeyer: (to therapist, laughing) You got me so interested I burnt my uniform, doggone it, anyway! I can't figure out what you're trying to get at here.

Dr. Zuk: You burnt your uniform?

Mrs. Dormeyer: I burnt my uniform.

Dr. Zuk: Oh, you burnt it. I thought you said at first you *brought* it. Well, with kids it's the worst thing in the world for them. In a way, of course, it's a wonderful thing too. Because we have to have people feel that they are important, and that they have done things in the world. But at each step he sort of trips himself up. And if you trip yourself too many times, of course, you never make anything.

Brenda: (sarcastically) You've lost us.

Dr. Zuk: And in a way, also, what does he need those things for? Who built those things up in his mind? Wonder who did that? (Brenda laughs)

Mrs. Dormeyer: Well, I don't know, Doctor. I don't think anything did it. All you hear on radio now is, "Take your trip now, have a wonderful vacation, and pay later."

Dr. Zuk: I never thought of that. I'm very glad you brought that up, because I think that *is* a dangerous thing.

Mrs. Dormeyer: They're just making everything so glamorous and beautiful.

Dr. Zuk: "Take your trip now and pay later in easy installments." Which is fine for those who are qualified to do it, but is a terrible temptation to those who aren't.

Mrs. Dormeyer: It doesn't tempt me. It's too hard to pay back. (laughs)

Dr. Zuk: You see, Hank, in a sense all kids . . . (to Mrs. Dormeyer) and he's still a kid . . . are subject to that kind of temptation.

Mrs. Dormeyer: Especially if they have a romantic nature.

Dr. Zuk: Yeah, and he does.

Brenda: "Romeo, Romeo, wherefore art thou?"

Dr. Zuk: The glamor of the airplane going off into the clouds is really too much, I'm sure. And all those TV pictures now at Fort Lauderdale, down in Florida, with all those pictures . . .

Hank: Yeah, with all them chicks walking down the beach.

Dr. Zuk: Yeah, that's almost too much to take.

Mrs. Dormeyer: And added to that, when the children were young we used to take them to see everything . . . educational places, beautiful places and, you know . . . and another thing, his oldest brother is now in Los Angeles, California. He started out for Florida and got as far as Daytona Beach. They don't like hippies down there, so he lit out of Florida before he got into trouble. He's already paid one 25 dollar fine.

Dr. Zuk: (referring to the older son) Bill? And he's a hippie?

Mrs. Dormeyer: Not really. Half a hippie.

Brenda: He's hip but he's not a hippie.

Dr. Zuk: He's in Los Angeles now? How do you know? Did you get a call from him?

Mrs. Dormeyer: Yes, he's been staying with a step-brother. They called last night.

Dr. Zuk: How old is Bill?

Mrs. Dormeyer: He'll be 19 in July. He wanted to go to this school, but apparently this school is not as legitimate as it should be.

Dr. Zuk: What kind of school is it?

Mrs. Dormeyer: Computer programming, in Upper Darby. He went to work as an orderly. When Bill gets up at 4 o'clock in the morning to go to work, he's very sincere. And he got all his money together to go to this school. And they cancelled the class but they still wanted his money. And from what I can gather now, their phone has been disconnected . . . so he's out his 50 dollars. So he said, "Well, mom, the army will have me next October." And he got the idea he wanted to see some of the country; and so I said, "Go ahead, see it."

Dr. Zuk: You see, Mrs. Dormeyer, I think you play a role in this. And you do inflate their dreams. You're in it.

Mrs. Dormeyer: Sure I'm in it. I'm all for it.

Dr. Zuk: What do you mean: you're all for it?

Mrs. Dormeyer: I want my children to enjoy life and taste it all.

Dr. Zuk: You're wrong. You're wrong. Because this boy has such inflated dreams for a boy his age that he doesn't know what to do with . . . he's bound to get into trouble. It's not so much with the law that I'm thinking of. It's just that he'll never be happy. He'll never be content. He'll never go in some kind of orderly path toward a goal. He'll never be a man if he continues in this path.

Hank: Oh, I'm 15 years old! Come on! What are you trying to do to me?

Dr. Zuk: Well, I want you to be a man someday.

Hank: Oh, well, thank you.

Dr. Zuk: That's what's required, you know. If he never sticks to anything; when there are so many . . . so many desires that have been planted in his mind. How can he stick to anything? Get anywhere? Do anything? How can anybody depend on him?

Brenda: You're wrong.

Dr. Zuk: They can't. You shouldn't take such pride in your . . .

Mrs. Dormeyer: I'm not taking pride in his trips.

Dr. Zuk: Well, I thought you were taking pride in that; and I thought maybe you shouldn't be.

Mrs. Dormeyer: No, no, the thing I'm taking pride in is, more or less, my realization of the way Hank was trying to show me that he is growing up; he is capable of taking care of himself.

Dr. Zuk: How did he do that, though? What are you talking about?

Mrs. Dormeyer: (sighing) He did go two places.

Dr. Zuk: You're talking about Hank, and I'm talking about you. Do you realize you've been a mischief-maker in this youngster's thinking?

Hank: (exasperated) Oh, God!

Mrs. Dormeyer: If I did so, it was deliberate from my own experience. Because I've always tried to teach my children, first of all, to get your education, get your job, and then . . .

Dr. Zuk: I'm telling you that your pride in his inflated dreamlike life . . .

Mrs. Dormeyer: Doctor, I don't know any boy that hasn't taken off at the age of 15 or 16 to try to be on their own.

Dr. Zuk: That's not what I'm talking about. You have such pride in his daydreaming capacity.

Hank: When did you establish the fact that I'm a wild daydreamer? And that I got all kinds of crazy notions in my head?

Brenda: Every kid wants to take a bite out of each and every cloud. I think you're nuts!

Mrs. Dormeyer: Brenda, that's not polite!

Brenda: Every kid has dreams. I want to do what Hank does, but I'm a girl and I can't do it . . .

Dr. Zuk: (commenting on Brenda's eyes being fixed on her mother) What are you looking at her for? Why aren't you looking at me?

Brenda: She's giving me this dirty look.

Mrs. Dormeyer: No, I'm not. I wasn't giving you a dirty look, honey.

Brenda: (to therapist) You're downing us for being kids.

Dr. Zuk: I'm what?

Brenda: Downing. Every kid has a wild dream.

Hank: He's trying to tell us we're making ourselves into somebody; we won't accomplish what we're looking for in life. I don't even know what we're looking for!

Mrs. Dormeyer: (inaudible) ... about a man sowing his wild oats before he settles down. You know, today's children are educated to a point they've got their families buffaloed as far as material knowledge is concerned. We've fed them so darn many vitamins that they're practically men before they're 15 and their bodies build up. Now we're dealing with an emotional need that takes a little bit longer to catch up with the other two.

Dr. Zuk: Is it his or yours that we're dealing with?

Mrs. Dormeyer: We're all together in this.

Dr. Zuk: That's right. That's why you're here. And that's why you should be here. But I'm talking about *your* emotional needs, not so much his at this time; we'll get to his. What is your emotional need? Why do you take the position on your son ... basically, you're saying that he won't accomplish anything. That's the only way I can understand what you are really doing. Intentionally or otherwise, I don't know. And you acknowledge it. You say, "Let them sow wild oats." And you say, "He has to strike off on his own." Well, that is not what is happening, though. It's not what happened to the other kids either.

Mrs. Dormeyer: I could be wrong, Doctor ...

Dr. Zuk: (interrupting, referring to his previous statement) You don't believe that, yet.

Mrs. Dormeyer: Oh, don't say that, please. It's difficult to find words to explain. When I was 15, as a punishment for not coming home, I was told to ... I was told to go to live with my step-father.

Dr. Zuk: As a punishment for ... would you say that again, please?

Mrs. Dormeyer: The cause isn't important. It's just the reaction. My grandfather told me to pack my bag and go to my step-father's to live. I packed my bags and I was gone for four months.

Dr. Zuk: How old were you?

Mrs. Dormeyer: Fifteen. But I was a mature 15. And I worked and I earned my way all the way down to Florida and back again. I traveled with my family to New York, to Maine, for summer vacations. I grew up very fast, physically, maybe because I was raised by grandparents. But there is nobody more settled down to a job that needs to be done than I am.

Dr. Zuk: I believe it.

Mrs. Dormeyer: I looked forward to my vacations; to traveling. I love this world and I want to see it. And I want my children to see all the beauty that's in it.

Dr. Zuk: Yeah, but, uh . . . you can't be entirely right.

Mrs. Dormeyer: Is anything ever entirely right?

Dr. Zuk: Well, but what you are doing is like saying to me that the only time one really lives is vacation time. You say that you are doing your work, and that you're responsible at work, and I believe that. But I believe that you do not consider that being alive.

Mrs. Dormeyer: I enjoy my work.

Dr. Zuk: That may be true. But from what you're doing, and what has happened with your children and yourself, there are some wild daydreams in your thinking . . . just wild. And the children pick them up; and they have their own, of course. But you're all together in that. You're a daydreamer! And you justify it by saying what a hard life you've had. It has been hard. But how is this boy and this girl . . . 15 years and 13 years . . . how are they going to grow up? Now you get a telephone call from your oldest boy. You don't know what he's doing. You have no idea of what he's up to. The other boy, Glen: you know what he's doing? Probably not.

Mrs. Dormeyer: Oh yes, I think I do.

Dr. Zuk: But in both those boys there is an aimlessness and lack of . . . that's what I asked before. (to Hank) You went up to New York for a sit-in. What'd you do it for? What is your position? What were you doing there? (to Mrs. Dormeyer) He's very resentful because somebody asked him why he participated.

Mrs. Dormeyer: Perhaps because he doesn't know how to explain it.

Dr. Zuk: I understood that. They're children. How does Hank grow up to be a man? Which means that in his life people will look to him for guidance; he must earn a living; he must take some position in the community. This is maleness, manliness; whether he likes it or not . . . that's life.

Mrs. Dormeyer: Nobody took more of an interest in their community than I did.

Dr. Zuk: Well, I'm talking about him. I'm talking about the two older boys. How are these boys to play the roles of men in our society? Do you have understanding of that need?

Mrs. Dormeyer: When there is somebody that needs us, Doctor, when we're really needed, or when we really give our love to somebody and we're needed . . . at least within me and I'm quite sure within an awful lot of other human beings . . . everything that we've learned, everything that we've been taught, our real values come to the fore, and that's when we settle down.

Dr. Zuk: All right. I think you said something that's true. So you have not felt that way.

Mrs. Dormeyer: No. I don't want my children to grow up to be vegetables. Working constantly; just existing. There's too much to be seen and felt and heard. I want them to open their eyes and know what's there.

Dr. Zuk: Is it true that this is what's happening to you? Can you really say that?

Mrs. Dormeyer: This is where I admit to being just a little bit confused myself.

Dr. Zuk: I can go along with you if this is really the outcome of your effort, but I don't think it is. I think what you're doing is, you're communicating and they're accepting. You are powerful in the family and influencing all the children. They look to you for leadership. And they're not growing up. You're saying that the reason for the whole thing is that you've never been needed. And so that gets you off the hook.

Mrs. Dormeyer: No, I'm not talking about me. When the time came and the need was there, there weren't any fancy dreams.

Dr. Zuk: Who needs you?

Mrs. Dormeyer: Who needs me? In my lifetime, a few people. My husband . . .

Dr. Zuk: Did you care whether he needed you or not?

Mrs. Dormeyer: Certainly I cared. Too much. I wasn't wise enough to allow him to keep the reins. He took my trying to help him and my pioneer spirit for competition, which it wasn't.

Dr. Zuk: But it was.

Mrs. Dormeyer: Not really.

Dr. Zuk: What were you trying to do?

Mrs. Dormeyer: Oh, I was trying to have a nice, normal, fairly successful family, so that we could enjoy the better things in life, because I never had . . . perhaps I wanted too much.

Dr. Zuk: I recall your ´saying you had great respect for your grandfather. When he told you to get out of the house . . . roughly . . . What was it again?

Mrs. Dormeyer: He told me to go live with my step-father.

Dr. Zuk: Who you did not like at all.

Mrs. Dormeyer: Uh huh.

Dr. Zuk: You hated this man.

Mrs. Dormeyer: Uh huh.

Dr. Zuk: Wasn't that a very unfair thing to do? ·

Hank: Maybe so, but there it was.

Mrs. Dormeyer: People aren't always fair. But at that time I didn't know it. But looking back now, I do. He was trying to punish me. And they came down two hours later to bring me back home, but it was too late.

Dr. Zuk: You were gone how many months?

Mrs. Dormeyer: Almost four months . . . the whole summer.

Dr. Zuk: Well, that . . . I don't know how you felt about it . . . I'm asking you . . . But it seems to me, particularly with the amount of love and respect you had for him . . .

Mrs. Dormeyer: I also had a deep-rooted inferiority complex . . . thinking they just tolerated me. I always felt that I was a little bit of a burden to them.

Dr. Zuk: But I was thinking that this man you said . . . the only person, the only male you ever respected . . . How could you respect a man who was so, uh, cruel? I mean, for really a little thing . . .

Mrs. Dormeyer: I, in my life, have said things that I didn't mean. Like telling Hank to "Go live with your father"; and I don't mean it.

Dr. Zuk: But at the time you obviously did react to it very strongly because you took off. Did anybody know where you were during that time? And you were where: Florida?

Mrs. Dormeyer: I went from Boston to Baltimore, to Washington . . .

Dr. Zuk: Without money. Did you have any money?

Mrs. Dormeyer: I had about 20 some odd dollars. But I worked.

Dr. Zuk: You worked. Must have been a very tough time.

Mrs. Dormeyer: No, I had a ball. Sorry!

Dr. Zuk: How old were you?

Mrs. Dormeyer: Uh, 15. I looked like I was 18.

Dr. Zuk: And you had a ball. Three, four months. What kind of a ball was it?

Mrs. Dormeyer: Well, I was a professional dancer.

Dr. Zuk: What kind of professional dancing?

Mrs. Dormeyer: Tap, acrobatic, ballet.

Dr. Zuk: That's still hard for a 15-year-old girl.

Mrs. Dormeyer: No, I had no trouble whatsoever. I looked like I was 18. I'm sorry to say so, but I had a wonderful time! Even in front of the children. I don't want to make it look so glorified to them that they go away for four months.

Dr. Zuk: What I'm concerned about is the way they're getting that from you in a steady diet.

Mrs. Dormeyer: If I had my way, I'd teach my children to get an education in a field where they could just go and explore everything.

Dr. Zuk: That's very admirable.

Mrs. Dormeyer: I don't know if it's admirable or not; but that's the way I feel.

Dr. Zuk: I think it's admirable, and I think you really want to do a good job. I think you really do; I'm not challenging that at all. I'm just saying you don't have the means, and never had the means to accomplish that; that the tools to do it are not at your disposal. You yourself do not have the confidence in yourself. And although today . . . I don't question for a moment that you're an able person . . . very able. It seems to me that some of the means are still lacking. And also, you've communicated those daydreams to them. So I'm concerned how they are to avoid the dangerous aspect of too much daydreaming.

Mrs. Dormeyer: You know, my grandfather used to say that there's nothing wrong with a daydream, so long as you build a foundation.

Dr. Zuk: Yeah. All right, I agree with that.

Mrs. Dormeyer: I'll give them the daydreams, and if they're good enough they'll build the foundation and reach them.

Dr. Zuk: All right, but I . . . you've already got to evaluate what's happened. You know, it probably sounds like I'm blaming you, but, uh . . .

Mrs. Dormeyer: You know, my biggest mistake, Doctor, is in the way I was raised. The woman is a complement to a man . . . she's secondary. And I believed it. So the best I could do with my talents is to try to help my husband. We built up a good business; we really did, the two of us. And, uh, it could have been quite successful if this hadn't happened.

(the next two comments of Brenda and Mrs. Dormeyer are deleted in order to preserve anonymity)

Dr. Zuk: You need more help, though. And I'm not sure you're willing to do that, because you are cautious of anybody else helping you. I think that still is a requirement for you, that you . . . You have worked hard, no question in my mind, to establish yourself as a person in your own right. I think you have. But you need help with these children and, uh, yourself too. Life requires dreaming, yes, and imagination, and wanting things. It's not wrong at all; it's what should be. But, uh, it can lead astray, because unless there is some anchor there . . .

Mrs. Dormeyer: I tried to make the home the anchor. And that's why I panicked so much when all this started within the home. The anchor seemed to be slipping.

Dr. Zuk: Yeah, well, that's true.

Mrs. Dormeyer: Life is such a wonderful thing, Hank, and I know it. Like the Doctor said, and I don't know how to communicate it to you: get your education; stay in one spot and grow; incubate!

Hank: Would you mind if I find out where I want to stay first? Please, man, like, don't push me!

Mrs. Dormeyer: I'm not pushing.

Hank: Like, this dude is. He's trying to say, "Yah, stay where you're at, man. Keep it cool."

Dr. Zuk: You don't know what I'm saying.

Hank: You're saying I got a wild imagination; and I keep getting dreams; and I have no foundation.

Dr. Zuk: For one thing, you just have to listen a bit more, and be willing to listen.

Hank: Would you state a point: where you're trying to push at?

Dr. Zuk: I just stated one point: that I wish you would listen with both ears to somebody beside your mother.

Hank: All right, I'm listening.

Dr. Zuk: Well good, then I'll have more time to . . .

Hank: Is somebody else here? (he is referring to another family scheduled for the next session)

Dr. Zuk: Yes.

Mrs. Dormeyer: Oh, darn it.

Hank: I feel like hassling with you some more.

Dr. Zuk: We have two or three more minutes. The other family was due but is not here. But I do have another meeting shortly, so we have to finish up the session. (referring to the fact that in today's session, Hank and Brenda have been seated next to one another, which is unusual) I was surprised to see you both so close together.

Brenda: He's my boyfriend.

Dr. Zuk: Six weeks ago I didn't think you could stand it. And I wasn't sure vice versa.

Hank: Whatever gave you that impression?

Mrs. Dormeyer: (changing the subject) Did you ever see a pure psychedelic room?

Dr. Zuk: Yes, I have.

Mrs. Dormeyer: You haven't until you've seen Hank's room. (laughs) I even enjoy going in there at night. He turns the lights off and everything sparkles. (laughs again)

Brenda: He has strobe lights . . . black lights.

Hank: Yeah, I built my own strobe light.

Brenda: He built his own stereo.

Dr. Zuk: That's good.

Brenda: He should be a mechanic.

Hank: Electrician.

Brenda: Yeah, electrician. I'm going to be a scientist.

Mrs. Dormeyer: (to Hank) If you want to go into electrics, go into *electronics.*

Nurse: I imagine he is very creative.

Brenda: He is. (to therapist) You're telling us we're always dreaming. Being an electrician, that's not such a big dream. I want to be a scientist.

Hank: I don't want to be an electrician.

Brenda: Yes you do; shut up. I want to be a scientist; that's not a very big dream.

Dr. Zuk: I don't know about that.

Brenda: Last time I talked to you, you said, like, I might think guys run after girls for sex and . . . But I don't know; I don't think I'm stupid, because if I was stupid . . . I'm taking college prep, and you've got to be smart to take that. So I don't think I'm stupid.

Dr. Zuk: I didn't say that you were.

Brenda: (inaudible)

Nurse: Yeah, but you were the one that sat in here and said, "I think I'm stupid."

Dr. Zuk: Uh huh.

Brenda: Now, I know I'm intelligent . . . (inaudible) People are nuts; sometimes they expect too much from you.

Nurse: Oh well, that's different. That makes sense.

Brenda: I'm great; I'm taking algebra.

Hank: (inaudible at first) . . . they're expecting too much from you.

Nurse: Is it hard to have people thinking you're older than you are?

Hank: No, I accept it. In fact, I like it, 'cuz I'm accepted with older people. It's the people in school that expect academic work from you; like, wow . . . I don't know, it's hard to keep up with the world.

Brenda: Like, you know how people are: saying us kids grow up too fast, and we're nonconformist, and we're . . . But in school, like my mom said, they teach us a lot more material than you learned when you were young. They're begging for our opinions. They're dragging it out of us. And, like, there is much more expected of us now than was expected of you. And you are always telling us, "Try and stay young." Well, it's not that easy any more, because . . .

Dr. Zuk: Who was telling you that?

Brenda: My mother. All grownups are saying, "Grow up in your own time."

Dr. Zuk: That's right, she is saying that. In effect saying, "Stay young."

Mrs. Dormeyer: It's such a nice time in their life.

Dr. Zuk: I'm not so sure. That's not what they're saying.

Nurse: They're saying, "It's a hard time."

Mrs. Dormeyer: Parents try to hold their children down to be young; and the schools are pulling them ahead. Parents and schools are going to have to get together.

Dr. Zuk: You sell them on being young.

Brenda: No she doesn't. You're wrong.

Nurse: You just said it.

Brenda: My mom's pretty understanding with it. You know, she tried to understand. You know, compromise. But, like, we're mature physically, maybe more so than we were before . . . intelligently . . . but mostly, we're just not ready for it. Nothing is going to speed that up.

Dr. Zuk: When will you be ready emotionally?

Brenda: When I'm ready, I'll tell you. I don't know.

Dr. Zuk: I think your mother does oversell you on staying young.

Hank: No, I don't think so.

Brenda: I don't think so.

Dr. Zuk: Seems that way to me. She just said it, in a way. She said that this is the best part of life.

Brenda: It is.

Dr. Zuk: But that's not what you're saying, is it?

Brenda: Yes!

Dr. Zuk: Is it the best time in life? How do you know? How could you possibly know?

Brenda: Because I'm living in it.

Hank: We haven't been to where you're at. Well, what do you think? What's your opinion?

Dr. Zuk: About what?

Hank: When was the best time of your life? What was the best age? When did you enjoy life the most?

Dr. Zuk: Not when I was your age.

Hank: Well, when was it?

Dr. Zuk: Now.

Hank: Well, I don't know where you think it's at. I couldn't picture it. I can't understand how you're trying to impress upon us . . .

Dr. Zuk: If I reached my age and I felt that the best thing in the world was to be your age, that would make me very unhappy. 'Course, it isn't true either. It isn't true that the best time of life is your age.

Hank: I don't think so. I'm thoroughly enjoying it.

Mrs. Dormeyer: I was having a ball when I was 15.

Dr. Zuk: (teasingly) You is?

Hank: I is. I am. If where you're at now is great, that would make us very unhappy.

Dr. Zuk: What do you mean, "Great"? What do you know about greatness to begin with? You're using words that don't mean a damn thing. You're using your language, which means something at this time to you. To me it doesn't mean very much.

Hank: Well, like, the way you're rapping right now, it's like circles, you know. I can't . . .

Dr. Zuk: I'm just telling you about your language. You're using words that I don't think are very appropriate for my understanding. The word "great" means everything to you. It doesn't mean anything to me.

Hank: What do you mean?

Dr. Zuk: Your mother says, "To have a ball." I don't know what that means, really.

Hank: You never had a ball? You never really enjoyed yourself?

Dr. Zuk: Oh, yes!

Hank: Well, then, that's where it's at. That's where it is.

Mrs. Dormeyer: I learned the vernacular of use, just so I could communicate.

Dr. Zuk: "Great" seems to me to encompass so much more than . . .

Hank: "Great" don't mean anything to me. "Everything" means everything to me.

Dr. Zuk: . . . than any one experience can be. You're building a terrific amount into any one expression. But we're getting too abstract now.

Hank: I think "great" means the ultimate, you know.

Dr. Zuk: What's that? How can you really know?

Brenda: Well, maybe it's our ultimate of happiness.

Dr. Zuk: What is that?

Hank: A good time; the best time.

Dr. Zuk: A good time is the ultimate?

Hank: No, the best time is the ultimate.

Dr. Zuk: What's the matter, you crazy or something? A *good* time is the ultimate?

Hank: Oh, that's not what I'm saying. I'm saying the best time that we have is "great."

Dr. Zuk: The *best* time you have is "great"? What is the ultimate?

Hank: What does that mean?

Dr. Zuk: Yeah. What does that have to do with a "good" time, the "best" time, and a "great" time?

Brenda: What does "ultimate" mean?

Hank: The highest.

Brenda: Oh, the supreme.

Hank: (to therapist) Would you say it again?

Dr. Zuk: Well, I don't recall it very well. I'm telling you, though, that your language slips around like, uh . . .

Hank: Putty?

Dr. Zuk: . . . a slippery pig, or something. You can't get hold of it.

Brenda: 'Cuz you don't know it. That's the trouble with
grownups today. We use language they don't know.
Dr. Zuk: Our experience is different than yours.
Brenda: Like, I don't know. One time I told my mom, "I made
out." She almost fainted.
Nurse: I dig your language, but I'm not with you either.
You're contradicting yourself everytime you . . .
Hank: Maybe I'm insane. (laughs)
Nurse: No. I think you're searching.
Brenda: Aren't all people?
Nurse: Yeah, always. All your life. Which makes you no
different from grownups. I think when you fight so hard with Dr. Zuk,
you're fighting yourself.
Brenda: We're having a hard time communicating. Like . . .
Nurse: No, no; when you're talking to him, I see you
struggling with yourself. You're throwing the words at him, but it's
really your own confusion that's coming out. He knows what you're
saying.
Mrs. Dormeyer: I've been thinking about it and thinking about it. And
you're right: maybe I'm wrong in what I base it on. But I've always
felt . . . my grandfather gave me a strong moral background to live up
to; which is wonderful because many, many times in the face of
temptation this has kept me out of trouble. At the point where I wasn't
at the age of reason; or I couldn't decide, "Well, I'm going to do this,"
and face the consequences; or I didn't have enough strength to face
what would be brought out of it. And I think I tried to instill this into
my children, too. Because all the moral codes are only based on things
that are natural with life. Well, for instance, take the Ten Commandments. If you live by them you live a nice, healthy, clean life, and you
don't have too many problems that you create for yourself. If you
break them, then you cause trouble for yourself; and a lot of it is
within your own psychological makeup. Not because society is going to
blast you for it . . . they may not even know about it . . . but your own
conscience, or whatever it is, it does bother you. And, like, I've tried to
teach Brenda as part of her moral makeup, that in adultery, or anything
like that, there's going to come a day in your life when if you really fall

in love, there's a part of you you want to give. And I've experienced it; where you just almost want to become one with the person, completely. And you feel as though ... what's the word? ... there can't be any adhesion unless the two things are pure. Are you following what I'm trying to say? Love is the most unexplainable thing in the world; but I do know one thing about it, sweetheart: when you've got it to give and it's given to you, there's nothing more powerful in this world. You try and find something nice and clean and pretty to give.

Dr. Zuk: You're jumping into stories, and I don't follow you.

Brenda: We follow her.

Hank: That's not what's important. We're listening.

Dr. Zuk: You sure you understand what she's saying?

Brenda: Positive. She means you want to be clean and pure and a virgin; and you want to give your virginity to a husband if you really love him. If you're not a virgin, it's just an empty, rotten feeling.

Mrs. Dormeyer: No, it's not rotten, honey, it's not rotten.

Brenda: It's bad.

Mrs. Dormeyer: Even though, let's say, as much as I love John now (referring to the man, not her husband, with whom she is emotionally involved at the present time) ... I've been married before.

Dr. Zuk: Is this the man you were talking about when you were talking about your love for a man?

Mrs. Dormeyer: John. I loved their father, but it wasn't the same kind of complete love.

Dr. Zuk: But you have found this with John?

Mrs. Dormeyer: Uh huh.

Dr. Zuk: All right, go ahead. Somebody ... I guess it was Brenda ... said she thought she knew what you were meaning. And I don't know whether she did or not.

Brenda: I'm not sure either.

Dr. Zuk: Legally you're still married, are you not?

Mrs. Dormeyer: Yes, sir.

Dr. Zuk: So, in a sense, you say you're in love with a man, and you're married to another man, right? How do you ...

Mrs. Dormeyer: ... explain that to the children? Well, the children know that I did everything I could to get my freedom.

Dr. Zuk: All right. But what she reported to you after your discussion was that she had to remain a virgin and pure and then that's the only time that she can, number one, be in love with a man; and that's the only time she can have sex with any man.

Mrs. Dormeyer: No, no . . .

Dr. Zuk: Well, better start to clear it up. You'd better clear it up with her. Because you're not very consistent.

Mrs. Dormeyer: Yes I am. I am in my own head, but perhaps my words aren't.

Brenda: But I feel that nobody is going to touch me or put their hands on my body, or pet with me until I'm married. That's how I feel.

Dr. Zuk: What was your mother saying?

Brenda: My mother was saying, like, "If you let other people touch your body . . . "

Hank: If you keep going around in free-love, man, and comes the time when you really dig someone, you know . . .

Brenda: I know what she means, but it's so hard to put into words.

Dr. Zuk: (to Mrs. Dormeyer) Would you make some effort to tell her what you meant? Exactly what you meant?

Mrs. Dormeyer: That by being promiscuous and, as you say, free-love, or to indulge in love-making lightly . . .

Brenda: Like Cathy? (referring to a girl friend)

Hank: No, like . . .

Dr. Zuk: (to Mrs. Dormeyer) Would you try, in a way consistent with your experience, to tell her what you meant? It should be consistent with your own experience in life. What you meant about men, love-making? Would you make some effort to do that? We don't have too much time, and I do want to hear what you say here.

Mrs. Dormeyer: (sighs) Well, you know how I feel about the Commandments being the natural laws of God. And they have meaning to us and purpose.

Brenda: Uh huh.

Mrs. Dormeyer: I was married and you children were born. I loved your father, but I since found out that there is another love, another kind of love, and it's deeper for me, perhaps because I'm older or perhaps because it came at a time in my life when I needed it so very badly. But whatever it is, it's as you put it, Hank: great, the ultimate. For me now . . . I don't say that it can happen again, I don't know . . . but as far as my experience is concerned, it's now. (a sentence is omitted here to preserve anonymity) I'm 43; I was 39 when I met John. And by the time you're 39, you have experience in life. What I'm doing is not correct by the standards of society. Everybody can rationalize and make things right in their own mind, because that's the way they want it. But deep in my heart, honey, what I am doing is wrong.

Brenda: Not to me.

Mrs. Dormeyer: I beg your pardon it's wrong. And I'll pay for it. This is the difference: I'm willing to pay for it. But when you're young, the price is much too high.

Brenda: I don't think it's wrong.

Mrs. Dormeyer: It is wrong. The way I was raised, what I am doing is wrong. And I pay for it; every day I pay for it.

Hank: Where did you get those thoughts in your head, that you put there by yourself! Just sit down and think about things; not listening to what other people tell you.

Mrs. Dormeyer: Honey, I do. This is what I feel. I am convinced because things have worked out that way. It is not just something that's written.

Dr. Zuk: Brenda, you feel that what your mother is doing is not wrong?

Brenda: No; if you love somebody. Nothing is wrong about love; I don't care how you put it or what you say about it.

Dr. Zuk: Hank, what do you think about it?

Hank: I don't have nothing to say about it.

Mrs. Dormeyer: I know Hank was very much ashamed of me in the beginning.

Dr. Zuk: Well, he's caught between . . . hard things to resolve.

Mrs. Dormeyer: And the only thing I hope is, when they become older and they understand life a little better, then they could understand why it could happen that way.

Dr. Zuk: Well, could you forgive yourself for what you are doing?

Brenda: She's not doing anything wrong! Not really!

Mrs. Dormeyer: To me it is, honey.

Dr. Zuk: In her mind she is.

Brenda: If she was really divorced . . . I mean she tried, God knows it, and really . . . she doesn't love my father. She has no inner feeling for him. Mentally and physically she's divorced from him. And I'm sure God understands. And if she loves John, I'm sure she'd marry him. Maybe she doesn't want to, but I think she loves him and . . . I don't know . . . if you really love someone, I don't see anything wrong with it.

Mrs. Dormeyer: That frightens me at your age.

Dr. Zuk: "That frightens you at her age?" What do you mean by that?

Mrs. Dormeyer: Well, you know how easily the human mind can justify its actions.

Dr. Zuk: Yes.

Mrs. Dormeyer: I'm afraid that too early in life she might justify the act . . . if she thinks she's in love.

Brenda: I know now that I'm not capable of loving anybody. In certain ways, but not in the way of a man and woman. I'm not emotionally mature enough for it. And like, uh, I've liked a boy really a lot and, like, got hung-up on him, but I know that that's not really love. It's just the feeling of having a guy around who cares. But I'm sure when I feel love, I'll know what love is, because I'm pretty wise and understanding, and I think I understand nature quite a bit for my age. But now I know for a fact that I'm not capable of loving any man, and I'm sure I won't be until at least 20 because, I don't know, I can't explain it good: but I guess I've learned by my mother's mistakes, sort of.

Dr. Zuk: Hank, what do you think?

Hank: I don't know what I want to say about that.

Mrs. Dormeyer: Does it bother you, Hank?

Hank: No, no.

Mrs. Dormeyer: Honestly?

Hank: Sure.

Dr. Zuk: (to Mrs. Dormeyer) Well, you can assume that it does.

Mrs. Dormeyer: I know it did, but (inaudible) . . . I was hoping he might give me an answer.

Dr. Zuk: He's not ready for one yet. It does bother him; there's no question about that. But it puts him in a more difficult position than Brenda. He's a little older; he's a boy.

Brenda: (sarcastically) Yeah, he's a boy! Guess what, Hank, you're a boy!

Hank: Really? I'm listening.

Dr. Zuk: There's a little different feeling about a mother's sharing her love for a boy than for a girl.

Mrs. Dormeyer: That happens even when the (inaudible) . . . even in the home.

Dr. Zuk: Yes. Uh, maybe not quite as much.

Mrs. Dormeyer: Well, you know something. I've always disliked hypocrisy and lying. Maybe . . . I've been told a lot of times that I'm brazen but I don't mean to be brazen, I just want to be honest. I don't want to be hypocritical. Does that make sense to you? I know there are times when . . . But when something is as basic as my position, and that has to be lived with daily . . .

Dr. Zuk: Well, what is it that you want most? You say you don't like to be hypocritical, and yet in your life you obviously have been. Everybody's a little hypocritical, and you've certainly had your share of it. What's the hypocritical area? In a way it's hypocritical to talk about strong moral beliefs and try to communicate these to others . . . to your children . . . and in your life, your dreams, you do the opposite to that. But you need both those things, obviously, in your life. You need the moralizing, and you need the dreams. How you gonna' fit them together?

Mrs. Dormeyer: Maybe that's why I get so upset . . . trying to juggle them.

Dr. Zuk: That's right. And sometimes you (inaudible) . . . But I think you're trying, and you should be given a lot of credit for making a terrific effort. (addressing Brenda) Boy, this girl has been terrific today. I'm surprised at her maturity; because she did try to hide her maturity. I'm very pleased to see that she has so much more capability. I'm sure this is true of Hank too, but he's a little more, uh, more . . .

Hank: More what?

Dr. Zuk: Well, I think you're a little more hung-up, to use that word . . .

Hank: (teasingly) He's a hippie! You dirty . . .

Mrs. Dormeyer: You know, Doctor, the moral side and the human need get to fighting within me sometimes, and I think I'm going to leave and build a completely new life. But I know if I do that, if I try to build on the moral side, the need of the woman in me . . . Oh, my goodness, I can't stand the feeling just thinking about it; I can't. I may have to resolve something somewhere.

Dr. Zuk: Yeah, right. Obviously you can't give up both sides . . . one side or the other. They're both with you. But how do you adjust; to make some kind of balance between them that makes life livable?

Mrs. Dormeyer: You know what I think I do: when I'm with John, I live the one life; and when I'm away from John, I live the other life. (sighs) I don't know. You know, the biggest problems in life, and the biggest fears . . . they're always resolved. Not always the way I wanted them to; but even when they didn't, it wasn't that bad. So from where I sit now, I know that no matter what way it ends, and (inaudible) . . . another door will open. They say you have to turn the knob, but (sighs again) it just seems that way. But you have to close the book. You can't leave any . . . Right now I'm in a quandary, and I don't know whether I'm in the quandary because I'm really that moral . . . moral . . . is the word "moralistic"? . . . or whether I'm trying to be the right moral guidance for the children. But I don't want them to grow up to be prudes either.

Brenda: (referring to Hank) He used to be a prude.

Mrs. Dormeyer: And there's still a puritanical part of Hank.

Brenda: My brother, the prude. (laughs)

Mrs. Dormeyer: Doctor, is there a possibility . . . (laughs) He's got Pilgrim shoes on. (referring to Hank's shoes)

Nurse: I think he's more sensitive than your other children.

Brenda: Yeah. No; I'm the sensitive one.

Mrs. Dormeyer: Oh, Hank has built up such a wall because he is so sensitive. All my children are. I have very sensitive children.

Hank: Well, it's time to go, people.

Mrs. Dormeyer: Do you think there might be a possibility of my speaking to either of you two at one time alone?

Dr. Zuk: Not now.

Mrs. Dormeyer: No, I don't mean today.
Dr. Zuk: Sometime later, maybe. See you next week.
(end of session)

EPILOGUE

The seventh session, which was held on April 9, 1969, was one in a series of thirty-two meetings with the Dormeyer family in the interval from January 22, 1969, through January 9, 1970, at which time meetings were suspended. Since it will add historical perspective to the transcript, I will present here an abstract of the progress notes I kept on the family.

In four sessions from January 22 through March 5, 1969, I focused on Hank and his mother. I sought to confront Hank on the issue of his glibness; his too-easy answers to difficult problems. I took up with Mrs. Dormeyer her inconsistency in moralizing to the children while at the same time departing in her personal conduct from the moral code she verbalized.

During March and April it seemed to me that the family settled into the treatment program, and that the engagement process was nearing completion. The Dormeyers attended sessions regularly, although at times certain members did not appear. In a session on March 26, for the first time I focused on Mrs. Dormeyer's attitude of distrust and hostility toward men, especially men in authority. She replied that she had to learn to be like a man herself for the sake of the children, since in effect they had no father. On April 11, Mrs. Dormeyer telephoned to say that Hank had received a poor report card, was depressed by it, and was threatening to leave school. (He had returned to school following release from a short hospitalization in connection with his taking drugs.) In a meeting on April 16 I dealt with the effect on Hank of his report card. I learned that Randy had also brought home a poor report card, but that Brenda had somewhat improved her grades. The session of April 23 focused on Randy: why he had to play the clown role in the family. I told the Dormeyers I thought they shut Randy up, and perhaps the only role left to him was that of the clown.

Toward the middle of May, Hank was expelled from school for several days because he was caught smoking and for some other minor mischief. At the end of May, Mrs. Dormeyer was called to the school to answer for an anonymous note received by school officials which accused both Hank and Brenda of bad behavior. Mrs. Dormeyer was quite upset about this and in a session during the latter part of May bitterly attacked the school officials for harboring prejudice toward her children. I asked Mrs. Dormeyer to return to the school and inquire specifically how seriously the school desired to treat the anonymous note. Mrs. Dormeyer did so and later reported to me that the school did not take the note seriously, but simply wanted to bring it to her attention. During the last week of May, Hank was picked up by the police at the New Jersey Shore and detained on a charge of trespassing.

During the last few days of the school term in June, Hank was again excluded from school because he was caught smoking. I got in touch by telephone with the school vice-principal who appeared fed-up with Hank and unwilling to accept him back in school for the next term. Later the vice-principal telephoned me to say he had relented somewhat and that Hank might be accepted back on a trial basis. On June 16 Mrs. Dormeyer informed me by telephone that Hank had again been picked up by the police at the New Jersey Shore on a curfew violation. During a session held in mid-June, I suggested that the Dormeyer children, Hank, Brenda, and Randy, might benefit from participating during the summer months in a daily program for adolescents. The children strongly rejected my idea, whereupon I warned them and Mrs. Dormeyer that by not cooperating with my treatment program they were risking termination.

The children continued in their refusal to join the adolescent program, but a difference in attitude was apparent in the session held on July 2. For the first time Hank acknowledged that the therapy had done him some good. Mrs. Dormeyer told me that Hank had been working evenings in the restaurant she managed, and his work there was good. I discussed with Hank the possibility of his starting in the fall a vocationally oriented school program, and he seemed interested. I told him I would make an initial contact with a program I knew about.

In a meeting on July 30, Hank appeared upset and said he wanted to tell me something but not in the presence of his younger brother. Reluctantly, I agreed to have Randy leave the room, whereupon Hank revealed that he visited his father's home during the previous week and found his oldest brother under the influence of drugs. Hank wanted my advice about whether he should turn his brother in to the police. Mrs. Dormeyer confirmed the incident and said she had already called a number of clinics where her son might receive help. I told Hank that I thought he had done his job by reporting the incident to his mother and then to me, and that his responsibility had ceased.

In a meeting on August 6, unexpectedly, the oldest Dormeyer son appeared with the family. He had come to live with his mother and she decided he should come to the session. He was somewhat disorganized in his thinking, and his attitude was lackadaisical. It was revealed during the meeting that he was not only taking drugs but selling them. I told Mrs. Dormeyer I was not sure I wanted to get involved with her son's problem at the time; and that it seemed to me she was sort of dumping him into an ongoing therapy in which he had not previously been a participant. I recommended several therapy programs that I thought might be appropriate for him.

There was a very dramatic event during the next week in August. I learned from Mrs. Dormeyer via the telephone that her oldest son had been arrested in connection with the death of a boy to whom, it was charged, he had sold drugs. Unexpectedly again, on August 27, Mrs. Dormeyer brought him, having just been released from jail, to the meeting. None of the other children but Brenda was present. Hank had gone to a music festival in Virginia and Randy was kept home because he had cut his foot on glass. Mrs. Dormeyer said that Hank was continuing to be cooperative at home and was doing good work in his job at the restaurant.

Mrs. Dormeyer's oldest son appeared quite different in the August 27 meeting, as compared with the time he was seen three weeks earlier. His hair had been cut; his mind was clearer; and he was less condescending. I was told that his lawyer was trying to have the charge against him changed to a lesser one, and that the chances for this seemed good. Again I told Mrs. Dormeyer that I questioned whether to accept her oldest son as a regular member in therapy sessions.

After a meeting on September 10—the oldest son did not make himself available for further meetings after August 27, although he continued to live with his mother for a while—contact with the family was broken for a period of about six weeks. Finally I established telephone contact with Mrs. Dormeyer, who informed me that she had been preoccupied with settling legal problems involving her oldest son, but that she had every intention to continue in family therapy. A meeting was arranged for October 24 at which I bluntly confronted Mrs. Dormeyer with my impression that, under pressures arising from the serious situation in connection with her oldest son, she had been manipulating the therapy to suit her own ends without real regard for my role or plan of guidance. Mrs. Dormeyer was angry with my challenge, then explained that she had been distraught due to her oldest son. Both she and Hank acknowledged again that family therapy had been helpful, and they agreed to try to follow my advice. However Hank, who had begun the special training program I had helped plan for him, was already complaining about its deficiencies. Mrs. Dormeyer revealed that she also learned of one or two instances during the previous few weeks in which Hank had used drugs, apparently LSD and marijuana. Hank acknowledged the incidents, but insisted he was not using drugs regularly and that they were isolated events.

Hank attended the special training program only for a few weeks and then dropped out. He made an effort to locate a job through a state employment service but, basically due to his youth, it was not successful. In sessions held during November and December—the family met with me quite regularly during these months—I dealt with Hank's failure to follow-through on the plan for a special training program. As an alternative I encouraged Mrs. Dormeyer to help Hank search for employment. In a meeting held during the latter half of December, Hank grumbled about continuing to come to meetings. I thought that "something was cooking" and decided to offer the family a temporary suspension of meetings rather than fight to convince Hank or others about their need to attend.

On January 9, 1970, Mrs. Dormeyer, Brenda, and Randy appeared for the meeting, but not Hank. Mrs. Dormeyer reported that in the interval Hank had decided to move to his father's home, and had actually done so. In this meeting the following information was forthcoming: Not only did Hank move in with his father, but he had also decided to return to public school in the district in which his father lived. The oldest Dormeyer son, the one seriously involved with drugs and the law, had returned to live with his father, was planning to get married the next summer, and had started a course of specialized training. The next oldest Dormeyer son, one also who had been with drugs, but never a participant in the meetings, came to live with his mother and had become engaged to be married. Brenda reported quite proudly that she was "going steady" with a boy of her own age. I was told by Mrs. Dormeyer and Brenda that Hank also had met a girl whom he had become attracted to, and who appeared to be exerting a beneficial influence on him.

I decided that the time might be ripe for a "breather," especially in view of Hank's move to his father's home and his stated reluctance to continue in therapy, and suggested a suspension of meetings for a period of six months, after which there would be a re-evaluation of the situation if Mrs. Dormeyer felt one was needed.

While there was no dramatic improvement that could be isolated in the Dormeyer family during the course of the year in family therapy, I believe changes did occur that were favorable. If Hank took any drugs during this period, I believe it was only on occasion. If he left public school, it was not simply to lead an aimless existence. With my help he made an effort to get specialized training and, when his motivation failed him in this effort, he did seem genuinely interested in securing employment. I believe his return to his father's home was a desire to test whether he could accept his father's guidance, which he had previously rejected completely. Whether he or his father would pass the test was of course unclear.

It was my impression that in the course of the therapy there was a change for the better in Mrs. Dormeyer's readiness to attack and undermine male authority and direction. One result of the many clashes I had with her regarding whether she would follow my direction was that she came to accept the legitimacy of my role as an advisor to the family. I think a further result of this was that, not having to be both mother and father to the children, she could be a better mother.

There was a reported improvement in Randy's reading skill during the course of the year and Randy could be more himself rather than the family clown. Brenda became less silly and giggly; and she evidenced a level of maturity that was not apparent initially.